Serapis
The Sacred Library and Its Declericalization

Stephen Bales and Wendi Arant Kaspar

Library Juice Press
Sacramento, CA

Copyright 2022

Published in 2022 by Library Juice Press.

Litwin Books
PO Box 188784
Sacramento, CA 95818

http://litwinbooks.com/

This book is printed on acid-free paper.

Publisher's Cataloging in Publication
Names: Bales, Stephen. | Kaspar, Wendi Arant.
Title: Serapis : the sacred library and its declericalization / Stephen Bale and Wendi Arant Kaspar.
Description: Sacramento, CA : Library Juice Press, 2023. | Includes bibliographical references and
   index.
Identifiers: LCCN 2023937551 | ISBN 9781634000970 (acid-free paper)
Subjects: LCSH: Academic libraries – History. | Academic libraries – Sociological aspects. | Libraries – History. | Libraries – Religious aspects.
Classification: LCC Z720.5 B35 2023 | DDC 027/009--dc23
LC record available at https://lccn.loc.gov/2023937551

We dedicate this work to the library faculty of Texas A&M University in College Station. They have long worked to uphold the values of information access and equity, expertise and innovation, and collaboration and dedication to education, constantly evolving their roles and their knowledge to meet the needs of faculty, researchers, and students in the university.

Long may they prosper.

Contents

ix	**Acknowledgements**
1	**Introduction** The Sacred Library
13	**Chapter 1** Information Institutions from the Dawn of History through the Early Iron Age
43	**Chapter 2** Information Institutions from Greece through the Medieval Period
79	**Chapter 3** The Early University Libraries, Modernity, and the Move Towards the Secular
103	**Chapter 4** Serapis and the Serapeum as Metaphors
123	**Chapter 5** Religious Ideology, Symbolism, and the Serapian MCAL
145	**Chapter 6** The "Cosmic" Serapian MCAL: Its Crypto-religious Symbolism
163	**Chapter 7** The Kynical Academic Library Worker
185	**Authors' Biographies**
187	**Image Copyright and Acknowledgments**
193	**Bibliography**
211	**Index**

Acknowledgements

Many people helped this book project come to fruition. The authors thank Rebecca Hankins, Professor, Archivist/Librarian of Africana and Women's & Gender Studies, Texas A&M University Libraries; Wyoma vanDuinkerken, Professor, Director of the Joint Library Facility, Texas A&M University Libraries; Bernardo H. Motta, PhD., Assistant Professor of Journalism, Roger Williams University; and Tyler Schmandt, Libraries Facilities Project Manager, University of Tennessee Libraries. Many thanks to Christopher Glass for taking the photographs of the University of Tennessee Hodges Library printed in Chapter Four and Daniel Welch, formerly of Texas A&M University Libraries Media and Reserves, for the photo of the Texas A&M University Libraries obelisk printed in Chapter Six.

Stephen Bales thanks his beautiful wife Mitzi, his daughters Stella and Irene, and his mother Cheryl Bales. He is very grateful to his co-author, Wendi Arant Kaspar, without whom this project would not have been realized.

Introduction   The Sacred Library

The Library exists ab aeterno. *No reasonable mind can doubt this truth, whose immediate corollary is the future eternity of the world. Man, the imperfect librarian, may be the work of chance or malevolent demiurges; the universe, with its elegant endowment of shelves, of enigmatic volumes, of indefatigable ladders for the voyager, and of privies for the seated librarian, can only be the work of god.*

Jorge Luis Borges[1]

In his short story *The Library of Babel*, Jorge Luis Borges describes a cosmic library of unfathomable dimensions. Borges's metaphor for the universe has existed *ab aeterno*, i.e., "from the beginning," and is a place that houses all knowledge. It is also where the deity itself takes up residence in the form of a book:

> We know, too, of another superstition of the time: The Man of the Book. In some shelf of some hexagon, men reason, there must exist a book which is the cipher and perfect compendium of *all the rest*: some librarian has perused it, and it is analogous to a god [...] to me it does not seem unlikely that on some shelf of the universe there lies a total book.[2]

Borges's literary creation can be seen as a sort of cheval mirror that, when tilted at just the right angle, allows the reader to glimpse humanity's near religious drive to grasp and organize information. *The Library is the Universe. The Library is Holy. The Library is God.*

---

1   Jorge Luis Borges, "The Library of Babel," in *The Mirror of Infinity: A Critics' Anthology of Science Fiction*, ed. Robert Silverberg (San Francisco: Canfield Press, 1970), 316.

2   Borges, "The Library of Babel," 320.

The library is also an ancient and much storied institution, and the realities of modern libraries and those that experience them are shaped by people's attempts over millennia to collect and organize recorded information for preservation and use. Entering a modern academic library, one feels the weight of history and culture bearing down. One also feels the press of something like the sublime or sacred, even if it can be difficult for the individual to put their finger on exactly what this sensation is or why they feel it.

David S. Porcaro wrote that: "Walking into the library today, one enters a sacred place. The atmosphere is hushed and books are handled with care. Many mysteries are to be found in the words inscribed in the multitude of books on the shelves: information at the fingertips of anyone willing to enter this hallowed world."[3] This notion that the modern library is a "hallowed world," is by no means a novel or even unconventional idea, but it involves something more than just the awestruck feeling that one gets when encountering massive buildings or gigantic collections of knowledge. It is more than the adoption of religious metaphors as a convenient way to capture in words one's adoration for an institution. Both religion as a system and the organization and dissemination of information are closely tied to issues of control and the equitable application of human power at historical, cultural, societal, and economic levels. What are the implications of the modern academic library embodying, in the same instance, both the organization of human knowledge and what might be called the sacred?

The arguments in this book comprise a critique of the modern academic library as a crypto-religious institution, a discussion initiated in "The Academic Library as Crypto-Temple: A Marxian Analysis,"[4] a chapter published in Estep and Enright's 2016 edited collection, *Class and Librarianship: Essays at the Intersection of Information, Labor and Capital*. The present elaboration argues that the modern capitalist academic library (MCAL),[5] including its buildings, collections, information

---

3   David S. Porcaro, "Sacred Libraries in the Temples of the Near East," *Studia Antiqua* 2, no. 1 (2002): 63.

4   Stephen Bales, "The Academic Library as Crypto-Temple: A Marxian Analysis," in *Class and Librarianship: Essays at the Intersection of Information, Labor and Capital*. Sacramento, ed. Erik Estep and Nathaniel F. Enright (Sacramento, CA: Library Juice Press, 2016), 5-24.

5   The "modern capitalist academic library" (MCAL) refers to all academic libraries operating under the capitalist mode of socioeconomic production that do not specifically challenge and subvert this social formation at an operational level through counter-hegemonic action. It is possible for individual units within the MCAL, however, to act counter-hegemonically.

technologies, online presences, faculty and staff, end users, and internal and external operational hierarchies, as well as the many connections that all these elements share among one another, comprises a poorly camouflaged but under-examined "crypto-temple" that has material consequences on human lives.

The word "Serapian," an adjective that points to both the Greco-Egyptian god Serapis and to that god's temple in Alexandria, the Serapeum, is used throughout the book and is explained in more detail in Chapter Four. Both deity and temple demonstrated the successful amalgamation of religion with other ideologies, and the authors use it herein to identify those institutions that incorporate religious ideology into what might otherwise be seen as secular structure. Since the first proto-libraries of ancient Mesopotamia,[6] there has existed an ideological confluence between information organizations, religion, and political power, a material and symbolical abutment that has become intrinsic to the reproduction of society regardless of particular historical social formation, be it ancient, feudal, or capitalist. In this book, the authors refer to this idea of the interwoven ideologies centering on information institutions using the term "Serapian ideological plexus" (SIP) as shorthand.

If one agrees with the notion that the religious is a significant element of the MCAL's material-ideological composition, it should not be difficult to convince them that the institution is an effective generative element in socio-cultural reproduction. Assuming a neo-Marxian stance that previous dominant socio-cultural formations have been essentially exploitative, the argument is made for the acknowledgement, challenge, and separation of the "ideology of the sacred" from the institution of the academic library through "declericalization." This institutional declericalization is defined as the MCAL worker's self-recognition of their heretofore unconsciously assumed role as a member of a "secular clergy," their unfolding understanding of the implications involved in maintaining this role, and their active resistance to this role. It is an awakening and response to an entrenched, systemic, and ideological element of the sociocultural superstructure that serves the interests of those in positions of power and many times works to the detriment of those who are not.

---

6 The term "proto-library" is used to include all information organizations prior to the Great Library of Alexandria (c. 300 BCE). The authors' reasoning for this choice of terminology is explained in Chapter One.

Note: the analysis in this book focuses on western academic libraries. This is done for two reasons. First, it makes the effort manageable. Second, because of western civilization's role as a crucible for modern capitalism and that system's near global hegemony, the authors concluded that an in-depth analysis of western libraries and their predecessors may offer some future insight into those non-western information institutions that currently or have in the past fallen under the domination of the Western capitalist societies. Further research concerning the relationship between religion and library should be conducted to better understand these relationships in non-western contexts.

Theoretical Framework

The authors adopt the theory of dialectical materialism as a framework for understanding the concept of the academic library as well as that institution's relationship to religious symbolism, ideology, and the state. Materialist dialectics is a powerful tool for analyzing social relationships and shining light upon the workings of change, stasis, and transformation both in modern society and throughout human history. Bertell Ollman described this approach to reality as a "philosophy of internal relations."[7] Dialectical materialism, he wrote "is best described as research into the manifold ways in which entities are internally related. It is a voyage of exploration that has the whole world for its object, but a world that is conceived of as relationally contained in each of its parts."[8] The heterodox view of dialectical materialism employed in this book is one that relies as much if not more on the philosophers Benedict Spinoza and Joseph Dietzgen as it does on Marx, Engels, and Lenin. It is presented in more detail in an earlier work by Bales.[9] Therefore, although a full recapitulation of this understanding of reality and its application to the problem at hand is not necessary here, readers may find a summary of its basic tenets useful.

As a theoretical framework, dialectical materialism offers the critical analyst a dynamic ontological means for situating and relating the

---

7   Bertell Ollman, *Dance of the Dialectic: Steps in Marx's Method*, (Urbana, IL: University of Illinois Press, 2003), 6.

8   Ollman, 127.

9   Stephen Bales, *The Dialectic of Academic Librarianship: A Critical Approach* (Sacramento, CA: Library Juice, 2015).

key elements involved in the objects of study, i.e., the processes and phenomena of the academic library and academic librarianship (i.e., it is a "philosophy of internal relations"), as an alternative to traditional ways of obtaining knowledge such as philosophical idealism and non-dialectical materialism (aka the traditional scientific method); dialectical materialism

> [...] is a philosophy and method that works as an integrative and monistic alternative to views of the cosmos that apply artificial metaphysical conditions to reality. It allows researchers and practitioners, and preferable, researchers as practitioners to understand and critique the academic library as a historically placed element of the matter/mind confluence.[10]

Dialectical materialism emerged independently and simultaneously out of the work of two nineteenth-century German philosophers, Karl Marx (1818-1883 CE) and Joseph Dietzgen (1828-1888 CE). Marx based his ideas on the work of German philosopher G.W.F. Hegel (1770-1831 CE) but, unlike the philosophical idealist Hegel, Marx was a materialist who rejected idealism while acknowledging the effectiveness of Hegel's dialectics as a means for understanding societal relations and change throughout history. Marx wrote that the development of society is not a reflection of the development of Hegel's "Ultimate Idea" but results from the inevitable conflict between material forces that are forever in motion and acting reciprocally upon one another. Contemporaneously with and independently of Marx, Dietzgen developed his own dialectical materialism, looking to the work of Spinoza instead of Hegel. Like Spinoza,[11] Dietzgen saw all reality as a singular substance that differentiates itself into various forms or modes.[12] Although ideas, concepts (as well as things like spirituality and God) are

---

10 Bales, 53.

11 Spinoza wrote in his *Ethics* that "But if anyone now asks by what sign, therefore, we may distinguish between substances, let him read the following propositions, which show that in nature only one substance exists, and that it is absolutely infinite. For this reason that sign would be sought for in vain." In Benedict Spinoza, *Ethics*, trans. W.H. White, rev. A.H. Stirling (London: Wordsworth, 2001), 10.

12 Bertrand Russell described Spinoza's metaphysical system as logical monism, "the doctrine, namely, that the world as a whole is a single substance, none of whose parts are logically capable of existing alone." In Bertrand Russell, *History of Western Philosophy* (London: Routledge, 2004), 528. Dietzgen would take this logical monism and layer it with a detailed analysis of movement and change.

the product of physically material things and processes,[13] they are no less material in their relations, effects, and interactions—either to other ideas or physical objects. Both Marx's and Dietzgen's dialectical materialisms rely firmly upon the notion that material nature is to be understood as relations and processes, and that nothing may be understood in and of itself outside of these relations and processes. All things, even if perceived via the senses as particulars, are only intelligible as expressions of multiple material relations.

These webs of relations have definite material impact. Writing on ideology, Popowich noted that "[…] social relations force people in a very real, material way—to think particular things in particular ways."[14] Since ideas have a material reality, there is the danger that *materially realized* "simple abstractions" will support the perpetuation of existing structures of hegemonic domination. A simple abstraction is one that has been effectively divorced from its material relations with other physical and mental phenomena due to the lack of sufficient dialectical consideration. It takes on a life of its own, being elevated to the level of "pure idea" while ignoring the "endless entanglement of relations and reactions, permutations and combinations in which nothing remains what, where, and as it was. But everything moves, changes, comes into being, and passes away."[15] One example of a simple abstraction is (big D) Democracy,[16] a concept that looms large in the western consciousness, and one that is often associated with libraries. Public libraries, for instance, are many times portrayed as "bulwarks of Democracy,"[17] a platitude that tends to curtail further discourse about what exactly "democracy" means. In an incisive critique

---

13   Similarly, Engels wrote that "the mind is the highest product of matter." In Friedrich Engels, *Feuerbach: The Roots of the Socialist Philosophy*, trans. Austin Lewis (New York: Mondial, 2009), 48.

14   Sam Popowich, *Confronting the Democratic Discourse of Librarianship: A Marxist Approach* (Sacramento, CA: Library Juice, 2019), 112.

15   Friedrich Engels, *Socialism: Utopian and Scientific*, trans. Edward Aveling (New York: International Publishers, 2004), 45.

16   Simple abstractions are capitalized throughout the book in order differentiate them from dialectically understood relations.

17   For example, the Texas State Library's *Public Library Advisory Handbook* states that "Libraries are one of the great bulwarks of democracy. They are living embodiments of the First Amendment because their collections include voices of dissent as well as assent. Libraries are impartial resources providing information on all points of view, available to all persons regardless of age, race, religion national origin, social or political views, economic status or any other characteristics." In Alvin R. Bailey, ed., *Public Library Advisory Board Handbook* (Austin, Texas: Texas State Library Development Division, 1992), 57.

of the democratic discourse of librarianship, Popowich identified this abstraction and called for rebuttal and resistance:

> The sacred mission of libraries, as "arsenals of democratic culture", "cornerstones of liberty", and the rest must be discredited if we want to participate in the creation of a world that is *truly* democratic. True democracy cannot be partial, cannot be exclusionary, and I will argue that this is precisely what "liberal democracy" has always been. The democratic discourse of librarianship, the idea that libraries are sacred to some actually-existing democratic reality, prevents us from working towards the achievement of this radical, total democracy.[18]

Library workers are themselves often guilty of perpetuating such abstractions through what Ettarh described as buying into the "vocational awe" surrounding library work, the "set of ideas, values, and assumptions librarians have about themselves and the profession that result in notions that libraries as institutions are inherently good, sacred notions, and therefore beyond critique."[19] In another example that is perhaps no less political, most conceptions of the Abrahamic deity are simple abstractions.

The problem with understanding the library in terms of simple, "sacred" abstractions is twofold. First, these abstractions ignore history, context, and culture by immortalizing and mythicizing the library without allowing room for the consideration of the possibility of change. Second, by making concepts like Democracy essentially inviolate, the simple abstraction cloaks inequities by invoking what is assumed to be a universal value and, thus, obscuring power relationships.[20] For example, an incomplete understanding of the library qua democratic apparatus (note the small d here) as a material idea, i.e., one that does not adequately account for its position in the web of relationships relating to the institution, makes it easier to ignore the ways in which institutions like the academic library may inhibit or even retard

---

18 Popowich, *Confronting the Democratic Discourse of Librarianship*, 49.

19 Fobazi Ettarh, "Vocational Awe and Librarianship: The Lies We Tell Ourselves, *In the Library with the Lead Pipe* (Jan. 10, 2018), https://www.inthelibrarywiththeleadpipe.org/2018/vocational-awe/.

20 The notion that Democracy is a sacrosanct concept does, in fact, make it antithetical to democracy as a complex of relations and processes. As such a tapestry, democracy contains within it its own contradictions, such as the tyranny of the majority, which the simple abstraction ignores.

democratic processes. The fixing and normalization of simple abstractions stifles critique and growth.

A dialectical approach identifies and contests simple abstractions and idealistic essentialism to support the revolutionary transformation of society. Engels wrote that:

> [...] once we understand [the active social forces in society and the relations they partake in], when once we grasp their action, their direction, their effects, it depends only upon ourselves to subject them more and more to our own will, and by means of them to reach our own end.[21]

According to dialectical logic, a change in any particular "thing," as we might conventionally see and name that thing, results in a change to every thing within that relationship as well as the whole (i.e., every thing determines everything, and vice versa). Ultimately, this approach to reality is revolutionary in design and intent. The goal of the dialectical analyst is not just to understand *what is*, but to realize *what is possible*.

This book analyzes the dialectical relation:

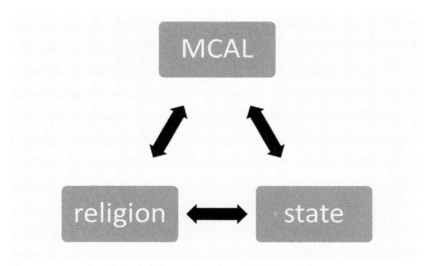

Figure 0.1 Serapian ideological plexus, the reciprocal relationship between MCAL-Religion-State

---

21 Engels, *Socialism: Utopian and Scientific*, 68.

A critique of this "concrete abstraction" (i.e., a concept with explanatory power because it considers the interaction of relationships) accomplishes two things. The approach adds to the emerging body of research concerning the intersection of library and information science and ideology. It also recognizes, through its consideration of the material nature of the existing academic library, that positive material change is possible.

Outline of the Book

The rest of this book consists of seven chapters that provide a narrative thread that moves from the ancient past to the modern day and then looks towards the future.

Chapter 1: Information Institutions from the Dawn of History through the Early Iron Age

Chapter One begins with a consideration of the contested use of the word "library" in the study of information institutions through history. Next, this chapter (as well as Chapter 2) expands upon the previous work of Bales concerning the history of libraries in the ancient world,[22] it considers the connections between information institutions, religion, and power in the Bronze Age and Iron Age civilizations of Mesopotamia and Egypt. This relationship is approached first by examining the "sacred nature" of the written word, a disposition that originated with these first civilizations. Three sections follow this analysis, the first dealing with Mesopotamian institutions in more detail, the second focusing on the Egyptian institutions, and the third offering concluding remarks.

Chapter 2: Information Institutions from Greece through the Medieval Period

This chapter picks up the historical thread with the pre-Alexandrian Greek information institutions. It then looks at the Great Library of Alexandria to understand how that institution transcended preceding proto-libraries while continuing their predecessors' basic

---

22 Stephen Bales, "Aristotle's Contribution to Scholarly Communication" (doctoral dissertation, University of Tennessee, 2008), https://trace.tennessee.edu/cgi/viewcontent.cgi?article=1539&-context=utk_graddiss.

sociocultural and religious functions. The post-Alexandrian libraries of Rome and late antiquity are accounted for as well as the ecclesiastical libraries of late antiquity and the Middle Ages. Continued attention is given to the close relationship of libraries to power throughout the periods.

Chapter 3: The Early University Libraries, Modernity, and the Move Towards the Secular

Chapter Three finishes the historical review with a look at the early western university libraries of the twelfth century CE "Medieval Renaissance," and considers the shift of education, and therefore the academic library, away from Christian monasteries to the more secular institution of the nascent universities. Next, a look at the European Renaissance proper and the Early Modern Period considers the impact of philosophical Humanism and the Enlightenment on the academic library's relationship to religious and temporal power. The chapter concludes with an examination of the Late Modern Period, neoliberalism, and the MCAL. It is argued that, although the religious ideology had, over a period of nearly 1000 years, become mystified under a cloak of secularity, it remained a substantive ideological force in that institution.

Chapter 4: Serapis and the Serapeum as Metaphors

Considering the preceding historical survey, this chapter proposes the great Ptolemaic god Serapis and the Serapeum of Alexandria as metaphors for those information institutions throughout history that employ religious ideology, symbolism, and ritual to manufacture hegemonic consent and maintain existing dominant power structures. It presents and explores the closely related concepts of the "Serapian ideological plexus" and the "Serapian information institution" as well as related terms. Depending on historical and sociocultural context, the Serapian information institution may contain multiple ideological structures, some of which are competing, but others that augment one another or work in tandem. The Serapian library, furthermore, has been historically attended to and managed by the Serapian library worker, i.e., a bureaucratic functionary that has in the past also been traditionally, and explicitly, a member of the clergy or priesthood as well as a member of the intelligentsia, professional elite, and a functionary of the state. To make these arguments, the chapter conducts two brief "virtual" tours: a tour of ancient Ptolemaic Alexandria and its Serapeum followed by a tour of the University of Tennessee Hodges Library of today.

Chapter 5: Religious Ideology and the Serapian MCAL

This chapter analyzes the MCAL using French structural Marxist Louis Althusser's concept of "ideological state apparatus" (ISA) and focuses specifically on the impact of religious ideology on the MCAL's role of both reinforcing the status quo and reproducing neoliberal capitalism. It considers the importance of understanding the MCAL in relationship to the dominant ideologies inherent in modern society. This analysis is performed to offer possible explanations for the MCAL's continuing existence as legacy ideological structures, arguing that these apparent anachronisms are material ideological motors with material consequences.

Chapter 6: Symbol, Ritual, and the Serapian MCAL

This chapter identifies and considers examples of the many times hidden, and many times overt, religious symbols and rituals found in the Serapian MCAL.

Chapter 7: The Kynical Academic Library Worker

The concluding chapter focuses on the role of the information worker within academic library qua crypto-temple as an adjunct to the dominant hegemonic forces found within society. It considers library work as a profession influenced by the information institutions' historical, long-lived, and persisting religious associations and proposes the concept of the "Kynical academic library worker" as a foil to traditional understandings of professionalism within the academic library. The Kynical academic library worker looks back to the ancient Greco-Roman philosophy of Cynicism (aka Kynicism) and that philosophy's modern-day interpreters for inspiration. Kynicism is a position from which modern academic library workers may respond to, challenge, and de-clericalize the dominant ideological structures found in the MCAL.

Chapter 1 Information Institutions from the Dawn of History through the Early Iron Age

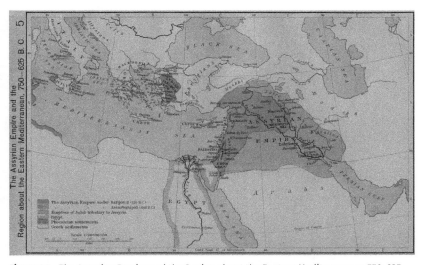

Figure 1.1 The Assyrian Empire and the Region about the Eastern Mediterranean, 750-625 B.C.E. from The Historical Atlas by William R. Shepherd, 1923

He who'd know what life's about
Three millennia must appraise;
Else he'll go in fear and doubt,
Unenlightened all his days.

Johann Wolfgang von Goethe[1]

---

1 Johann Wolfgang von Goethe, in *West-Östilicher Diwan* (Stuttgard: Stuttgard Cottaische Bucandlung, 1819), quoted in Ernst Posner, *Archives in the Ancient World* (Cambridge, MA: Harvard University Press, 1972), 12.

It has only been in recent human history that the secularization of many libraries has obscured the once obvious connections between religion, library, and state. Before considering the modern capitalist academic library (MCAL) as a tenacious and consequential reverberation of sacred space, symbol, and ritual, it is necessary to examine information institutions through history. The creation of a sightline extending from the earliest organized collections of information to those of the present day will allow for a better understanding of contemporary manifestations of the academic library. Through such an analysis, the critical analyst engages in the process of historicization, a technique that Ollman said is a necessary element of Marx's dialectical method. Historicization allows the analyst to understand the constellations of social relations found in present day social phenomena: "[...] the second step Marx takes in his quest to unlock the future is to examine the preconditions of this present in the past" (the first step of Ollman's understanding of Marx's method being to identify a present situation for study).[2]

The MCAL is just the latest manifestation in a long line of information institutions, the chain of proto-libraries, libraries, archives, special collections, museums, etc. These are the religious and crypto-religious—i.e., where religious influences are muted or masked—institutions in which the ideological pull of the sacred (or what is perceived as sacred) makes demands on the people within their orbits. These ideological institutions stretch back to the earliest temple collections of the ancient Mesopotamians in a historical chain of ideological state apparatuses (ISAs): institutions that reinforce hegemonic norms through ideologically persuasive means instead of intimidation or violence.

With the MCAL, there appears to be no appreciable departure, evolutionary leap, or shift away from the information institutions that preceded the modern institution regarding its role as a conservative ideological construct. Most information institutions, regardless of the historical mode of socioeconomic production within which they operated or presently operate, actively supported, and still support, the dominant forms of sociocultural and political control. As place and space, the information institution is unrivaled in its capacity to

---

2 Bertell Ollman, *Dance of the Dialectic: Steps in Marx's Method* (Urbana, IL: University of Illinois Press, 2003), 163.

perpetuate what A. Leo Oppenheim described as the "stream of tradition,"[3] i.e., the persistent body of conservative literary customs, professional training, and beliefs passed down through the millennia from the Mesopotamian scribal elite for the purpose of maintaining the established architectures of power, both earthly and celestial. Furthermore, this stream of tradition supported the scribes' own continued status as societal elites and gatekeepers within these hegemonic centers of power.

Although Oppenheim was referring explicitly to the Mesopotamians when writing about the stream of tradition, this concept of "curation for control" by elite gatekeepers who are organic to the dominant classes may be seen in any cultural/historical context. The Great Library of Alexandria, and those institutions that followed it—such as the library of the Serapeum, the Library of Pergamum, the monastery libraries of the Middle Ages, the early western university libraries, and the modern academic and public libraries—were qualitatively different than the Near Eastern proto-libraries in that they moved more obviously into the realm of knowledge production. Nonetheless, these later, post-Alexandrian institutions never completely abandoned their role as conservators of entrenched power and class structures.

The information institutions' long held associations to religion and their remarkable continuity across history challenges the notion that the MCAL's religious associations are nothing more than an interesting but ultimately vestigial curiosity or throwback, i.e., it is not merely something that points towards the past in terms of aesthetic elements or seemingly hollow ritual only. Instead, with a consideration of the MCAL in the context of the institutions that preceded it, one might reasonably conclude that religious elements have survived in the form of a still persuasive material ideological construct that has important ramifications to its modern-day users. The MCAL maintains the preceding institutions' religious function of ideological control, even if this function appears to have become obscured and more agnostic over the centuries.

Despite the existence of these religious survivals over the entire span of human history, there remains the possibility for meaningful change, and the fact that such discussions are taking place concerning the

---

3 A. Leo Oppenheim, "— Assyriology—Why and How?" *Current Anthropology* 1, no. 5/6 (1960): 410.

MCAL's and other modern capitalist libraries' relationship to dominant ideologies augurs well for such change. It suggests that the subversion and refutation of dominant ideologies is possible. Indeed, the increasing tempo and forcefulness of the critical discourse surrounding libraries and archives of all types suggests that such counter-hegemonic subversions are presently underway. These ramifications apply to present society, through the information institution's function as a tool for the hegemonic control of dominant power structures and its implications on the equitable distribution of economic and social justice as well as human rights. Indeed, the MCAL is an ideological engine of great importance and reach, and though religion certainly does not make up the entirety of the current institution's ideological content, a significant portion of this ideological content derives from a history which is rooted in the sacred.

About the Word "Library"

The word "library" signifies a complex concept. It is also an easy word to get hung up on, particularly when researching and writing on the information institutions of the ancient world. It is beneficial, therefore, to consider the terminology used in such scholarship before looking further at institutions both ancient and contemporary. Doing so will set parameters for the usage of specific terminology and help prevent confusion.

The history of written language, as well as the history of the collection and organization of written language, begins with the ancient Sumerians in the mid-third millennium BCE. Assyriologists, a confusing label referring to those scholars that study ancient Assyria as well as the other ancient Mesopotamian civilizations stretching back to the Sumerians, tend to be inflexible as to what constitutes a "library." For instance, Morris Jastrow, who was both an eminent nineteenth century Assyriologist and a librarian at the University of Pennsylvania, chided scholars over what he considered to be the careless use of the word library when dealing with ancient Near Eastern collections. According to Jastrow, with few exceptions such as the sixth century neo-Assyrian king Ashurbanipal's Great Library of Nineveh, the Mesopotamians had no "libraries" "in any proper sense of the term" because the temple and scribal school libraries had notably smaller numbers of literary texts when compared to those societies' collections of what we today would consider to be "archival material."[4]

Figure 1.2   Tablets from the Great Library of Ashurbanipal

The key words in Jastrow's critique of the non-technical use of the word library are "smaller numbers" and "literary texts." Oppenheim, one of the most distinguished Assyriologists of the twentieth century, reinforced Jastrow's viewpoint. In his landmark study, *Ancient Mesopotamia: Portrait of a Dead Civilization*, Oppenheim wrote that "[...] the temples played a rather important role in keeping up the literary tradition, even though they had no libraries of their own."[5] Oppenheim dismissed those ancient collections which did not look like modern libraries—either for being too small or for not being "literary enough"—or were not collected and organized by processes like those of modern

---

4   Morris Jastrow, Jr., "Did the Babylonian Temples Have Libraries," *Journal of the American Oriental Society* 27 (1906): 173. The definition of archives is also open to criticisms of over-rigidity and the influence of anachronistic understandings superimposed on the diverse collections of the past. Posner wrote that: "Except for a few isolated cases, the general archives is a product of the last two hundred years. Although the Tabularium, the archives of Republican Rome, showed a tendency to absorb records of various administrative origins, the idea of concentrating in one place the archives of different creators was alien to ancient and medieval times. The ancient world did not even have the concept of an *archivio di deposito*, for nowhere are there to be found arrangements revealing an intention to differentiate administratively between current records and those no longer regularly needed for the dispatch of business. It was only in the Middle Ages that a discriminating attitude toward the value of records developed." In Posner, *Archives in the Ancient World*, 4-5.

5   A. Leo Oppenheim, *Ancient Mesopotamia: Portrait of a Dead Civilization* (Chicago: University of Chicago Press, 1964), 107.

libraries. To him, the Great Library of Ashurbanipal was the only "true" pre-Alexandrian library:

> But one should stress that a library in our sense, a systematic collecting of texts copied for the purpose of being included in such a collection, existed in Mesopotamia solely in Nineveh. Here, at the instance of Assurbanipal [a variant rendering of Ashurbanipal], king of Assyria, such a library was assembled, and large sections of it have been preserved.[6]

This dogmatic approach to what is and what is not a library in the ancient world is problematic for those both seeking to trace information institutions back to their inception and to develop an overall understanding of the library throughout history. It imposes modern assumptions of what makes a library onto the ancient institutions. Nevertheless, while widespread, the position is not universally held by Assyriologists. Wendel, in contrast to Jastrow and Oppenheim, wrote that "in the ancient Orient no distinction was made, between record and literary product, between archival establishments and libraries. Every accumulation of clay tablets would start from archival holdings and possibly expand by taking in literary pieces."[7] Ernest Cushing Richardson, a theologian and librarian, wrote that, when dealing with ancient information institutions, the strict application of the term "library," as Jastrow preferred to use it, and as Assyriologists like Oppenheim have generally adopted it, is too confining:

> A library then "in the proper and ordinary sense of the term" or "in the sense in which that term is ordinarily understood" [by the Assyriologists] is very big, wholly literary, gathered from various geographical sources, not associated with schools. No such library is known save that of Ashurbanipal and no other is likely save for Babylon—(Marduk temple) and perhaps Borsippa (Nebo temple).[8]

Again, the reader encounters spatial terms like "very big" and genre keywords like "wholly literary." Following this rigid definition, besides

---

6   Oppenheim, 244.

7   Posner's translation of Carl Wendel, *Die Griechisch-römische Buchbeschreibung Verglichen mit der des Vorderen Orients* (Halle, 1949), 11-12, quoted in Posner, *Archives in the Ancient World*, 27.

8   Ernest Cushing Richardson, *Biblical Libraries: A Sketch of Library History from 3400 BC to AD 150* (Hamden, CT: Archon Books, 1963), 22.

the three listed above by Richardson (two of which Oppenheim would have dismissed because they were housed in temples), the only "library" to appear between c. 3500 BCE and c. 300 BCE is the Great Library of Alexandria. The rest are simply "book collections" or archives. Richardson noted the absurdity of such a restrictive definition and contended that the Assyriologists' definition of what makes a library is, by no means, the accepted common usage of the term. Collection size, for instance, does not figure significantly into modern understandings of whether a library is, in fact, a "library": "The Report of the United States Commissioner of Education for 1912, for example, recognizes 10,329 public high school libraries having an average of only 600 volumes each [...] Size of course does not count."[9]

Another problem with determining what an ancient "library" consists of, in any strict sense, is that the scope and topical boundaries of what made up the collections are oftentimes ambiguous. The belief that "true" libraries contained solely literary material is untenable, considering that, if one applies this criterion to all collections, even today's collections, there would be relatively few true libraries. Richardson said that "every [Mesopotamian] temple had at least a collection of school textbooks and reference books, amounting also at least to several hundred tablets, with a collection of religious texts amounting also at least to several hundred texts, while in the case of the largest collection, there may have been thousands."[10] Collections might and often did contain archival material as well as literary material,[11] and both types of documents might be heavily used by scribes. At least half of Ashurbanipal's Library was composed of archival materials,[12] and the predominating texts in the "literary" portion of the collection were divination texts used for ensuring the well-being of the king himself.[13] When viewing such divination texts, or the numerous recorded Mesopotamian and Egyptian incantations and spells, it can often be difficult to see them as much more than recipes or

---

9   Richardson, 24-25.

10 Richardson, 26.

11 Archival materials in the ancient sense being business, governmental, and historical records kept for active use.

12 Richardson, *Biblical Libraries*, 35.

13 Gerald E. Max, "Ancient Near East," in *Encyclopedia of Library History*, ed. Wayne A. Wiegand and Donald G. Davis, Jr. (New York: Routledge, 1994), 27.

algorithms. Incantations and spells, said Posner, "are intimately related to the process of government and could be of record rather than literary character."[14] There are also differences of opinion among Assyriologists as to whether all Mesopotamian religious texts qualify as literature.[15] Olmstead wrote, when describing Ashurbanipal's Nineveh collection, that the Assyrians made little distinction between material types for the purposes of organization: "Nearly a thousand business documents, fifteen hundred letters, a large group of omen texts, are firmly dated to the last Assyrian century. Today we call them archival material, but the Assyrians saw no reason why they should not be placed side by side with the other writings."[16] According to Richardson, the Shamash/Utu temple collection of Neo-Babylonian Sippar, which contained approximately 50,000 tablets, included, "temple archives, public and private business documents like those of Lagash, but they include 'some hundreds' at least of 'literary texts,' hymns, prayers, incantations, a deluge of narrative and other religious texts as well as a school outfit."[17] The main palace archive at Ebla (an ancient Syrian city state) contained correspondence, international and internal legal regulations, management records for the holdings of the palace and of the state, records for the administration of palace goods, religious documents, and education and literature texts.[18] The ancient archive contained all sorts of records, and was not limited exclusively to the materials expected to be found in modern archives.[19]

Finally, investigators must consider the lack of available evidence when settling upon a definition of what constitutes a "library." Even though there is an enormous corpus of recovered Mesopotamian documents, relatively few of these artifacts have been translated and categorized. In addition, there were many documents written on perishable

---

14   Posner, *Archives in the Ancient World*, 27.

15   Tammi J. Schneider, *An Introduction to Ancient Mesopotamian Religion* (Grand Rapids, MI: William B. Eerdmans, 2011), 91.

16   A.T. Olmstead, *History of Assyria* (New York: Charles Scribner's Sons, 1923), 493.

17   Richardson, *Biblical Libraries*, 46.

18   Walther Sallaberger, "The Management of Royal Treasure: Palace Archives and Palatial Economy in the Ancient Near East," in *Experiencing Power, Generating Authority: Cosmos, Politics, and the Ideology of Kingship in Ancient Egypt and Mesopotamia*, ed. Jane A. Hill, Philip Jones, and Antonio J. Morales (Philadelphia, PA: University of Pennsylvania Museum of Archaeology and Anthropology, 2013), 219-255.

19   Posner, *Archives in the Ancient World*, 5.

materials such as papyrus, wood, wax tablets, parchment, and leather, the majority of which have been lost to time. Oppenheim himself implicitly recognized this lacuna in the archaeological evidence and written record when he wrote that alternative Mesopotamian media like wax tablets, papyrus, and leather scrolls were used because they were much more convenient than clay tablets.[20] A lack of evidence precludes the application of any precise definition of what makes a "library" in ancient Mesopotamia, Egypt, and the surrounding areas, and the draconian use of the Assyriologists' definition of the concept risks one falling into the fallacy of anachronism, uncritically viewing the past through the lens of contemporary beliefs.

With the understanding that ancient information institutions might and often did contain a combination of different types of written materials, be they literary, administrative, archival, and otherwise, the present authors have chosen to use the word "proto-library" to refer to all "official" information institutions that existed prior to the Great Library of Alexandria. Although referring to some pre-Alexandrian private collections, particularly the nearly entirely literary/scholarly collections of Greeks like Plato and Aristotle, as "libraries" seems more appropriate because such collections more closely match modern understandings of the term, "proto-library" is used as a matter of convenience to clearly delineate those institutions that came before the Great Library of Alexandria and those that came after. The present authors agree with Richardson that, "In a sense modern library history begins with Aristotle, Alexander and Alexandria."[21] When discussing the post-Alexandrian information institutions, the reader will note the usage of words like library and archive when referring to collections that tend to adhere more closely to the modern understanding of the institutions, i.e., a collection of solely or primarily literary material (library), or one dedicated solely or primarily to an accumulation of historical records (archive). Post-Alexandrian information institutions which remain "fuzzy" in terms of their contents or functions, i.e., more in keeping with the pre-Alexandrian institutions, are flagged and explained. Nevertheless, despite the occurrence of any paradigmatic shift between proto-library and library, this book contends that there has always been a central feature in the constitutional makeup of what

---

20 Oppenheim. *Ancient Mesopotamia*, 242.
21 Richardson, *Biblical Libraries*, 148.

defines any "official" information institution throughout history: religion. This criterion remains largely consistent over the millennia as well as, as will be shown, this criterion's sociocultural ramifications, despite either the size of the collection or the types of items that sit on the shelves.

The Utterances of Ra: The Sacred Origins and Nature of Recorded Language

Since its beginnings with the earliest Sumerian and Egyptian civilizations, and up until relatively recent times, written language has been closely associated with the divine. Writing was explainable, as was most everything else to the Bronze Age mind, in terms of this relationship to the gods:

> So awesome was the concept of taking speech—and, even more astonishing, thought—and making it visual and preserving it through time that the concept and the capability could not be credited to mere mortals. Man knew it to be a divine gift. This unquestionable recognition was shared by almost every early civilization.[22]

While the development of writing appears to have occurred over a relatively short period of time when compared to the 300,000 or so years that humans had already been on the planet, the written word was seen by the Mesopotamians and Egyptians as having always existed. It was a primordial power capable of weaving together the fabric of reality itself. To disrespect the written word was to profane the holy.[23] Robinson wrote that divine origin would remain the most popular explanation for the birth of writing systems up until the Age of Enlightenment, after which time the dominant explanation shifted to one where

---

22 Marc Drogin, *Biblioclasm: The Mythical Origins, Magic Powers, and Perishability of the Written Word* (Savage, MD. Rowman & Littlefield Publishers, 1989), 11-12.

23 Mesopotamian tablets, for example, are renowned for their inscribed curses meant to dissuade careless handling or thievery. A tablet found at the site of the ancient Ashur (today Qalat Sherqat), for example, contained the curse: "Whoever breaks this tablet asunder or puts it in water and rubs (?) it, until you cannot recognize it and cannot make it hear (i.e., read it aloud)—may Ashur, Sin, Shamash, Adad and Istar, Bel, Nabu, Nergal, Ishtar of Arbela, Istar of Bit Kdmurri, the of the heavens and earth, and the gods of Assyria, may all these curse him with a curse which cannot be relieved, terrible and merciless as long as he lives, may they let his name, his seed, (i.e., his kin) be carried off from the land, may they put his flesh in a dog's mouth." In Erster Band, *Keilschriftexte Aus Assur Religiösen Inhalts*, (Leipzig, J.C. Hinrichs'sche Buchhandlung, 1919), translated in Mogens Weitmeyer, "Archive and Library Technique in Ancient Mesopotamia," *Libri* 6, no. 3 (1956): 230.

the technology was seen as having developed as a means for accounting for business transactions and administrative recordkeeping.[24]

The Power of the Written Word

The Mesopotamians had scribe deities of both sexes. Although these patron divinities evolved over the millennia and were identified by different names across several civilizations, they were largely variations of the Sumerian goddess Nisaba and her consort Nabû. According to the Mesopotamian religious texts, Nisaba invented writing and bestowed it upon humankind for their benefit. The following text is taken from a hymn of praise to the goddess supposedly written in the 19th century BCE by the Sumerian king Lipit-Estar. The king's verse implies a link between knowledge and joy as personified by the goddess and, at the same time, relates such joy directly to celestial authority:

> Nisaba, the woman radiant with joy,
> The true woman scribe, the lady of all knowledge,
> Guided your fingers on the clay,
> Embellished the writing on the tablets,
> Made the hand resplendent with a golden stylus.[25]

The Sumerians and their successor civilizations saw recorded language as their gods' means of exerting power and maintaining control of all creation. Writing essentially served as a divine scaffolding for reality. Lipit-Estar's hymn to Nisaba illustrates the association of recorded script with authority, suggesting that the words inscribed by the mortal scribe are, in fact, the words of the immortal scribe. It is not he, the scribe, that moves the stylus but her, the deity. The Sumerian writer becomes a cipher for the goddess and a direct link between ultimate authority and that authority's earthly bureaucratic realization.

---

24 Andrew Robinson, "Writing Systems," in *The Book: A Global History*, ed. Michael F. Suarez, S.J. Woudhuysen, and H.R. Woudhuysen (Oxford: Oxford University Press, 2013), 3. Morenz, however, noted that pictorial compositions in the Near Eastern inscriptions dealt with both religious ritual and royal power. In Ludwig D. Morenz, "Texts before Writing: Reading (Proto-)Egyptian Poetics of Power," in *Experiencing Power, Generating Authority: Cosmos, Politics, and the Ideology of Kingship in Ancient Egypt and Mesopotamia*, ed. Jane A. Hill, Philip Jones, and Antonio J. Morales (Philadelphia: University of Pennsylvania Museum of Archaeology and Anthropology, 2013), 121-149. This might suggest a confluence of factors in the development of script.

25 H.L.J. Vanstiphout, "Lipit-Estar's Praise in the Edubba," *Journal of Cuneiform Studies* 30, no. 1 (1978): 37.

The irony is inescapable when one considers that the celestial mother figure that birthed both written language and the information professions was a female even though most women would be excluded from both higher education and the literate professions for millennia.

Nabû, the son of the creator god Assuru (or the son of Marduk for the Babylonians)[26] was, like his wife, a patron of literacy and the scribal arts. When one considers the Mesopotamian religious texts that feature Nabû, writing's mystical function to structure reality again becomes apparent. In some myths, the scribe god was "controller of the Tablet of Destinies guarded by the Seven Sages and sealed with the Seal of Destinies."[27] The words inscribed on the mythic tablet were fundamental for maintaining order in the cosmos by ensuring the supreme position of the god Enlil, and thus preventing the triumph of chaos and the dissolution of the cosmos.[28] The Tablet was also the document in which the fates of both humans and the gods themselves were recorded.

The fact that writing was given to humans by the gods "underscores the magic with which these early societies regarded writing. It also suggests their dependency upon a well-working system of written communication, one implicitly controlled by the gods' representatives on earth, the priesthood."[29] The recognition of the cosmic power of writing and this power's extension into mundane spheres of administration and sociopolitical control is seen throughout the ancient world, beyond the Mesopotamian and Egyptian societies. Shalom M. Paul, for example, finds instances of references to myths like the Mesopotamian Tablet of Destinies in multiple Hebrew works including the books of Exodus, Isaiah, Jeremiah, Malachi, Daniel, the Psalms, Pseudepigrapha, Enoch, Apocalypse of Zephania, Dead Sea Scrolls, and the Talmudic Literature, as well as the Christian New Testament books of Luke, Philippians, Hebrews, and Revelations.[30]

---

26 Drogin, *Biblioclasm*, 12.

27 Stephanie Dalley, "The Sassanian Period and Early Islam, c. AD 224-651," in *The Legacy of Mesopotamia*, ed. Stephanie Dalley (Oxford: Oxford University Press, 1998), 166.

28 Jeremy Black and Anthony Green, *Gods, Demons and Symbols of Ancient Mesopotamia: An Illustrated Dictionary* (Austin, TX: University of Texas Press, 1992), 173.

29 Max, "Ancient Near East," 24.

30 Shalom M. Paul, "Heavenly Tablets and the Book of Life," *Janes* 5 (1973): 347-350.

Like the Mesopotamians, the ancient Egyptians also considered recorded language to have a heavenly pedigree and to embody Truth and Order in opposition to Chaos. To the ancient Egyptian, writing and recorded texts absolutely were physical manifestations of the utterances of Ra, the falcon-headed deity of the sun, the creator god, and progenitor of the pharaohs themselves.[31] Ra shone forth the Truth by means of his sacred speech: pronouncements which were recorded in hieroglyphics (a word that literally translates to "sacred carvings") by his royal scribe, the sometimes ibis-headed and sometimes baboon-headed god Thoth.[32]

Figure 1.3 and 1.4 Illustrations of Thoth in two guises: Thoth illustration from Pantheon Egyptien (1823-1825) by Leon Jean Joseph Dubois (1780-1846) and Cynocephalus, emblem of Thoth illustration from Pantheon Egyptien (1823-1825) by Leon Jean Joseph Dubois (1780-1846).

Also like the Mesopotamians, the Egyptians considered language not only to be the script that detailed every human's fate but held that it structured human reality itself and "was basic to the nature of life."[33] A prayer to Thoth in the *Book of the Dead* offers a vision of holy writing as creating and constituting the human self:

---

31 George Hart. *Routledge Dictionary of Egyptian Gods and Goddesses*, 2nd ed. (London: Routledge, 2005), 133.

32 The Egyptians saw baboons as being intelligent and capable of writing. See Ernest Cushing Richardson, *Some Old Egyptian Librarians* (Berkeley, CA: Peacock Press, 1964), 20.

33 Drogin, *Biblioclasm*, 13.

> Hail Thoth, architect of truth, give me words of power that I may form the characters of my own evolution. I stand before the masters who witnessed the genesis, who were the authors of their own forms, who rolled into being, who walked the dark circuitous passages of their own becoming, who saw with their eyes their destinies and the shapes of things to come.[34]

The Egyptians worshiped Thoth—with whom they would later come to identify the Mesopotamian Nabû and the Greek god Hermes through cross-cultural exchange—[35] as the god and patron of writing and scribes, and they recognized his heavenly wife Seshat as the corresponding patron goddess of these same things. Illustrating both his own power and, by association, the elevated position of the literate in Egyptian society, Thoth proclaimed in the *Book of the Dead* (Theban Recension):

> I am Thoth, the perfect scribe, whose hands are pure, the lord of the two horns, who maketh iniquity [to be destroyed], the scribe of right and truth, who abominateth sin. Behold, he is the writing-reed of the god Nebertcher [Ra], lord of laws, who giveth forth the speech of wisdom and understanding, whose words have dominion over the two lands.[36]

As with the Mesopotamian scribe and the goddess Nisaba, the Egyptian scribe might be seen as a direct conduit for celestial authority. Thoth's influence would extend beyond the Egyptians. The Greek historian Philo of Byblos, for example, attributed the Phoenicians' creation of their proto-alphabet to the god.[37]

The Divine Collection of Documents

For these ancient civilizations, the sacred had a definite material constitution and form, and this conception of reality would continue to hold sway in the West throughout the Greco-Roman period and into late antiquity. To some degree, this material nature of the gods

---

34 Normandi Ellis, trans., *Awakening Osiris: The Egyptian Book of the Dead* (Grand Rapids, MI: Phanes Press. 1988), 101-102.

35 Richardson, *Some Old Egyptian Librarians*, 13.

36 E.A. Wallis Budge, trans., *The Book of the Dead: The Chapters of Coming Forth By Day* (London: Kegan Paul, Trench, Trubner & Co., 1898), 341.

37 Eusebius, *Preparation for the Gospel*, 9.

remains to the present day. Witness, for example, the concept of the transubstantiation of Christ, the veneration of icons in the Greek Orthodox Christian Church, the Shinto kami, and the offering of physical sacrifices in faiths like Voudon and Santería.

For the Mesopotamians and Egyptians, writing was viewed both as recorded evidence of the sacred and as a tool for demonstrating and asserting the authority of the gods and their earthly peers—the kings and pharaohs. The physical book, the receptacle in which the script was compiled, might itself become a sacred artifact. For the Egyptians, a sacred book represented "order, unity and perfection."[38] Writing, however, could be much more than an artifact deemed sacred merely by association to the gods. Writing could also be, and this was especially the case for the Egyptians, worshipped as a god itself.

Physical objects *were the gods themselves*, substantiating their essences or geniuses. They were tied to place with the temples, which were not seen as merely representations of celestial abodes or places to provide obeisance but as the actual earthly homes where a god like Nabû "lived in the temple sanctuary with his family."[39] Dunand and Coche wrote that, for the Egyptians, the gods were rooted spatially in specific places, and that to

> [...] misapprehend the nature of an Egyptian temple is to misunderstand its role and function. It cannot be compared to a synagogue, a church, a mosque, or a Hindu temple. It was not a place of assembly where the community of the faithful came to proclaim its faith, to pray and praise its unique and unrepresentable god, to commemorate ritually the sacrifice of Jesus, or to make offerings to its gods of Brahmanic origin. Moreover, in Egypt, no one was ever required to make a declaration of faith, and it was a specialist, an indispensable intervener, who had the job making the offerings within the temple. A temple was not a place where assembled people proclaimed the existence of the divine, but rather the place where the divine was

---

[38] Carl Olson, "The Sacred Book," in *The Book: A Global History*, ed. Michael F. Suarez, S.J. Woudhuysen, and H.R. Woudhuysen (Oxford: Oxford University Press, 2013), 19.

[39] Oppenheim, *Ancient Mesopotamia*, 186.

rooted and manifested itself directly and visibly on earth, its permanent receptacle and thus itself divine.[40]

The holy statuary of the gods or goddesses was cared for by religious personnel as if it was a living thing. Among the Mesopotamians, access to the chambers of the temple where the statues sat was often restricted to only the highest-ranking religious functionaries;[41] indeed, it would be gravely insulting for members of the rabble to disturb a god's reverie. Priests and priestesses were even responsible for feeding the statues two meals a day.[42]

Material writing shared directly in the divine, perhaps even more so for the Egyptians than it did for the Mesopotamians. Writing, for the former, was synonymous with the gods and worshipped accordingly. Richardson wrote that Thoth "factually is writing [...] Thoth is the moon in nature, writing (or expression) in human affairs, and creator and regulator in the religious world because expression is creation."[43] During the earliest period of Egyptian recorded history, Richardson said, there is evidence that the "holy of holies" found at the heart of the Egyptian temple may well have been a chest of books, and that the temple priests would address their prayers directly to these caches of documents.[44] The writings themselves, he contended, "were the real god. They constituted his person. When the god was carried in the procession, it was his words not his statue which was carried."[45] Furthermore, the sacred book, just like the anthropomorphic or zoomorphic gods, possessed the power to control and transform humanity.[46]

If the inscribed words were the emanations of the god or even the god itself, and if physical objects like statues and papyri might become an object of worship, then it seems natural that the physical location of the

---

40   Francoise Dunand and Christiane Zivie Coche, *Gods and Men in Egypt: 3000 BCE to 395 CE* (Ithaca, NY: Cornell University Press, 2004), 83.

41   Heather D. Baker, "From Street Altar to Palace: Reading the Built Environment of Urban Babylonia," in *The Oxford Handbook of Cuneiform Culture*, ed. Karen Radner and Eleanor Robson (Oxford: Oxford University Press, 2011), 544.

42   Schneider, *Introduction to Ancient Mesopotamian Religion*, 103.

43   Richardson, *Some Old Egyptian Librarians*, 61.

44   Richardson, 73.

45   Richardson, 79.

46   Olson, "The Sacred Book," 19.

physical objects qua god was destined to become a sacred space, what Mircea Eliade described as "the only real and real-ly existing space" that "ontologically founds the world" by establishing a fixed point of Truth for people to orient themselves too.[47] It takes no great intellectual leap to see how, just as inscribed words would become holy, *organized collections* of "divine" inscribed words, whether those documents reflected the stability of the universe, were worshipped in their own right, or both, might also become closely associated with the supernatural. By virtue of either their intimate relationship to the gods and/or due to some inherent divine status of its own, a collection of books might be said to transform its immediate surroundings, to be, in Eliade's words, "an irruption of the sacred that results in detaching a territory from the surrounding cosmic milieu and making it qualitatively different."[48] The information institution itself becomes a sacred space because it is a temple housing these collections of "hierophantic" documents. Writing on the religious orientation of ancient libraries, Gerald E. Max saw the library as religious institution as a means by which political relationships, identities, and ideologies are constructed and maintained:

> Above all, the part played by religion in the history of both education and libraries is especially significant. The purpose of all rites and ceremonies is basically that of communication; both on the phylogenetic level in the animal world and on the cultural level among men, ritual and recorded tradition, the forces by which tribes and nations are held together and given a continuing and dominant personality. The written word wields a magic power over the populace, both in primitive terms and to some extent today also; and the leaders of the tribe or nation a common focus in some sacred grove, temple oracle, or church. It is thus no accident that such places should become the centers of recorded tradition that almost all institutional libraries in early times should be associated with temples.[49]

Until the European Enlightenment, to enter a library was to enter either the home of the god or the home of the ruler who might themselves be considered a god, avatar of a god, demi-god, or, at the least,

---

47 Mircea Eliade, *The Sacred and the Profane: The Nature of Religion*, trans. Willard R. Trask (San Diego, CA: Harcourt, 1957), 20-21.

48 Eliade, 26.

49 Max, "Ancient Near East," 399.

the home or property of a god's chief representative on Earth. Whatever the case, the Serapian ideological plexus (SIP) is a knot worth untangling. The following two sections of this chapter look first at the Mesopotamian proto-libraries and then at their pre-Hellenistic Egyptian counterparts. This is done for the purpose of understanding the development between the ideological knot's three elements—a relationship that would serve as a basic criterion for all "official" information organizations that followed.

The Mesopotamian Proto-libraries

It would be presumptuous to conclude that the Sumerians (c. 3350–c. 1900 BCE), a culture that is many times also credited with founding the earliest known civilization, invented writing. Nevertheless, the earliest evidence of recorded language that may truly be called writing (as opposed to being simply pictograms) comes from Sumerian archaeological digs, with caches of proto-cuneiform tablets being discovered in predynastic Late Uruk period archaeological sites dating to approximately 3200 BCE. This proto-cuneiform script would develop into the

Figure 1.5   Photo of Sumerian cuneiform clay tablet

cuneiform script proper, a complex system of ideograms (characters symbolizing ideas) and syllabograms (characters representing individual syllables). There were well over a thousand of these cuneiform characters, many of which possess multiple possible meanings. The same Sumerian word, in fact, might be written in several different ways using various combinations of characters. So why did the Sumerians develop their written language, go to great lengths to inscribe it on clay and other media, and organize it into collections? Posner described the Sumerians as a "a gifted people endowed with a remarkable talent for organization and a sense of orderliness that approached a national characteristic."[50] They were a pragmatic people and their development of written language came about as a necessary tool for the organization and administration of their complex civilization, leading Oppenheim to conclude that the "very invention of writing owes its existence to the needs of bureaucracy."[51] The Neolithic Mesopotamians had begun developing the rudiments of their text as early as 8000 BCE with the development of inscribed clay accounting tokens meant for economic record keeping,[52] and this passion for preserving the evidence of business transactions would, with the Sumerians, eventually lead to the development of proto-libraries dedicated primarily to providing access to these records.

The oldest evidence for a Sumerian temple proto-library, known as an *e dub ba* ("tablet house") in Sumerian,[53] was discovered in the ruins of the temple in Uruk, located in southern Mesopotamia and dating to around 3100 BCE,[54] making the oldest known collections of writing not much younger than the earliest known proto-cuneiform inscriptions. Evidence for Sumerian proto-libraries have been found throughout Sumerian archaeological sites including those at Ur, Lagash, and Kish.

The Sumerians' economic orientation—it is estimated that more than 90% of the recovered Bronze and Iron Age Mesopotamian items relate

---

50 Posner, *Archives of the Ancient World*, 23-24.

51 A. Leo Oppenheim, "The Position of the Intellectual in Mesopotamian Society," *Daedalus* 104, no. 2 (Spring, 1975): 39.

52 Denise Schmandt-Besserat, *How Writing Came About* (Austin, TX: University of Texas Press, 1996), 29-31.

53 Weitmeyer, "Archive and Library Technique in Ancient Mesopotamia," 214.

54 Weitmeyer, 224-25.

Figure 1.6 Sumerian clay counting tokens

directly to economic activity and business transactions —[55] as well as their cultural practices, literary, and artistic forms, became implanted in the post-Sumerian civilizations of the Fertile Crescent and the Levant. Indeed, the Mesopotamian civilizations that followed, namely the Akkadian, Assyrian, and Babylonian, looked to Sumer as a sort of cultural Prometheus. The Sumerian language would serve as the "classical" written language of the ancient Near East for thousands of years, filling much the same purpose that Latin did in western Europe during the Middle Ages, used by both contemporaneous and post-Sumerian civilizations to record religious and scientific knowledge.

In addition to keeping the Sumerian language alive for millennia, the Mesopotamian civilizations which followed Sumer adopted many of the Sumerian scribes' tools, including their cuneiform writing technology. The vast influence of Sumer is evidenced by the hundreds of thousands of baked clay tablets created by the Bronze and Iron Age

---

55 Rod Barker, "Ancient Libraries: The Early Evolution of Cataloging and Finding Tools," *Cataloguing Australia* 24, no. 1/2, (1998): 3.

Mesopotamian civilizations discovered thus far.[56] These successor civilizations modified the Sumerian's symbol system for use in recording their own languages. Most notable among these adoptions is Akkadian, a script which served as the *lingua franca* for business transactions and diplomacy in the Near East during most of the Bronze Age. In addition to adopting and modifying the Sumerian script, the many heirs to Sumer took their predecessor's approach to organizing their documents. And although there is no recorded evidence of any Sumerian "library philosophy" per se beyond the implicit understanding that the documents were to be organized for the purpose of maintaining the "stream of tradition" and the peaceful continuation of society, the basic techniques and technologies that the culture developed, such as record-level metadata and collection catalogs have been used up to the present day.[57] Further attesting to the reach of Sumerian culture, language, and writing technology, one early (c. 2300-2500 BCE) cuneiform proto-library containing thousands of administrative documents as well as word lists and tablets recording Sumerian myths was discovered during the excavation of the palace complex at the site of ancient Ebla in northeastern Syria.[58]

Besides the records of economic, business, and administrative transactions found in these ancient Mesopotamian collections, the majority of the rest of the material contained in the tablet collections might be classified as divinatory texts (an important tool used for the purposes of state decision-making) as well as a small percentage of what we would refer to today as "literature," such as hymns written in praise of the gods and recorded myths like the *Epic of Gilgamesh*, the *Epic of Zu*, and the *Myth of Adapa*. It is important to note that the earliest Mesopotamian texts to be classified as literature were explicitly related to religion,[59] and that this orientation would remain a defining characteristic of literature throughout ancient Mesopotamian history. This orientation of Mesopotamian literature to the religious demonstrates

---

56 Clay tablets that bear some resemblance to the tablets of the Late Predynastic Uruk period have also been found as far away as Tartaria, Romania. See M.S.F. Hood, "the Tartaria Tablets," *Antiquity* 41, no. 2 (1967), 99-113. Neo-Babylonian tablets have been found in El-Amarna in Lower Egypt at the site of a mid-fourteenth Century BCE Egyptian proto-library. See Victor H. Matthews, "El-Amarna Texts," in *Near Eastern Archaeology: A Reader*, ed. Suzanne Richard (Winona Lake, IN: Eisenbrauns, 2003), 357.

57 Barker, "Ancient Libraries," 10.

58 Lionel Casson, *Libraries of the Ancient World*. New Haven, CT: Yale University Press, 2001), 3.

59 Andrew Dalby, "The Sumerian Catalogs," *Journal of Library History* 21, no. 3 (Summer, 1986): 476.

both the close bond of recorded language to the sacred dating back to the earliest period of human history and the importance of maintaining an easily accessible collection of material necessary for the continued welfare of the state.

The "official" Mesopotamian proto-libraries, as opposed to privately held collections, were nearly always found attached to temples, palaces, or other buildings that were property of a ruler. Since their earliest beginnings in Sumer, these official proto-libraries could be categorized as being either *princely* or *priestly*,[60] demonstrating the inextricable tie between political and religious authorities. In a study of Near Eastern proto-libraries existing from 1500- 300 BCE, Pedersėn identified a total of 253 known proto-libraries, while recognizing that potential sites may have been overlooked or not properly documented by preceding archaeologists.[61] Of the 253 proto-libraries, six to eight percent consisted of between 1000 to 30,000 texts, with the remainder of the sites containing less than 1000 texts.[62] Pedersėn classified "palaces, temples, and other public buildings" as "official buildings."[63] Of the 253 proto-libraries, 127 were found in official buildings, and 36 of these were located in temples or associated buildings.[64] The ninety-one other proto-libraries were found in "palaces and other official secular buildings."[65] These "secular" official proto-libraries, Pedersėn wrote, were ultimately the property of the king.[66] Although Pedersėn's survey covers just about half of the pre-Alexandrian lifespan of the Near East, the remarkable continuity of both Mesopotamian and Egyptian cultures suggests that this state of affairs likely remained consistent throughout the Bronze and early Iron Ages.

The differentiation between princely and priestly proto-libraries seen among the Mesopotamians would serve as the basic division of official information institutions until the modern age. But, while this

---

60 E. Jiménez. "Cities and Libraries," in *Cuneiform Commentaries Project*, ed. E. Frahm, E. Jiménez, M. Frazer, and K. Wagensonner, 2013-2021, https://ccp.yale.edu/introduction/cities-and-libraries.

61 Olof Pedersėn, *Archives and Libraries in the Ancient Near East: 1500-300 B.C.* (Bethesda: MD: CDL Press, 1998), 238.

62 Pedersėn, 244-245.

63 Pedersėn, 258.

64 Pedersėn, 261.

65 Pedersėn, 262.

66 Pedersėn, 265.

distinction appears on first sight to be a binary means of classification, in the ancient world, there is little appreciable difference between these two types of institution. Both the princely and priestly proto-libraries served both government administrative and religious functions simultaneously. The former was established by a ruler to serve the state and were typically located within palaces or in the vicinity of palaces. The latter served religious cults and were located within temples or in the vicinity of temples. However, when one considers that the ruler of the ancient Mesopotamian state or empire was, in fact, the ultimate mortal representative of the gods, and that they were sometimes even worshipped as deities themselves (as was also the case with the Egyptian and Greek pharaohs), it is arguable that the princely proto-libraries were in the same instance priestly proto-libraries, and it is equally possible to contend that the priestly proto-libraries ultimately served the interests of the state.

De Vleeschauwer confidently wrote that "Every temple was a place of sacrifice, a school, and an economic domain."[67] Indeed, the Mesopotamian temples were powerful politico-economic entities that were substantial actors within the economy of the state. Jursa noted, for instance, that the temples of the Neo-Babylonian era (seventh through sixth century BCE) might have thousands of dependents.[68] There is also evidence of interaction between the palaces and temples. The Mesopotamian kings, according to de Vleeschauwer, could and would draw upon the resources of the temples in terms of both written and human resources.[69] The temple schools, scriptoria, and proto-libraries also served as training grounds for administrative officials throughout the Near East. Finally, there was also little differentiation between the princely and priestly nature within the administrative structure of the temple when considering who held on to the reins of power. For example, within the Neo-Babylonian empire, temple priests usually came from what Jursa termed "'prebendary' or priestly families" and governed the institutions with secular royal officials.[70] Because of this

---

67   H.J. de Vleeschauwer, "History of the Western Library: History of the Library in Antiquity," *Mousaion*, (Pretoria: University of South Africa, 1963), 1:9.

68   Michael Jursa, "Chapter 9: Cuneiform Writing in Neo-Babylonian Temple Communities," in *The Oxford Handbook of Cuneiform Culture*, ed. Karen Radner and Eleanor Robson (Oxford: Oxford University Press, 2011), 184-185.

69   de Vleeschauwer, "History of the Western Library," 1:15.

70   Jursa, "Chapter 9," 187.

blurring of lines between prince and priest, it is not surprising to find that the temple proto-library collections served a fundamentally utilitarian nature of cultural and political maintenance.[71] All official Mesopotamian proto-libraries essentially had the same interlocking objectives, to appease the gods and to maintain the state.

The more explicitly princely proto-libraries were likewise linked intimately with Mesopotamian religious life. A case in point is the Great Library of Ashurbanipal at Nineveh—possibly the most famous Mesopotamian proto-library—which was rediscovered in the nineteenth century excavation of Nineveh by Austen Henry Layard and Hormuzd Rassam. Ashurbanipal ruled the Neo-Assyrian Empire from 668 BCE-631 BCE and is generally considered by historians to be that empire's last great ruler before its eventual fall to the Persians in 605 BCE. The king took great pride in the fact that he was literate, and his most ambitious project during his long reign was the creation of his palace library, an impressive collection of over 20,000 clay tablets.[72] Ashurbanipal's Library contained the extent of Mesopotamian document types, including business and administrative documents, divinatory texts, and literary documents and, unlike all earlier proto-libraries, it is historically notable in that it was universal in scope.[73] Such a universal collection would only be fitting for a ruler that stylized himself as "King of the World" and would be a major reason for Assyriologists like Jastrow and Oppenheim considering it to be the only true "library" before Alexandria.

When proto-libraries were housed within the royal palaces, religious iconography was often also found; Ashurbanipal's Library was part of the palace complex and included impressive sculptures of fish gods (popular zoomorphic Mesopotamian deities that represented wisdom) that were likely set there to act as the collection's supernatural guardians.[74]

---

71 de Vleeschauwer, "History of the Western Library," 1:17.

72 Pedersèn, *Archives and Libraries in the Ancient Near East*, 164.

73 D.T. Potts, "Before Alexandria: Libraries in the Ancient Near East," in *The Library of Alexandria: Centre of Learning in the Ancient World*, ed. Roy MacLeod (London: I.B. Tauris & Co., 2010), 23.

74 Dennis M. Gormley, "A Bibliographic Essay of Western Library Architecture to the Mid-Twentieth Century," *Journal of Library History* 9, no. 1 (January 1974): 5.

Figure 1.7 Modern Reconstruction of Ashurbanipal's Library at Mosul (since destroyed in conflict)

If, as Gormley wrote, the architectural remains of the library of Ashurbanipal likely represent the "prototype of the style [i.e., royal proto-library] in the area at this time,"[75] and one takes into consideration that the Neo-Assyrian scribes were firmly ensconced in the "stream of tradition," holding the Sumerian culture, language, literature, and religion in high esteem and often emulating it, it would not be controversial to contend that similar features were found in both temples and palaces stretching back to the dawn of recorded history.

Ashurbanipal even recognized himself as being ultimately in the thrall of the divine word, proclaiming in an Assyrian cuneiform to his patron god Nabû: "My life is inscribed before you."[76] He would dedicate the library at Nineveh to Nabû and other gods. A colophon appended to a tablet found in the archaeological excavation at the palaces at Nineveh reiterates this connection in its statement of ownership: "Palace of Ashurbanipal, King of the World, King of Assyria, who trusts in Ashur and Ninlil, whom Nabû and Tashmetu gave wide open ears, and who was given profound insight."[77]

---

75   Gormley, "A Bibliographic Essay of Western Library Architecture," 5.

76   M. Streck, *Assurbanipal*, VAB 7/2 (Leipzig, 1916), 347:21, quoted in Shalom M. Paul, "Heavenly Tablets and the Book of Life," *Janes* 5 (1973), 346.

77   Weitmeyer, "Archive and Library Technique in Ancient Mesopotamia," 228.

Ancient Egyptian Proto-libraries

Avoiding clay tablets, the ancient Egyptians chose to write most of their texts on sheets of papyrus glued together end-to-end to form scrolls. However, this medium was expensive to construct, and its production was tightly controlled by the state,[78] demonstrating both the value and importance of recorded knowledge among the Egyptians as well as the close bond between religion, the state, and knowledge production and control. Unfortunately for archaeologists and historians, papyrus decays much more rapidly than clay which, when baked hard, has lasted for millennia. As a result, there are few existing documents from ancient Egypt besides those lucky few papyri documents that did survive, inscriptions on stone monuments, and notes jotted down on ostraca (potsherds).

Nevertheless, like the Mesopotamians, the Egyptians were obsessed with writing, and there is archaeological evidence for the existence of proto-libraries in both Upper and Lower Egypt in the form of the actual proto-library spaces themselves with tell-tale features like inscriptions and physical features such as wall-niches and other containers used for holding scrolls.[79]

As with the Mesopotamians, the Egyptian collections might be either official, i.e., princely or priestly, or privately owned. The official pre-Alexandrian Egyptian proto-libraries were attached to temples or palaces where they served as scribal schools, cultural repositories, and stockpiles of information for conducting science such as medicine and astronomy. Gormley, in fact, wrote that "Nearly every work on Egyptian architecture, however, makes at least some reference to a library, either fixed or portable, in their discussion of temples."[80] The Egyptians loved to promote their supremacy through the monolithic design of their architecture and writing was meant to "provide lasting and impressive inscriptions suitable for monuments, for writing was believed to glorify kings, and the inscriptions on monuments and on the walls of the temples were meant to impress the world"[81]

---

78   Edward F. Wente, "The Scribes of Ancient Egypt," in *Civilizations of the Ancient Near East*, ed. Jack M. Sasson (New York: Charles Scribner's Sons, 1995), 4:2212.

79   Michael H. Harris, *History of Libraries in the Western World*, 4th ed. (Metuchen, N.J.: Scarecrow Press, 1995), 33.

80   Gormley, "A Bibliographic Essay," 6.

81   Jean Key Gates, *Introduction to Librarianship*, 2nd ed. (New York: McGraw-Hill, 1976), 9.

Egyptian proto-libraries are many times associated with the famous Egyptian institution known as the "House of Life," or *Per Ankh* (the ankh being the Egyptian symbol of life), although there were many other temple and palace proto-libraries with names like "House of Books." The House of Life served multiple roles in Egyptian society throughout both the pharaonic and Hellenistic periods and is thought to have been a widespread institution, possibly being in "every city of importance" in Egypt.[82] Held to have been first created by Thoth himself, the place was simultaneously a scribal school, scriptorium, and medical institution, and it was always connected to a temple. Gardiner wrote that the House of Life was a "place of learned discussion and composition,"[83] and that the scribes employed within the House of Life possessed the title of priest.[84] There was a close connection between religion and pharaonic rule in the institution:

> The priestly character of the said scribes [of the House of Life] did not prevent them from being active in the service of the Pharaoh, and the Peteēse [high ranking Egyptian official] just mentioned accompanied the king on his journey to Syria together with many others like him from different places. We have seen how Ramesses IV used a scribe of the House of Life in connexion with his funerary monuments. In important matters touching religion or medicine the king was apt to convoke priests from all parts of Egypt, including the scribes of the House of Life, and Ptolemy VI on one occasion made a long journey together with this multitude of theologians in order to induct a new Buchis bull. Or again, the entire body of priests including the staffs of the Houses of Life, ostensibly on their own initiative, assemble in solemn conclave at a given city, and thence issue a decree. In earlier times we find the title 'scribe of the House of Life of the two Lands', and there are other titles of a similar kind or cases where a scribe concerned with religious writings is shown by his titles to have been in the direct employment of the king.[85]

So, as was the case with the Mesopotamian proto-libraries, the Egyptian proto-libraries blurred the line between princely and priestly.

---

82 Alan H. Gardiner, "The House of Life," *Journal of Egyptian Archaeology* 24, no. 2 (1938), 177.
83 Gardiner, 176.
84 Gardiner, 176.
85 Gardiner, 176

Redford wrote, for example, that when "the king [of Egypt] wished to discover the 'truth' about the gods and their cults and images, he repaired, not to his wise men, but to the library."[86] The Egyptian proto-library essentially took on the role of a composite wise man consisting of the body of esteemed learned opinion.

Another example of the indistinct borderline between religious and royal Egyptian proto-libraries could be found at Rameses II's (reigned c. 1279–c. 1213 BCE) monumental royal proto-library attached to the Ramesseum, the mortuary temple of that same pharaoh. This was the largest Egyptian proto-library before Alexandria and contained over 20,000 papyrus rolls.[87] Despite its grand scale, the Ramesseum was like other "official" Egyptian proto-libraries in terms of its clear religio-political affiliations. As with most other Egyptian proto-libraries, it was most likely run by priest-scribes.[88] In his *Library of History*, the first-century BCE Greek historian Diodorus Siculus wrote that the fifth century BCE philosopher Hecataeus of Abdera had visited

> the sacred library, which bears the inscription "Healing-place of the Soul," and contiguous to this building are statues of all the gods of Egypt, to each of whom the king in like manner makes the offering appropriate to him, as though he were submitting proof before Osiris and his assessors in the underworld that to the end of his days he had lived a life of piety and justice towards both men and gods.[89]

Conclusion

The divine origin of written language, whether it be an emanation of a god like the Egyptian Ra or synonymous with deity itself à la Thoth, was taken for granted by the ancients. In one fascinating Assyrian myth, the Tablet of Destinies was fought over by the forces of the good gods and the forces of evil as represented by the demon storm-bird Zu:

---

86 Donald Redford, "Ancient Egyptian Literature: An Overview," in *Civilizations of the Ancient Near East*, ed. Jack M. Sasson (New York: Charles Scribner's Sons, 1995), 4:2225.

87 Charles L. Nichols, *The Library of Rameses the Great* (Berkeley: Peacock Press, 1964), 28.

88 Mohammed Aman, "Egypt, Libraries In," in *Encyclopedia of Library and Information Science*, ed. Allen Kent and Harold Lancour (New York: Marcel Dekker, 1972), 7:574

89 Diodorus Siculus, *Library of History*, 1.49.

In the Epic of Zu (or Anzu), Zu, a winged storm god, steals from the sovereign God Enlil the Destiny-Tablet, which, besides serving as a talisman of divine power, can determine the fate of the gods themselves. The importance assigned to the "Tablet" (in the parallel Greek Myth of Prometheus, it is fire) underscores the magic with which these early societies regarded writing. It also suggests their dependency upon a well-working system of written communication, one implicitly controlled by the gods' representatives on earth, the priesthood.[90]

Figure 1.8 Storm God Zu steals the Destiny Tablet from the God Enlil by L. Gruner

Fortunately for everyone except Zu, the god Ninurta (himself a Mesopotamian god associated with scribes) was able kill the evil stormbird and retrieve the Tablet of Destinies. Reflections of this myth may be seen in the constitution of the Mesopotamian official proto-libraries themselves. These institutions were essentially charged with keeping sacred knowledge in the hands of the "good people," i.e., the priests and the kings. These "bearers of the word" acted as subalterns of divine authority and, as a result, as gatekeepers of knowledge and guardians of Truth. Doing so ensured the continuing prosperity

---

90   Max, "Ancient Near East," 24.

of the city-state or empire while it worked to maintain the "stream of tradition" and dominant power structures. The same general *modus operandi* is also apparent with the ancient Egyptians, whose scribes imitated Thoth and were even referred to as that god's prophets.[91] One may even extend the Myth of Zu to the present day by substituting the often-repeated idea introduced in the preceding chapter that the modern library, as well as those people who work to maintain the modern library in its present form, comprise the bulwark of modern Democracy—a simple abstraction that is depicted as the zenith of societal good (a stand-in for a god even). And, as with its predecessors, this place-associated abstraction is maintained by gatekeepers which comprise a professional elite.

Although the ancient Mesopotamian and Egyptian proto-libraries were not academic libraries in the sense that academic libraries are understood to be in the present day (that association most likely started to gel during the Hellenistic period), these earliest information institutions may be seen as prototypical, in a broad manner, of all the information institutions that followed after them. With the Mesopotamian and Egyptian proto-libraries, the basic outline of the information institution was drafted, not only in terms of fundamental organizational techniques but also in regard to their internal, external, and political power structures and ideological relationships.

---

91 Gardiner, "The House of Life," 173.

Chapter 2 Information Institutions from Greece through the Medieval Period

The priest smiled at the housekeeper's simplicity, and ordered the barber to reach him the books one by one, that they might see what they treated of, for perhaps, they might find some that might not deserve to be chastised by fire.

Cervantes[1]

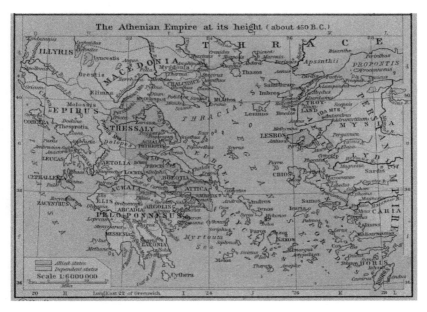

Figure 2.1 The Athenian Empire at its Height (about 450 B.C.E.) from The Historical Atlas by William R. Shepherd, 1923.

---

1 Miguel de Cervantes Saavedra, "Don Quixote de la Mancha," trans. Milan Kundera (Oxford: Oxford University Press, 1999), 57.

The Greek Proto-libraries before Alexandria

The proto-libraries of the Bronze Age Mycenaean civilization (c. 1600-1100 BCE) are an interesting anomaly when viewed in the company of the other ancient information institutions outlined in this book. The Mycenaean script, known as Linear Class B, developed from a Cretan hieroglyphic system and appears to have been used entirely to record economic and administrative transactions.

Figure 2.2 Linear Class B Tablet from Pylos

Collections of tablets have been found only at palaces or citadels and do not seem to deal with any affairs outside of those relating to the political seat of power.[2] The Mycenaean records that have been recovered are hyper-functional,[3] leading some archaeologists to conclude that the Mycenaean scribes were semi-literate, having developed their writing only to record business and administrative transactions.[4] Reflecting this hyper-functionality, religious documentation found in palace collections deals with "the economics of offerings, festivals,

---

[2] Rosalind Thomas, *Literacy and Orality in Ancient Greece* (Cambridge: Cambridge University Press, 1999), 12; Lionel Casson, *Libraries of the Ancient World* (New Haven, CT: Yale University Press, 2001), 17.

[3] The basic pattern for Linear B records found in Crete is "—Personal name, geographical name, OVIS 100, e.g., Hector, at Phaistos (has a flock of 100 sheep)." In J.P. Olivier, "Cretan Writing in the Second Millennium B.C.," *World Archaeology* 17, no. 3 (February 1986): 379.

[4] Michael Ventris and John Chadwick, *Documents in Mycenaean Greek: Three Hundred Selected Tablets From Knossos, Pylos, and Mycenae with Commentary and Vocabulary* (Cambridge: Cambridge University Press, 1956), 109-110; J.P. Olivier, *Les Scribes de Cnossos: Essai de Classement Des Archives D'un Palais Mycénien, Incuanubala Graeca* (Rome: Edizioni Dell'Ateneao, 1967), 135-136.

shrines and cult personnel."⁵ The earlier and contemporaneous Cretan Minoan civilization (c. 3000-1100 BCE), produced clay tablets c. 1800-1450 BCE in the still undeciphered Linear Class A script (also derived from the Cretan hieroglyphic script).

Figure 2.3   Linear Class A Tablet

Like the Mycenaeans, the Minoans seem to have used writing mostly for accounting and administrative purposes,⁶ although a few Linear Class A inscriptions have been found at religious sites and chiseled into religious artifacts like offering tables.⁷

There is no firm connection, largely due to a lack of evidence, between either Bronze Age Greek priests and literacy or sacrality and the

---

5   Lisa Maria Bendall, *Resources Dedicated to Religion in the Mycenaean Palace Economy* (Oxford: Oxford University School of Archaeology, 2007), 3.

6   Konstantinos Sp. Staikos, *The History of the Library in Western Civilization*, trans. Timothy Cullen (New Castle, DE: Oak Knoll Press, 2004), 1:12.

7   John G. Younger and Paul Rehak, "Minoan Culture: Religion, Burial Customs, and Administration," in *The Cambridge Companion to the Aegean Bronze Age*, ed. Cynthia W. Shelmerdine (Cambridge, NY: Cambridge University Press, 2008), 175.

written word as it is seen among the Mesopotamians and Egyptians. There is evidence, nonetheless, of organized religion's integration into the political milieu in Bronze Age Greece. In addition to the economic and administrative records mentioned above, a limited amount of evidence for shrines and the remains of religious artifacts has been found in citadels such as those at Pylos and Mycenae.[8] It is clear, nonetheless, that while the connections between religion and writing for both the Mycenaeans and the Minoans remains obscure for modern scholars, the script was connected to the maintenance of political power.

The twelfth century BCE saw the destruction of both Bronze Age Greek civilizations for reasons which have alternatively been attributed to outside invasions, local uprisings, and crises brought on by climate change.[9] For a period of several hundred years, the Greek peninsula and islands plunged into a "Dark Age." This Greek Dark Age, typically considered to have spanned c. 1100- 800 BCE, was a "time of poverty, isolation, and illiteracy."[10] Desborough wrote that during these troublesome years "The art of writing had been lost to the Greeks for nearly half a millennium, and was recovered only during the eighth century, in other words over a hundred years after the end of our period [the Greek Dark Ages]."[11]

During the Archaic period (c. 800-480 BCE) which followed the Greek Dark Age, the Greeks developed their alphabet, an inestimable advance in the history of communication and information matched only by the invention of written language, moveable type, and the digital revolution of the late twentieth century. The simplicity of the alphabet, which reduced the number of symbols for expressing language from the thousands found in Mesopotamian cuneiform and Egyptian hieroglyphs to just 24 letters, made learning to read and write a much easier task. By the mid-seventh century BCE, literacy in Greece, while still mostly restricted to the upper classes, had become "somewhat widespread."[12] Kallendorf wrote that by the sixth century BCE the "average Athenian male citizen [still a minority group in the ancient Greek

---

8   Rodney Castleden, *Mycenaeans* (New York: Routledge, 2005), 245-246.

9   V.R. d'A Desborough, *The Greek Dark Ages* (New York:St. Martin's Press, 1972), 21-22.

10   J.M. Coldstream, *Geometric Greece*, 2nd ed. (London: Routledge, 2003), 17.

11   d'A Desborough, *Greek Dark Ages*, 321.

12   Harris estimated that in ancient Greece never reached over 15%. In William V. Harris, *Ancient Literacy* (Cambridge, MA: Harvard University Press, 1989), 328.

polis] knew his alphabet, girls could get enough of an education to run a household, and slaves were also sometimes literate."[13] Classical Greece (c. 480- 323 BCE) would see a subsequent explosion of the book trade[14] and, by the end of the fourth century BCE, there were many proto-libraries in Greece both official and private.

The reader will note the continued use of the term "proto-library" to refer to the Archaic and Classical Greek collections. The official proto-libraries were not academic or public "libraries" as understood in the modern era, i.e., as institutions tasked both with preserving history and culture and producing new knowledge. The official proto-libraries of the Archaic and Classical Greece were, just as with the Mesopotamians and Egyptians, found attached to temples (usually in the town or city agora).[15] Here they housed archival records often written on papyrus, parchment, and wooden boards[16] related to the city states in which they sat. In a study of fifth century CE Athenian archives, Sickinger found that the Athenian Metroon, a temple dedicated to a mother goddess (possibly Cybele), archived city laws and decrees, administrative, financial, and land records, treaties, alliances, and interstate agreement documents.[17]

The Metroon also collected some works of literature, including that of the tragedians Aeschylus, Sophocles, and Euripides, which the temple was required by law to keep an official copy.[18] Official proto-libraries throughout Greece might also contain documents (both literary and documentary) of important people within the community.[19] Diogenes Laertius (ca 180- 240 CE), for example, wrote that the philosopher Heraclitus (fl. ca 500 BCE) deposited his work "in the temple of Artemis [at Ephesus], as some say, having purposely written it in a

---

13   Craig Kallendorf, "The Ancient Book," in *The Book: A Global History*, ed. Michael F. Suarez, S.J. Woudhuysen, and H.R. Woudhuysen (Oxford: Oxford University Press, 2013), 44.

14   Casson, *Libraries of the Ancient World*, 26.

15   John K. Davies, "Greek Archives: From Record to Monument," in *Ancient Archives and Archival Traditions: Concepts of Record-Keeping in the Ancient World*, ed. Maria Brosius (Oxford: Oxford University Press, 2003), 337.

16   Davies, 327-328.

17   James P. Sickinger, *Public Records and Archives in Classical Athens* (Chapel Hill, NC: University of North Carolina Press, 1999), 114-138.

18   Sickinger, 134.

19   Davies, "Greek Archives," 330.

Figure 2.4 Metroon in Athens

Figure 2.5 Temple of Artemis at Ephesus

rather obscure style so that [only] the competent might approach it, and lest a common style should make it easy to despise."[20] Religious documents, of course, were housed in the temple collections for use by the priesthood.

---

20 Diogenes Laertius, *Lives of the Eminent Philosophers*, 9.6.

There were also private book collections which appear to have been oriented around literary and scholarly materials. There is however, except for the case of Aristotle's library, little information provided concerning the actual contents of these proto-libraries.[21] The private collections might be owned by political leaders, the rich, or the heads of philosophical schools like Aristotle's collection at the Lyceum or Plato's collection at the Academy. Many times, these were prestige collections, broadcasting the wealth and power of the owner to those who visited. Pisistratus, tyrant of Athens c. 561-527 BCE, whom the Spanish scholar Isidorus of Seville (c. 560 CE- 636 CE) wrote "is thought to have been the first to establish a library,"[22] was a scholar of Homer renowned for his personal proto-library.[23] According to Aulus Gellius, Pisistratus's collection was also a "public library":

> The tyrant Pisistratus is said to have been the first to establish at Athens a public library of books relating to the liberal arts. Then the Athenians themselves added to this collection with considerable diligence and care; but later Xerxes, when he got possession of Athens and burned the entire city except the citadel, removed that whole collection of books and carried them off to Persia. Finally, a long time afterwards, king Seleucus, who was surnamed Nicanor, had all those books taken back to Athens.[24]

It is not certain what is meant here by the word "public" as it is used in conjunction with "library."

Since these large collections were privately owned, their users were given access to the books at the pleasure of the owners and were likely visiting scholars of at least some means. Pisistratus's collection was essentially a research collection used for compiling the work of Homer, an effort that is reported to have taken the intellectual labor of 72 learned men.[25] Polycrates, tyrant of Samos (c. 540- 522 CE), also collected a large personal proto-library of literary works which was likely used similarly for scholarly production.

---

21 Edward Alexander Parsons, *The Alexandrian Library: Glory of the Hellenic World* (Amsterdam: Elsevier, 1952), 8-18.
22 Isodorus of Seville, *Etymologies*, 6.33.
23 Anonymous, *Greek Anthology*, 442.
24 Aulus Gellius, *Attic Nights*, 7.17.3.
25 Timothy W. Boyd, "Libri Confusi," *The Classical Journal* 91, no. 1 (1995): 44.

To some degree, as is argued in later chapters, the paradigm of the academic library in the modern mind owes a debt to the pre-Alexandrian Greek temple collections, as well as the Mesopotamian and Egyptian proto-libraries that preceded and existed side-by-side with them. All of these proto-libraries may be seen as being cut from similar cloth; they were organs of institutionalized religious ideology used to cement a cultural, political, and economic "stream of tradition" that ensured the continuation of the status quo and the established network of power relations within the society. The Archaic and Classical Greek temple collections are notable, however, in that the increased literacy rates among the Greeks resulted in the weakening of the tight relationship between literacy and the priesthood—many more people, even non-elites, were able to read and write. The stream of tradition, in a sense, had become less focused on preserving a literate class of elite information gatekeepers, being centered instead on preserving the ideological integrity of the polis. As one might expect to happen with a general increase in literacy, the sacrality of the written word also shifted as its use became wider spread. Although books in the temple remained under the sponsorship of the gods, they were not themselves the gods.

The pre-Alexandrian Greek private proto-libraries are likely more conceptually familiar to modern people than the Mesopotamian and Egyptian institutions. The invention of the Greek alphabet, with its ease of use and its added facility for expressing abstract concepts,[26] did much to shift the role of private collections from primarily housing archival type records and/or as markers of wealth and prestige to serving as apparatuses for scholarship. The Great Library of Alexandria, however, through its aims at universality, use of monumental architecture, and use as a tool for engaging in shared intellectual endeavors, falls even closer to deserving recognition as the first realization of the familiar academic library model. Nevertheless, like all information institutions before it, religion remained the specter that lurked continually in the Great Library's background.

---

26 Robert K. Logan, *The Alphabet Effect: A Media Ecology Understanding of the Making of Western Civilization* (Creskill: New Jersey, 2004), 4-5.

The Great Library of Alexandria and the Post-Alexandrian Hellenistic Model

Alexander III ("the Great") of Macedon (lived 356-323 BCE) founded the city of Alexandria in 331 BCE during his conquest of Egypt, after which he left to continue his eastern campaign, only to die before being able to return.

Figure 2.6 Illustrated map of Alexandria by Goerg Braun, 1575

Ptolemy I Soter (the "Savior") (367/6- 282 BCE), one of Alexander's satraps and his lifelong friend, claimed Egypt during the conflicts following Alexander's demise and reigned in Alexandria until his own death in 282 BCE. Both Egypt and Alexandria remained under the control of Ptolemaic pharaohs until the Roman conquest in 30 BCE. Soter was a master propagandist and political strategist who saw the immense political and cultural capital that he might amass through supporting the arts and sciences. While the thread of this discussion is picked up in Chapter Four's consideration of the god Serapis and the Alexandrian Serapeum as a metaphors, this section focuses on the ways in which the Great Library of Alexandria, Soter's fantastic cultural/intellectual achievement, differed from and resembled its proto-library forebears.

The Great Library of Alexandria did not exist apart from the Great Museum of Alexandria. Soter founded the Museum—a religious community of scholars and scientists (an ancient "Museum" being a "Temple of the Muses")—sometime during the first few decades of his reign. the geographer Strabo of Pontus (64/63 BCE- 24 CE) provided this description of the Museum in his famous *Geography* of the Greco-Roman world:

> The Museum is also part of the royal palaces; it has a public walk, an Exedra with seats, and a large house, in which is the common mess-hall of the men of learning who share the Museum. This group of men not only hold property in common, but also have a priest in charge of the Museum, who formerly was appointed by the kings, but is now by Caesar.[27]

Soter and his successors gave a great deal of financial support to the Museum and provided the scholars who were its members with many rights and privileges. As a result of this patronage, the list of imminent scholars who worked in Alexandria at this center of knowledge from the late fourth to the mid-second century BCE is not surprising. Among these men were the mathematician Euclid (fl. c. 323- 285 BCE), the poet Theocritus (fl. early to mid-third century BCE), the historian Manetho (fl. late fourth to mid third century BCE), the Peripatetic philosopher and physicist Straton of Lampsacus (fl. early third century BCE), and Callimachus of Cyrene (fl. c. mid third century BCE) the creator of the Library's catalog, the Pinakes. The Ptolemies supported so many intellectuals that the philosopher Timon of Phlius (fl. c. third century BCE) referred to the Museum as "the Muses' bird-cage."[28] This was both a religious and scholarly institution that, except for not having a clear-cut curriculum (although higher education certainly took place there), contained the germ of the modern university.

Soter founded the Great Library of Alexandria in c. 297/6 BCE with the aid of Demetrius of Phalerum (c. 350- c. 280 BCE), the former tyrant of Athens and a student of Theophrastus (c. 371- c. 287 BCE), Aristotle's successor at the Lyceum. The first Greek pharaoh had himself been a direct student of Aristotle, attending philosopher's lectures with Alexander before the latter two set off on the Persian conquest. A clear

---

27 Strabo, *Geography*, 17.1.8.

28 Athenaeus, *Learned Banqueters*, 1.22d.

link between the Library to the Peripatetic philosophy is also demonstrated in the manner in which the Library's collection was used to support knowledge creation.

Figure 2.7   19th century illustration of the Library of Alexandria by O. von Corven, 19th c.

As part of his rigorous method for producing new knowledge, Aristotle developed and employed a dialectical method that relied on the collection and synthesis of *endoxa*, i.e., "esteemed opinions," to act as a foundation for making scientific deductions and scholarly conclusion. This dialectical method provided a philosophical underpinning for the creation and use of the Great Library:

> Prior to Aristotelian science, the consideration of others' opinions was not a formalized part of scholarship or had any clearly defined epistemological purpose in the creation of knowledge. Aristotle's dialectic validated the careful manipulation of *endoxa* as a means

of gaining a perspicacious view of a subject. The [Aristotle's] use of his own library suggests that the methodical consideration of expert *endoxa* in the form of recorded material had become increasingly *de rigeur* by the end of the fourth century BCE. Museum scholars regardless of scientific discipline, and even if they were not performing dialectic in a strictly orthodox Peripatetic sense, were using the Library collection as a post-Aristotelian tool for preliminary analysis, abstraction, and theory building.[29]

As a tool for engaging in science and scholarship, the Library's collection of books was indisputably the largest of its kind in the ancient world; although the total number of the Library's books is not definitively known, Aulus Gellius wrote that it contained nearly 700,000 rolls.[30] In fact, it would not be bested in terms of total volume of gathered knowledge until modern times.

The Great Library of Alexandria was emulated by contemporary Hellenistic states. While it was such a success at home that it resulted in the building of what came to be known as its "daughter library,"[31] the Serapeum (a topic returned to in Chapter Four)—possibly to contain overflow books and/or act as a sort of branch library—it was also envied and aped by other Mediterranean kings. Arguably, the most famous ancient library to adopt the model of the Great Library was the Library of Pergamum, founded by the Hellenistic King Eumenes II (ruled 197-160 BCE) in western Anatolia (now western Turkey).

Figure 2.8 Library at Pergamum

---

29 Stephen Edward Bales, "Aristotle's Contribution to Scholarly Communication" (hD. Diss, University of TennesseeKnoxville,2008, 191. https://trace.tennessee.edu/cgi/viewcontent.cgi?article=1539&context=utk_graddiss.

30 Aulus Gellius, *Attic Nights*, 7.17. 3.

31 Epiphanius, *Treatise on Weights and Measures*, 2.53c.

This project was an attempt to compete with Alexandria, and Pergamum possibly even stole some of the latter city's intellectual capital by enticing Museum scholars to switch allegiances. Like the Great Library, Pergamum acted essentially as a database for engaging in Aristotelian dialectic and supporting shared scholarly endeavor. Plutarch wrote that the Pergamum library contained a massive collection of 200,000 scrolls/volumes.[32] Finally, as was the *modus operandi* of both the earlier proto-libraries of antiquity and the Great Library of Alexandria, the Pergamum collection was housed in a temple, that of Athena Nikephoros.[33]

With the Great Library of Alexandria, the academic "library" transcended the preceding "proto-libraries" by incorporating the Greeks' rigorous mode of theoretical inquiry. Although the post-Alexandrian academic libraries retained this basic function as an apparatus for knowledge synthesis and creation, the legacy of the pre-Alexandrian information institutions also persisted within them. The Great Library kept elements of the proto-library qua crypto-temple, and some of these legacies remain obvious in the Library's successors while others persist under camouflage.

While de Vleeschauwer noted the most popular explanation for the origin of the Library is the "Greek thesis," i.e., the argument outlined above that the Museum was founded by Demetrius of Phalerum on the model of the Lyceum,[34] he proposed the competing or possibly even concomitant "Ptolemaic thesis."[35] According to this view, Soter established the Library after encountering and being impressed by the great cuneiform proto-libraries of the Near East with their sometimes massive collections housed in monumental temples and palaces:

> These "charnel houses" of colored clay would have been imposing, especially in their massiveness; indeed, the impression of mass must have become familiar to them. [Alexander and his generals]

---

32 Plutarch, *Lives*, 58.5.

33 Gheorge Vais, "The House of Books: The Metamorphosis of the Library Space," *Philobiblon* 17, no. 1 (2011): 18.

34 H.J. de Vleeschauwer, "Afterword: Origins of the Mouseion of Alexandria," afterword to *The Oral Antecedents of Greek Librarianship* by H. Curtis Wright (Provo, UT: Brigham Young University Press, 1977), 176.

35 de Vleeschauwer, 177.

probably learned too, that Assurbanipal had actually essayed to gather the whole of oriental literature into his library, and may have sensed their own document inferiority in relation to these "barbarians"—their subjects of tomorrow.[36]

The "Ptolemaic thesis" holds that Soter built the Museum and Great Library as part of an ideological strategy to assimilate a subjugated people into his kingdom by introducing Greek cultural hegemony in the guise of the traditional Near Eastern proto-library institutions: awe-inspiring buildings that supported the conquered peoples "veneration of writing and the book, which seemingly appeared as a the natural manifestation of the political, religious, intellectual, and economic life of a society destined to become part of Alexander's empire."[37] This is a compelling theory, and one that de Vleeschauwer recognizes as not necessarily mutually exclusive. It is possible that both the Greek thesis and the Ptolemaic thesis describe important inputs into the Library's founding, what de Vleeschauwer termed a *Zweistrombegriff*, or the convergence of multiple streams to form a new whole.[38] This Alexandrian *Zweistrombegriff* makes sense intuitively when one considers that both the introduction of Greek culture and ideology as well as the general tolerance of local culture and tradition occurred during the process of Hellenization in the post-Alexandrian world. While the Library was something new, it was also something quite ancient, and this ideological confluence made it at once both a powerful force for intellectual progress and apparatus for reproducing power structures.

Roman Libraries and Archives

Like the Greeks, the Romans enjoyed a higher level of literacy than their Near Eastern neighbors and they also engaged in a considerable book trade.[39] According to de Vleeschauwer, Roman proto-libraries before Rome's third century BCE expansion were similar to those of the Archaic and Classical Greeks. Typically, they consisted of archival records housed in temples or they were wealthy Romans' private collections of literary material and were often housed at their

---

36   de Vleeschauwer, 182.

37   de Vleeschauwer, 181.

38   de Vleeschauwer, 176.

39   H.L. Pinner, *The World of Books in Classical Antiquity* (Leiden: A.W. Sijthoff, 1948), 34.

country villas.⁴⁰ During the Republic's expansion efforts, the Romans, who were rabid Hellenophiles, encountered the Greek proto-libraries during their Eastern campaigns and either took over their operation entirely or packed the collections up and shipped them home as the spoils of war.⁴¹ De Vleeschauwer concluded that the Roman official collections of the era were, in fact, little more than imitations:

> The Roman library is probably the least independent of history. The Diadochi [successors of Alexander] undoubtedly saw Eastern Libraries and this contributed much to their own creations. Yet the Hellenistic library remained a typical and original Greek creation. The Romans, on the other hand, came across the Greek collections and simply adopted them without any creative imagination or adaptation. Actually, the Roman library was as to its character, purpose and organization a Greek library for Roman citizens. Even its content was for the most part composed in Greek the language of scholarship.⁴²

This adoption of the Greek model is in line with the typical Roman manner of operating because, despite the Roman people's often exaggerated chauvinism, it readily absorbed cultural elements from those that it conquered.

In his *Tristia*, the poet Ovid (lived 43 BCE- 14 CE) described his personal library in Rome which, although it had probably been collected during the early imperial period, gives insight into what a private library looked like in both Republican Rome and Hellenistic Greece, i.e., a (usually) small collection of literary materials with some kind of organization for retrieval:

> But when you find refuge in my sanctuary, reaching your own home, the round book-cases, you will behold there brothers arranged in order—brothers whom the same craftmanship produced with toil and waking. The rest of the band will display their titles openly, bearing their names on their exposed edges, but three at some

---

40   de Vleeschauwer, "History of the Western Library: History of the Library in Antiquity," *Mousaion*, (Pretoria: University of South Africa, 1963), 1:108.

41   de Vleeschauwer, 1:106-107.

42   de Vleeschauwer, 1:104.

distance will strive to hide themselves in a dark place, as you will notice—even so, as everybody knows, they teach how to love.[43]

These collections were owned by elites for their personal use. The owners were typically wealthy male citizens, and de Vleeschauwer noted that the collections were usually kept in urban villas, reflecting this wealth.[44] Johnson's description of the collection of Paulus Aemilius (fl. c. 219 BCE), owner of the "first notable Roman library," provides an idea of both who owned these collections and how they were sometimes obtained: "The Roman general, who was also a scholar, defeated King Perseus of Macedonia in 168 B.C. While his victorious soldiers ransacked the palace for everything of value, Aemilius himself claimed only the library, saying that he preferred it to gold for the benefit of his sons."[45] The Roman library owners, nonetheless, might be generous in allowing outside researchers access to them much in the same way as did Pisistratus or Polycrates. Such was the case with the politician Lucullus (lived 118- 56 BCE), who provided extensive access to his private library to the Greeks of Rome who "privately repaired thither as to an hostelry of the Muses."[46]

The shift from republican to imperial control brought with it the creation of the first true Roman public library by Asinius Pollio in 39 BCE.[47] The emperor Augustus (reigned 27 BCE- 14 CE) followed Pollio's lead by founding two impressive imperial public libraries in the city. These libraries were, like their predecessors, erected in or near temples, and Savage noted that one of these Augustan collections, the *Porticus Octaviae* (Portico of Octavia), was heavily influenced in its design by the Library of Pergamum and the Temple of Athena at Athens.[48]

With these imperial collections, libraries were, for the first time, not just Greek appropriations but something uniquely Roman:

---

43 Ovid, *Tristia*, 1.105-110.

44 de Vleeschauwer, "History of the Western Library," 1:106.

45 Elmer D. Johnson, *History of Libraries in the Western World* (Metuchen, NJ: Scarecrow Press, 1970), 69.

46 Plutarch, *Lives*, 42.1.

47 Pliny the Elder, *Natural History*, 35.2.10.

48 Ernest A. Savage, *The Story of Libraries and Book Collecting* (New York: Burt Franklin, 1969), 15-16.

Figure 2.9 Portico of Octavia

The imperial library was characterized by three features. In the first place the imperial foundations were all temple libraries in the sense that Augustus erected them all in or in the vicinity of sacerdotal sanctuaries. There is little doubt but that the example of the Serapeum and of Pergamum which the Romans knew well, was decisive. In the second place they were all dual libraries in the sense that the Greek and Latin literature were separated and were kept and arranged as distinct libraries. This was simply a survival from the republican age when it was common practice for all private libraries. In the third place they were public libraries and in the true sense of the word perhaps the first public institutions to be met within antiquity. Neither the [Alexandrian] Mousaion, nor the Serapeum, nor the Diadochian libraries were generally open to the public at large. It is possible that the Serapeum acquired a public character at about the same time as Augustus's innovation.[49]

The Roman public libraries are likely more recognizable to modern library users than the "public" libraries of the Hellenic and Hellenistic Greeks. The collections were housed in monumental buildings built to

---

49 de Vleeschauwer, "History of the Western Library," 1:113.

impress visitors, much in the same way as today's large public libraries are designed to be shown off, acting as marketing tools for the communities they serve. Unlike their Greek predecessors, and like today's libraries, the Roman public libraries also included reading rooms.[50] One such public library—Augustus's other great imperial library in Rome—was housed the Temple of the Palatine Apollo.

Figure 2.10 Temple of Palatine Apollo

The Library of Palatine Apollo was surrounded by impressive columns and contained a large hall flanked on one side by a collection in Latin and on the other by a collection in Greek,[51] and it was said to be large enough to have occasionally housed meetings of the Roman Senate.[52]

The Roman emperors that followed Augustus also constructed public libraries as part of their public works projects; libraries were seen as worthy of construction as expressions of Roman philanthropy and *euergetism* (elite benefaction). They were prolific throughout the Roman world, with there likely being twenty-eight public libraries in the city of Rome alone in the mid-fourth century CE.[53] The emperor Hadrian

---

50 Casson, *Libraries in the Ancient World*, 83.

51 John Edwin Sandys, *A History of Classical Scholarship: From Antiquity to the Modern Era* (London: I.B. Taurus, 2011), 1:99.

52 Suetonius, *Lives of the Caesars*, 29.1.

53 Laura Townsend Kane, "Access Versus Ownership," in *Encyclopedia of Library and Information Science*, 2nd ed., ed. Miriam A. Drake (New York: Marcel Dekker, 2003), 1:51.

(reigned 117- 138 CE) built one of the most magnificent imperial public libraries in the early second century CE on the Acropolis. Hadrian's Library was, as might be expected, associated with a temple, that of Olympian Zeus.

Figure 2.11 Hadrian's Library in Athens

Pausanius described the building in a manner reminiscent of descriptions of Hellenistic temples like the Alexandrian Serapeum: "The walls too are constructed of the same material as the cloisters. And there are rooms there adorned with a gilded roof and with alabaster stone, as well as with statues and paintings. In them are kept books."[54]

Romans used these public libraries for study, although it is believed that books were not allowed outside of the temples that housed them, attesting to both the expensive nature of books as well as to the fact that the library books were located within a sacred precinct. One library, built by Titus Flavius Pantainos in Athens c. 100 CE and dedicated to the goddess Athena, provided instructions for its use engraved into the building itself: "No book shall be taken out, since we have sworn thus. [The library will be] open from the first hour until the sixth."[55]

---

54 Pausanius, *Description of Greece*, 1.18.9.

55 R.E. Wycherley, *The Athenian Agora: Results of Excavations Conducted by the American School of Classical Studies at* Athens (Princeton, NJ: American School of Classical Studies at Athens, 1957), 3:150.

The imperial public libraries associated with the great temples likely served a relatively small portion of Roman society, those "people with professional interest in, or deep-seated feeling for literature and learning—writers, lawyers, philosophers, teachers, scholars, and the like,"[56] and there was also likely some animosity towards the libraries from peasants and the poor who tended to see them as institutions of the privileged.[57] Public access to library collections would increase in the first century CE with the building of the first great imperial public baths, which also often incorporated library collections and were frequented by members of all strata of Roman society.[58] The Roman baths were themselves sacred spaces, being built adjacent to temples or being considered temples themselves.

This age of remarkably progressive libraries, progressive for the ancient world at least, lasted several centuries. The period maintained the historical model of previous official information institutions as being either princely or priestly (the imperial public libraries were both at once), and these associations were not veiled by pretensions of public "ownership." Nevertheless, in the same instance the imperial public libraries subverted the traditional model by making the books physically available to non-elites, removing even more of the sacral aura surrounding the written word than did the Greeks. Unfortunately, this situation would come to an end with the political, religious, and cultural upheaval of late antiquity. Libraries would, once again, become cloistered and tightly controlled.

Information Institutions of Late Antiquity and the Middle Ages

Late antiquity and the dissolution of the Western Roman Empire in the fifth century CE, as well as the protracted decline and decay of the Eastern Roman Empire, ushered in a period of political and social upheaval in Europe and the Near East that would last for centuries. This was not a particularly happy time to be alive for many people, and William Manchester wrote that these centuries,

---

56 Casson, *Libraries in the Ancient World*, 85-86.

57 Sidney L. Jackson, *Libraries and Librarianship in the West: A Brief History* (New York: McGraw-Hill, 1974), 20.

58 Casson, *Libraries in the Ancient World*, 89-91.

[...] were stark in every dimension. Famines and plague, culminating in the Black Death and its recurring pandemics, repeatedly thinned the population. Rickets afflicted the survivors. Extraordinary climatic changes brought storms and floods which turned into major disasters because the [Roman] empire's drainage system, like most of the imperial infrastructure, was no longer functioning. It says much about the Middle Ages that in the year 1500, after a thousand years of neglect, the roads built by the Romans were still the best on the continent.[59]

The label "Dark Ages" is an unfashionable and somewhat misleading term denoting the period comprising late antiquity and the Early Middle Ages, usually seen as spanning from around the fourth century CE to the conclusion of the tenth century CE, with some historians considering it to extend all the way to the fourteenth century Italian Renaissance. The moniker has been rejected by many modern historians who point to the period's vibrant art, literature, and architecture, as well as to important advances in some technologies (such as the development of stirrups for riding horses). Even so, a large portion of the cultural highlights of the Middle Ages were created by and monopolized by the elite classes of society, demonstrating a step back from the "progressive libraries" of the Roman Empire.

What is difficult to dispute, and what is germane to the present study, is that there were enormous setbacks in learning and education during late antiquity and the Early Middle Ages. The West entered into a grim period of a decline in learning that lasted "some six centuries–between the dark days when the last of the great academies of antiquity were shut down and the exciting times when the first universities began their work"[60] The great research libraries of Alexandria were either long gone or greatly diminished by the late fifth century CE, as were other great Hellenistic libraries like the one at Pergamum, the libraries of the pagan philosophical schools, and the Roman public libraries.

---

59 William Manchester, *A World Lit Only by Fire: The Medieval Mind and the Renaissance: Portrait of an Age* (Boston, MA: Little, Brown and Company, 1992), 5.

60 Willis Rudy, *The Universities of Europe, 1100-1914: A History* (Rutherford, NJ: Fairleigh Dickinson University Press, 1984), 14.

The Ecclesiastical Collections

Literacy rates were generally abysmal throughout the Middle Ages and, although they would begin to increase in the eleventh century CE, Bäuml concluded that "the majority of the population of Europe between the fourth and fifteenth centuries was, in some sense, illiterate."[61] During the Early Middle Ages, Latin served as the primary language for reading and writing in Western Europe, with Greek fulfilling that function in the Byzantine East. Education in Latin and Greek remained largely in the hands of the unified Christian Church until 1054 CE, then in the divided Roman Catholic and Orthodox Churches. Although monasteries were where most education occurred—providing schooling to the clergy, those training for the clergy, and lay people—time considerations, cultural norms, and the typically out of the way locations of the schools generally limited those non-clergy attending school largely to wealthy males. Literacy, in fact, was so associated with the regular clergy during the Early and High Middle Ages that the Latin word *clericus* (clergyperson) was sometimes used as a synonym for *litteratus* (literate), while *laicus* (layperson) was a synonym for *illiteratus* (illiterate).[62]

During the Middle Ages, the reasons for providing education shifted away from ancient models. While the classical Greek and Roman worlds viewed education as a means of preparing people for taking part in public life, and those that were educated in the Greco-Roman world were largely secular and not members of a professional clergy, the Early Middle Ages saw education primarily as a necessity for maintaining religious continuity.[63] Moore listed the methods for realizing this religious continuity as including (1) Latin instruction for the purpose of reading the Bible and ministering to the community, (2) instruction in astronomy to facilitate rituals and coordinate the liturgical calendar, (3) the provision of access to the works of early Christian writers, and (4) providing monastics with the ability to understand the written rules of their orders.[64] The age of the liberal arts education

---

61 Franz H. Bäuml, "Varieties and Consequences of Medieval Literacy and Illiteracy," *Speculum* 55, no. 2 (1980): 237.

62 M.T. Clanchy, *From Memory to Written Record: England, 1066-1307* (Cambridge, MA: Harvard University Press, 1979), 181-187.

63 John C. Moore, *A Brief History of Universities* (Cham, Switzerland: Palgrave Macmillan, 2019), 9.

64 Moore, 10-11.

was essentially over, and would not be restored until the Italian renaissance and the birth of civic humanism in the late 14th century CE.

Another setback to both literacy and the collection and organization of knowledge was the loss of great swathes of documents to the myriad manmade and natural disasters that occurred throughout the Middle Ages. Late antiquity and the Early Middle Ages were a particularly notorious time for biblioclasms, i.e., the destruction of library collections, whether by calculated effort or by natural disaster. The monastery libraries acted as a guard against complete disaster but as will be argued, kept the library in the firm grip of religion and the dominant ideologies that religion supports.

During the chaotic transitional period between late antiquity and the Early Middle Ages, large research collections were replaced by modest collections of primarily religious materials held firmly in the grasp of monasteries or with royal and private personages of wealth, privilege, and power, returning to a basic geography of official information institutions that looked almost Bronze Age in composition. However, even though there were royal and privately owned libraries, *The Encyclopedia of Library and Information Science* asserts that most libraries in the Middle Ages were nearly "exclusively ecclesiastical."[65] Despite the seemingly endless wars, conflagrations, and hardships of late antiquity and the Early Middle Ages, recorded knowledge, and therefore collections of recorded knowledge, had a staunch defender in the Western Christian Church. Indeed, the monasteries deserve a large amount of the credit for keeping scholarship and the written record alive during the Middle Ages. In *The Name of the Rose*, Umberto Eco illustrates the vital importance of the monasteries in the preservation of knowledge throughout the medieval period with the words of the Benedictine abbot Abo of Fossanova:

> "[...] And our order, growing up under the double command of work and prayer, was light to the whole known world, depository of knowledge, salvation of the ancient learning that threatened to disappear

---

65 Raymond Irwin, "Ancient and Medieval Libraries," in *Encyclopedia of Library and Information Science*, ed. Allen Kent and Harold Lancour (New York: Marcel Dekker, 1968), 1:411. There were, of course, private libraries throughout the Middle Ages in the hands of aristocrats and influential churchmen.

in fires, sacks, earthquakes, forge of new writing and increase of the ancient…. Oh, as you well know, we live in very dark times […]"[66]

Being a light to the whole known world was not an easy task, as ecclesiastical wealth in all its forms, including books, is tempting to marauders. As a result, the monasteries were often built as self-contained fortresses to withstand the hostile milieus in which they squatted.[67] It was in these religious strongholds that, until the rise of the medieval universities in the twelfth century CE and the transformations in education that these new institutions ushered in, the cloistered monastics quietly worked to preserve knowledge. Although they may not have used their libraries often to create new knowledge (science particularly suffered in these times), centuries of monks and nuns sat in their scriptoria engaged in the tedious work of copying manuscripts by hand. As a testimonial to the long-lived fortitude of the Christian monastery, several Medieval European monasteries, including Senanque Abbey in France (opened 1148 CE) and Santa Maria de Montserrat Abbey in Spain (founded 11th century CE) have continuously operated since their beginnings.

Figure 2.12 Abbey of Senanque

---

66 Umberto Eco, *The Name of the Rose*, trans. William Weaver (Boston, MA: Mariner Books, 2014), 40.

67 Charles L. H. Coulson, *Castles in Medieval Society: Fortresses in England, France, and Ireland in the Central Middle Ages* (Oxford: Oxford University Press, 2003), 84-85.

Figure 2.13 Abbey of Montserrat

The monastery libraries tucked within their walls, tiny as they might be, were precious to the monastery as well as the societies which those institutions served in terms of sociocultural continuity. In his examination of the Byzantine and Near Eastern monastic libraries, de Vleeschauwer reinforced the importance of the Christian monasteries on post-classical civilization:

> Did the monastic library have any significance for the civilization of the future? I do not think there can be the slightest doubt on that score. The Greek, Syrian and Coptic literature of the Fathers which has come down to us and on the strength of which we can reconstruct the earliest history of Christian dogma and theology, was for a considerable part the work of monks. Admittedly no manuscript of note of any size has been preserved from this early period we are considering, but when from the 8th to 9th centuries more sources come to view, they derive in the main from monasteries. This suggests a settled tradition from which existed without interruption.[68]

---

68 de Vleeschauwer, "History of the Western Library," 1:211.

The same might be said for the monastery libraries of the West as well as for their caretakers, who were many times operating under considerably more dire circumstances than the Near Eastern religious houses.

Within the monasteries, the library collections were closely associated with the scriptoria where books were faithfully copied by cenobite scribes, as well as being closely associated with the monks' educational training. The scriptoria were many times in the same room as or near the libraries, and the two units were central to the daily life of the institutions, what Horn and Born describe as "the intellectual nerve centers of the monastery."[69] The prominent place of the monastery libraries and scriptoria is shown in the Plan of Saint Gall, a ninth century CE Carolingian architectural drawing of a proposed, but never built, Benedictine monastery.

The Plan clearly designates spaces for both a scriptorium and a library in close proximity (and both are housed within the monastery church).[70] The size of this scriptorium/library combination was impressive, with the library being located at the top of a two-story structure set above the scriptorium,[71] a space estimated at approximately 3200 sq. ft. combined.[72] If one assumes that the Plan of Saint Gall depicts an aspirational model for monastic compound of the Carolingian age—and there is evidence that it influenced the design of later medieval monasteries[73]—then it becomes possible to extrapolate the importance, at least conceptually,[74] of the scriptorium and library collection to the medieval institution. Also described in the design for Saint Gall was a building intended to house a school, further illustrating the

---

69 Walter Horn and Ernest Born, *The Plan of St. Gaul: A Study of the Architecture & Economy of, & Life in a Paradigmatic Carolingian Monastery* (Berkeley, CA: University of California Press, 1979), 1:147.

70 Horn and Born, 1:xxiv.

71 Horn and Born, 1:147.

72 Horn and Born, 1:149

73 Carolyn Marino Malone and Walter Horn, "The Plan of St. Gall & Its Effect on Later Monastic Planning," in Walter Horn and Ernest Born, *The Plan of St. Gaul: A Study of the Architecture & Economy of, & Life in a Paradigmatic Carolingian Monastery* (Berkeley, CA: University of California Press, 1979), 2:315-359.

74 It should be noted that despite the grand ambition shown in the Plan of Saint Gall, the monastery libraries of the Early Middle Ages were typically of modest size. Gormley, wrote that the Cistercian order, founded 1098 CE, was probably the first monastic order to dedicate a room solely for use as a library). In Dennis M. Gormley, "A Bibliographic Essay of Western Library Architecture to the Mid-Twentieth Century," *The Journal of Library History* 9, no. 1 (1974): 8.

central role of the Christian monastery in medieval intellectual life and production.

The monastery was the place where information and knowledge were collected, preserved, and imparted in a cyclical, iterative process that worked for centuries. The following poem, On the Scribes, composed by Anglo-Saxon scholar and courtesan of Charlemagne Alcuin (c. 735–804 CE), shows the ideological importance of the monastic scriptoria

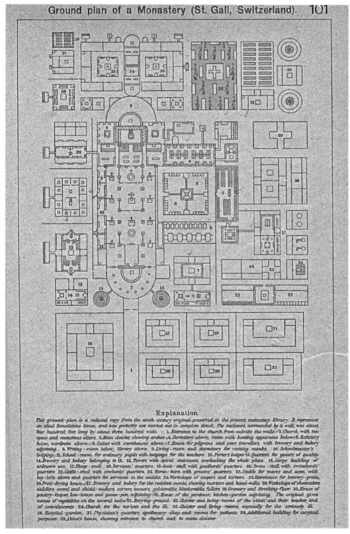

Figure 2.14 Plan of St. Gall

and libraries in the Early Middle Ages, linking books with the concepts of Law, Truth, Authority, and Noble Labor:

> Here should the writers sit, transcribing sacred Law,
> Together with the inspired Father's gloss.
> Here let no empty words of writers' own creep in —
> Empty, as well, when hand or eye betray.
> By might and main they try for wholly perfect texts
> With flying pen along the straight-ruled line.
> Per cola et commata [By colons and commas one] should make clear the sense
> When scribes insert right punctuation marks
> To prevent the lector, before reverend monks in church,
> From reading false, or stumblingly, or fast.
> Our greatest need these days is copying sacred books;
> Hence every scribe will thereby gain his meed.
> To copy books is better than to ditch the vines:
> The second serves the belly, but the first the mind.
> The master—whoe'er transmits the holy Fathers' words —
> Needs wealthy stores to bring forth new and old.[75]

Alcuin's poem affirms the underlying sanctity of what is being produced in the scriptorium and what ultimately makes the monastery collection sacred. The personal intellectual agency of the scribes reproducing the information is heavily discouraged and discounted with, ideally, "no empty words of the writers' own" degrading the integrity of the collection. Cassiodorus (c. 485—c. 585 CE), a Christian statesman serving under Theodoric the Great, mid-sixth century CE king of the Ostrogoths and Italy, would comment on Christian monastic life, work, and education in his Institutes, i.e., the intellectual guidelines that he set for the monastery which he founded at the Vivarium in Calabria, Italy:

> I admit that among those of your tasks which require physical effort that of the scribe, if he writes correctly, appeals most to me; and it appeals, perhaps not without reason, for by reading the Divine Scripture he wholesomely instructs his own mind and by copying the precepts of the Lord he spreads them far and wide. Happy his

---

75 Charles W. Jones's translation of Alcuin's *On the Scribes*, quoted in Horn and Born, *Plan of St. Gaul*, 1:145.

design, praiseworthy his zeal, to preach with the hand alone, to unleash tongues with the fingers, to give salvation silently to mortals, And to fight against the illicit temptations of the devil with pen and ink. Every work of the Lord written by the scribe is a wound inflicted on Satan. And so, though seated in one spot, with the dissemination of his work he travels through different provinces.[76]

Once again, after centuries of the humanistic thought found with the classical Greeks and Romans, the scribe was a cipher for the deity. This situation no doubt dampened creativity while it reaffirmed the bond between knowledge collection and organization and religious authority.

One sees with Cassiodorus that the Christians not only embraced book culture, but they also wrote book culture into the day-to-day operating procedures of their orders. These religious orders included instructions for the reproduction of texts and the maintenance of collections into the monastic rules of the period; copying books in scriptoria "soon became recognized as a meritorious form of labor:"[77]

> The Cluniacs freed the copyists from service in the choir, and Abbot Peter the Venerable urges copying as superior to work in the fields. The Cistercians relieved their scribes from agricultural labor, save at harvest time, and permitted them access to the forbidden kitchen for the tasks necessary to their occupation. The Carthusians required copying from the monks in their several cells. Flagging zeal was stimulated by hope of eternal rewards: "for every letter, line, and point, a sin is forgiven me," writes a monk of Arras in the in the eleventh century; and Ordericus tells of an erring monk who gained salvation by copying, being finally saved from the Devil by a credit balance of a single letter over his many sins."[78]

A directive to copy texts can be found in the Rule of Saint Benedict. Written in 516 CE, Benedict's Rule is one of the earliest monastic rules, and it was later approved in 816 CE "as the official monastic rule for the Western Church."[79] The Rule sets down a regimen for communal re-

---

76 Cassiodorus, *The Institutes*, 1.30.
77 Charles Homer Haskins, *The Renaissance of the Twelfth Century* (New York: New American Library, 1976), 72-73.
78 Haskins, 72-73.
79 Staikos, *History of the Library*, 4:36.

ligious life based on the guiding principles of work and obedience under the complete authority of the abbot and church,[80] and it suggests in multiple places that the common occupation of the monk is to work in the scriptorium.[81] The Rule also touts the benefits of reading holy and edifying books after the final church service of the day.[82]

The earliest discovered document that details the responsibilities of the medieval librarian is the twelfth century CE *Antiquae Consuetudines Canonicorum Regularium* ("The Old Customs of the Canons") of the Royal Abbey and School of Saint Victor near Paris. The *Antiquae Consuetudines* sets down practices for managing the library collection, including its cataloging, shelving, and circulation.[83] This document also outlines the role of the monastery librarian, the *armarius* (master of the wardrobe), who is notably of a higher ecclesiastical rank than the rest of the scribes, serving also in the office of cantor and leading the music in religious services.[84] Once again, the connection between the written word and the religious offices had tightened.

Religion, Power, and the Medieval Library

A shift of power between religious systems may, to some degree, be understood as a shift in the control of information and the control of the established canon of knowledge, even if a substantial portion of that appropriated learning is despised by whoever is in authority or it is considered dangerous or obsolete by whomever engages in them. Such bibliographic power grabs are prominent throughout history, whether they are through (1) sheer destruction, (2) crass theft, or (3) cultural assimilation. Battles considered the first of these power grabs in his *Libraries: An Unquiet History*, noting that the purposeful destruction of books—most often accomplished through conflagration—are the results of calculated historical revision on the part of the conquerors, where the new power holders aim to "to erase [the

---

80 Count de Montalembert, *Monks of the West* (Edinburgh: William Blackwood and Sons, 1861), 2:45.

81 Sister Mary Alfred Schroll, *Benedictine Monasticism as Reflected in the Warnefrid-Hildemar Commentaries on the Rule* (New York, Columbia University Press, 1941), 125.

82 Benedict, *Rule of Benedict*, 42.

83 Karl Christ, *The Handbook of Medieval Library History*, ed. and trans. Theophil Otto (Metuchen, NJ: Scarecrow Press, 1984), 20-21.

84 Christ, 21.

books'] authors and readers from history."[85] The destruction of the Great Library of Alexandria is one particularly memorable biblioclasm and, depending on which version is accepted of its final destruction, represents power shifts from Greek to Roman, or from Byzantine to Arab. There are many other examples of the intentional mass destruction of books as a means of asserting political and cultural domination. Battles, for instance, writes about conflagrations in the ancient world to the present: "[Book burning] stalks the history of the library from Alexandria to Tenochtitlán, from Cappadocia to Catalonia, from China's Qin dynasty to the dissolution of the English monasteries."[86] Drogin chronicled efforts at book destruction at the hands of many different aggressors, many of which were driven in the same instance by religious and political motives, such as the English suppression of monasteries in the mid-16th century.[87] One only has to look as far back as the Nazi book burnings of the 1930's or the Islamic State of Iraq and the Levant's (ISIL) destruction by explosives of Mosul's central public library in 2015 to demonstrate that the ideologically driven biblioclasm remains very much a modern practice as well.

As the grip of paganism waned in the West, pagan temples were either ransacked of their books or their collections were simply destroyed. Later in the period, the Catholic inquisitions continued to limit access to literature through force. The Church was particularly fond of burning heretical and controversial material, and they did not always show much discrimination when selecting fuel for conflagrations. Polastron wrote, for example, that

> When in doubt, the library destroyers of the sixteenth century were not satisfied applying the torch to the clearly designated titles, but would sometimes hazard a guess as to which ones needed to be burned. Their goodwill ensured, for example, the disappearance of an incalculable number of scientific books with positive or evil implications that they were incapable of determining.[88]

---

85   Matthew Battles, *Libraries: An Unquiet History* (New York: W.W. Norton, 2003), 42.

86   Battles, 152.

87   Marc Drogin, *Biblioclasm: The Mythical Origins, Magic Powers, and Perishability of the Written Word* (Savage, MD. Rowman & Littlefield Publishers, 1989), 97.

88   Lucien X. Polastron, *Books on Fire: The Destruction of Libraries throughout History*, trans. Jon E. Graham (Rochester, VT: Inner Traditions, 2004), 116.

In *Books on Fire*, Polastron references the destruction of Don Quixote's private library by a priest, a barber, a niece, and housekeeper in Cervantes' novel.[89] "Of course," Polastron commented, "this is a vicious affair; just like the inquisitors, the priest removes and keeps the best works for himself."[90] The actual text from The *Adventures of Don Quixote* comes across as lighthearted, but it serves as an incisive approximation of the acts of the Church during the Late Middle Ages. Furthermore, the passage portrays the ongoing role of the clergy as gatekeepers of knowledge who, as described above, had over the course of centuries acquired a monopoly on literacy, the provision of education, the determination of what constitutes truth, the collection of knowledge, and the disposition of that knowledge.

The second form of power grab listed above, i.e., the crass appropriation of knowledge through theft, is a grim thread that also runs throughout world history. The Neo-Assyrian king Ashurbanipal, for instance, would send out his agents to confiscate the proto-library collections of his conquered enemies to add to his Great Library at Nineveh.[91] In more recent times, the Israelis looted captured Palestinian libraries and archives during their occupation of Palestine:

> During the 1948 Nakbah ["the Catastrophe"], however, as Zionist militias ethnically cleansed the area, and as the indigenous Palestinians fled the violence, Palestinian possessions–including their books, personal papers, and photographs–were subject to looting. This looting occurred first by partisan Zionist fighters and then, a few hours later, by the "official" looters, as Ilan Pappe calls them, i.e., those hired to "collect" what became known as "abandoned property" (Al Jazeera, 2012).[92]

Such rapacity was baldly on display throughout the Middle Ages. When they weren't burned to the ground, pagan temples were many times

---

89 Polastron, 301.

90 Polastron, 301.

91 Mogens Weitmeyer, "Archive and Library Technique in Ancient Mesopotamia," Libri 6, no. 3 (1956): 229.

92 See Blair Kuntz, "Stolen Memories: Israeli State Repression and Appropriation of Palestinian Cultural Resources," *Journal of Radical Librarianship* 7 (2021): 27, https://journal.radicallibrarianship.org/index.php/journal/article/view/54. At the end of this quotation Kuntz cites Al Jazeera, "The Great Book Robbery," https://www.youtube.com/watch?v=myvobIkwkNMl-.

converted into Christian churches, and their libraries were sometimes stolen for use by the new owners.

In addition to biblioclasm and outright theft, one of the defining features of Christianity in late antiquity, and a feature that would help ensure the political and intellectual dominance of the religion into the Middle Ages and beyond, was Christianity's cultural absorption of pagan literature and book culture. What remains interesting about this transition between dominant religions is that, despite the confiscation and assimilation of pagan books, there was a general ambivalence among the Medieval clergy towards the pagan literature which they many times valued but did not respect. Staikos noted that "Christians were not forbidden to read pagan writings, but they were forbidden to propagate pagan teachings."[93] Furthermore, starting in the late fifth century CE, the pagans were most definitely forbidden to propagate their own teachings in the now Christian dominated world.

There were, however, notable exceptions among the Church leaders and Christian scholars that saw value in the pagan books and appropriated the ideas found in them to strengthen Christian theology and, as a result, Christian hegemony. These men included luminaries like the maverick Christian theologian-philosopher Origen (c. 184- 253 CE), and preservationists of the classics like Cassiodorus, Boethius (c. 480- 524), and the Venerable Bede (c. 673-735).[94] There were also churchmen like Ambrose of Milan (c. 340- 397 CE) and Augustine of Hippo (c. 354—c. 430 CE) who at times decried classical learning while, at other times, either advocated for it or drew upon it for their own work.[95] There was, in fact, a significant uproar among Christians when the fourth century CE pagan emperor Julian the Apostate (reigned 361-363 CE) forbade Christian teachers from teaching Roman classical literature. Losing access to the pagan works, the "core of fourth century culture," [96] meant losing a full stake in the educational system. The control of knowledge and culture through the control of the book remained a terrain of conflict throughout the Middle Ages, as it remains today.

---

93 Staikos, *History of the Library*, 4:4.

94 Staikos, 4:17.

95 Staikos, 4:4-5.

96 G.W. Bowersock, *Julian the Apostate* (Cambridge, Harvard University Press, 1978), 83.

Conclusion

The proto-libraries of the Mesopotamians and Egyptians operated as religio-political tools for the maintenance of the status quo by supporting and perpetuating a stream of tradition. Considering the evidence of the cultural continuity of these civilizations, these ancient institutions were remarkably effective in what they did. Even though the evidence for the connection between writing, proto-libraries, and religion is less decisive for the Mycenaean and Minoan civilizations, written language remained in the hands of the state and elites.

In many ways, the Greek proto-libraries that followed the Greek Dark Age were similar to their Near Eastern counterparts, with official collections being located in temples. An increase in literacy, however, saw the rise of collections consisting primarily of literature and scholarship, and meant for the purpose of research and knowledge creation. The Great Library of Alexandria represented the pinnacle of this conjunction of philosophy, science, and material body of knowledge, while at the same time supporting the information institution's role as a conservative ideological force. The Roman imperial libraries were novel in that they were the first true "public" libraries while they built upon the innovations made at cities like Alexandria and Pergamum. The Roman imperial libraries might, in fact, be considered at the same time the most progressive and ideologically forthright information institutions of the ancient world.

Upon the fall of the Western Roman Empire, Christian churches and monasteries became the primary repositories of book collections and works of art, both of which Black, Pepper, and Bagshaw said "served as memorials to the intellectual achievements of the past."[97] The libraries, their administrators, and their benefactors may be seen as complicit in a knowledge grab, a process which involved the destruction and theft of knowledge, as well as less violent methods like cultural appropriation such as the absorption of pagan literature by the Christian intelligentsia.

Although it may chafe library workers to liken the information institutions of any age to some sort of poison dwarf, the Christian library continued where the pagan one left off. It was back to business as usual

---

97 Alastair Black, Simon Pepper, and Kaye Bagshaw, *Books, Buildings, and Social Engineering: Early Public Libraries in Britain from Past to Present* (New York: Ashgate, 2009), 272.

or, as Pete Townshend would write: "Meet the new boss, Same as the old boss."[98] In fact, the Christian domination of collections of knowledge up to at least the twelfth century CE was nothing if not a reversal of the movement towards more publicly accessible collections during Greco-Roman period. Staikos wrote that during the Middle Ages,

> There is no doubt that the world of books in the Middle Ages, at least up to the twelfth century, was dominated by monks. Preachers, missionaries, advocates of the communal life, ascetics and others who renounced material pleasures founded thousands of monasteries following the rules of one order or another. Then, to give each and every monk a common intellectual grounding regardless of the order he belonged to, schools, scriptoria and libraries were established in the monasteries so that the superiors could control not only the monks but the laity as well.[99]

This situation, as is discussed in the following chapter, would not last. The Late Middle Ages would see some return to the intellectual ideals of the classical age with the start of the first Western universities. Furthermore, it would see religion, while still a force in information institutions, become increasingly camouflaged in the emerging academic library as crypto-temple and the academic librarian as crypto-priest, a subterfuge which continues to the modern day.

---

98 Pete Townsend," Won't Get Fooled Again," with The Who, recorded April 1971–May 1971, Decca 088 113 056-2, 1971, vinyl long playing record.

99 Staikos, 4:7.

Chapter 3 The Early University Libraries, Modernity, and the Move Towards the Secular

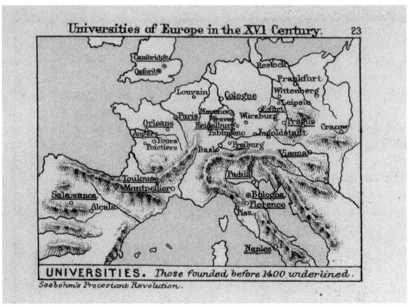

Figure 3.1 Map of Universities in Europe in the 16th Century from "The Public Schools Historical Atlas" by Charles Colbeck

Yow shall promise and sweare in the presence of almightie God, that whensoever you shall repaire to the publique Librarie of this Universitie, you will conforme your self to studie with modestie and silence, and use both the books and every thing else appertaining to their furniture, with a carefull respect to their longest conservation; that neither your self in person, nor any other whosoever, by your procurement or privitie, shall either openly or underhand, by way of embezeling, changing, razing, defacing, tearing, cutting, noting, interlining, or by voluntarie corrupting, blotting, slurring or any other maner of mangling, or misusing, any one or more of the saied books, either wholly or in part, make any alteration: but shall hinder and impeache, so much as lieth in yow, all and ever such offendour or offendours, by detecting their demeanour unto the Vice-chancellour, or to his Deputie then in place, within the next three daies after it shall com to your knowledge, so helpe you God by Christes merites, according to the doctrine of his holy Evangelistes. – Thomas Bodley "oath of fidelity" to the Bodleian Library.[1]

The Twelfth Century Renaissance and the Rise of the Universities

The twelfth century CE is sometimes portrayed as an intellectual and cultural Spring for the European civilization, and some scholars refer to the period as the "Medieval Renaissance."[2] This moniker comes as a result of the leaps in learning and artistic expression that occurred in the Western world during that century, where higher education[3] had for centuries been (literally) cloistered away in the monasteries—a situation which helped the Roman Catholic Church keep their tight grip over knowledge as well as that knowledge's transmission by the monastic rule. The notion of the Medieval Renaissance was promoted and popularized in the early twentieth century by historian Charles Homer Haskins who wrote that the twelfth century CE "left its signature on higher education, on the scholastic philosophy, on European systems of law, on architecture and sculpture, on the liturgical drama, on Latin and vernacular poetry."[4]

Up until the twelfth century CE, a typical monastery collection might contain a few hundred volumes and a palace library not many more,

---

1 Thomas Bodley quoted in *Trecentale Bodleianum: A Memorial Volume* (Oxford: Clarendon Press, 1913), 51-52.

2 Charles Homer Haskins, *The Renaissance of the 12th Century* (New York, NY: New American Library, 1976), vi.

3 The concept "higher education" itself is suggestive of societal elitism, with Cowley and Williams writing that "Higher educational institutions enroll those who presumably seek to acquire the more complex skills and knowledge of their societies and also prepare them by 'rites of passage' for membership in elite groups." In W.H. Cowley and Donald T. Williams, "The Meaning of Higher Education," *The Educational Forum* 33, no. 4 (1969): 507.

4 Haskins, *Renaissance of the 12th Century*, vi.

although royal collections would not come into fashion until the fourteenth century CE.[5] Throughout the eleventh century CE, schools operated primarily in monasteries and cathedrals. A seismic event in higher education, however, occurred with the founding of the University of Bologna in 1088 CE. By the close of the twelfth century CE, Europe had seen the founding of several major universities,[6] including those in Paris (1150 CE), Oxford (1167 CE), and Modena (1175 CE), with more to follow in the thirteenth century CE. The number of universities continued to multiply across Europe during the Late Middle Ages, with over 70 universities in existence by 1500 CE.[7]

The origins of the new universities may be attributed to several factors. One driving force for their development was the need for urban students (mostly at the cathedral schools) to band together as corporate entities (in a way presaging academic unions), much in the same way that tradespeople of the Middle Ages had organized before them to form guilds. Writing about the University of Bologna, credited as the oldest existing university in the world, Rudy wrote that life for students could be difficult to navigate, and student incorporation provided safety in numbers against

> [...] avaricious landlords, heavy municipal taxes, compulsory militia service. How were the students as outlanders, to defend themselves against such impositions? Organization was the obvious answer, for it would enable them to make use of a form of collective bargaining.[8]

According to Rudy, other factors influencing the development of the universities included the growth in numbers of a non-cloistered, urbanized secular clergy; the reintroduction of the West to the works of classical philosophers, and particularly that of Aristotle following his rediscovery by the scholastics' through the commentaries of the Muslim philosopher Ibn Rushd (Latinized in the West as Averroes); the rise of the guild system in Europe; and the increasing societal need for "trained administrators, lawyers, notaries, physicians, and

---

5   Haskins, 85.

6   Haskins, 369.

7   John C. Moore, *A Brief History of Universities* (Cham, Switzerland: Palgrave Macmillan, 2019), 29.

8   Willis Rudy, *The Universities of Europe, 1100-1914* (Rutherford, NJ: Fairleigh Dickinson University Press, 1984), 18.

ecclesiastics."[9] Bologna saw large numbers of lay law school students organize themselves into corporate entities or guilds called *universitates*,[10] and these groups sometimes engaged in direct action, including student strikes (e.g., by physically removing themselves en masse from Bologna) in order to have their desires regarding their education and general welfare met.[11] The word *universitates*, in fact, may be roughly translated as "student guild."[12] The emerging universities of the High Middle Ages, Haskins wrote, were not derived from the ancient Greco-Roman model of higher education, instead representing something new with the collectives' organization "into faculties and colleges with the mechanism of fixed curricula and academic degrees," a design which has served as the model for higher education ever since.[13]

The development of the universities was accompanied by a shift in higher education that saw the power centers of western learning moving away from the control of monasteries to that of the "secular clergy in the cathedral and urban schools [i.e., the universities]."[14] This shift in power from the monasteries and, then cathedrals, to the universities came about partly from the monasteries' inability to deal with growing numbers of non-monastic students.[15] Raitt wrote that "The men who came to study law at Bologna were not schoolboys; some of them were ecclesiastics, others were lawyers, and most them were possessed of adequate means of living."[16] Schwinges wrote that medieval European university students came from the middle and upper classes, although the former group included both the poor and well-to-do.[17] Many students were *clerici vagantes* (nomadic clerics) that went "from town in

---

9 Rudy, 15-16.

10 Rudy, 18.

11 Rudy, 19.

12 Moore, *Brief History of Universities*, 16.

13 Haskins, *Renaissance of the Twelfth Century*, 369.

14 L.D. Reynolds & N.G. Wilson, *Scribes & Scholars: A Guide to the Transmission of Greek & Latin Literature*, 2nd ed. (Oxford: Clarendon Press, 1975), 97.

15 Haskins, *Renaissance of the 12th Century*, 395.

16 Robert S. Rait, *Life in the Medieval University* (Cambridge, Cambridge University Press, 1918), 13.

17 Rainer Schwinges, *Studenten und Gelehrte: Studien zur Sozial- und Kulturgeschichte deutscher Universitäten im Mittelalter* (Leiden: Brill, 2008): 431-488.

search of learning and still more of adventure, nominally clerks but leading often very unclerical lives."[18]

Higher education would eventually be dominated by the universities. Within a relatively short time, many of the universities, and therefore many of the major academic libraries, would be on their way to becoming nominally secular institutions. The move towards secularization was due in part to the introduction of laws like the *Authentica Habita* (1155 CE),[19] issued by the Holy Roman Emperor Frederick Barbarossa (1122- 1190 CE), which bestowed rights upon the new universities including those traditionally held by the clergy. These rights provided new protections for lay students (an emerging class of scholar), as well as the right of faculty members to choose to be tried in judicial proceedings by either the Church or a body of their peers.[20] The rise of the universities also saw an increase in student agency within higher education and society. With the monastic rule, novices had been under the strict control of their clerical superiors and were expected to be ever obedient to these superiors. Within the nascent university systems, the lay students were responsible for paying their professors' wages and, as a result, were empowered to fire these men when they did not perform to their standards. There are even reports of students pelting their professors with stones during lectures if they did not live up to expectations.[21]

The modern university system, therefore, to a large part evolved as the result of a student-led revolution seeking redress for inequalities resulting from the domination of the Church over scholarship and education as well as the maltreatment of students by urban society. Essentially, the power of the Church over education had been shaken but not broken. Although the universities saw a marked decline in

---

18 Charles Homer Haskins, *The Rise of the Universities* (Ithaca, NY: Great Seal Books, 1957), 111.

19 The *Authentica Habita* is also called the *Privilegium Scholasticum*, which translates to "Scholastic Privilege." Considered today, this may be seen as a loaded term that not only refers to the special rights of professional academics within higher education, but also to their status as sociocultural elites within society in general.

20 Kibre wrote that "The *authentica Habita* provided further that scholars who committed offenses against local laws had a right to decline the ordinary jurisdiction of the town and to choose instead as judge either their own teachers or the bishop of the diocese. Similarly, where a scholar was the plaintiff, the case must be tried before either of these judges, according to the scholar's choice and at the place of the schools." In Pearl Kibre, "Scholarly Privileges: Their Roman Origins and Medieval Expression," *The American Historical Review* 59, no. 3 (1954): 550.

21 Nathan Schachner, *The Medieval Universities* (New York: A.S. Barnes and Co., 1962), 372-375.

organized religion's influence over the new institutions, they were not then, nor would they ever become, completely free of its influence. The University of Paris, for example, still required all members of its faculty of arts to receive the tonsure and take up clerical orders (albeit a non-monastic commitment to a religious entity),[22] and student life was sometimes marked by a near monastic discipline:

> Attendance at Chapel (the only meeting-place of students in different Faculties in the same College) came to be strictly required. Punctuality at meals was frequently insisted upon, under pain of receiving nothing but bread. Silence was enjoined at meal times and the Bible was read. Latin was, from the first, the only lawful medium of conversation. All the members of a college, had to be within the gates when the curfew bell rang. Bearing arms or wearing unusual clothes was forbidden, and singing, shouting and games were denounced as interfering with the studies of others [...].[23]

However, possibly more important than these two examples of lingering ecclesiastical influence—both of which would fade over time—was the fact that elements of the Church's ideological structures remained intact within these education institutions. The physical manifestations of ideology persisted in things like iconography and ritual, as did their material effects and consequences, even as they became increasingly muted or hidden.

The rise of the medieval universities can be, at least in part, attributed to a burgeoning resistance to a status quo amounting to an elitist monopoly/embargo on knowledge which had been remarkably consistent for centuries; the resulting synthesis retained influential elements of the prior dominating societal force: the Church. Although the Church's authority had taken a hit, and it would continue to lose political and cultural clout over the succeeding centuries, it remained an important influence on higher education and the academic library.

---

22 William J. Courtenay, *Rituals for the Dead: Religion and Community in the Medieval University of Paris* (Notre Dame, IN: University of Notre Dame Press, 2016), 4.

23 Robert S. Rait, *Life in the Medieval University* (Cambridge, Cambridge University Press, 1918), 82-83.

The Persistent Influence of Religion in the New Universities and their Libraries

The medieval university libraries were different than their monastic counterparts in that the collections were meant primarily for *"ad hoc"* research and study as opposed to being used "merely for storage,"[24] i.e., holding books until they were needed either for the scriptorium or the school lesson. However, there is scant information as to what they looked like in terms of their architecture and fittings. The influence of the Church on practical aspects of the library, however, persisted. Staikos wrote that the college and university libraries of the Late Middle Ages were characterized by elements like chained books, regulations mandating silence,[25] and lecterns "exactly the same as what was used in churches for mass" used as "desks-bookcases-bookstands."[26]

Despite the shift of the provision of education away from the monastics to the lay clergy, many university professors reached positions of high authority within the Church establishment. Among these illustrious cleric/professors were "Thomas Aquinas, Albertus Magnus, Bonaventura, all the great array of doctors angelic, invincible, irrefragable, seraphic, subtle, and universal. That these were also Dominicans or Franciscans withdrew them only partially from the world."[27] The head librarians at both Oxford and Cambridge were also their respective library's chaplains and were "entrusted with the joint, indeed inseparable task of caring for its books and praying for the souls of its benefactors."[28] The students at the new universities were themselves given a form of clerical status which offered them additional legal protections and status within the Church, particularly against violence at the hands of local city or townspeople. In addition, while the medieval institutions furthered the development of a reverence for academic freedom, these academic liberties were comprised of the freedom

---

24 Konstantinos Sp. Staikos, *The History of the Library in Western Civilization*, trans. Timothy Cullen and Doolie Sloman (New Castle: DE, 2010), 4:411; Roger Lovatt wrote that "For monks, books were an aid to devotion; for scholars, they were of the essence." In Roger Lovatt, " College and University Book Collections and Libraries," in *The Cambridge History of Libraries in Britain and Ireland*, ed. Elisabeth Leedham-Green and Teresa Webber (Cambridge: Cambridge University Press, 2006), 1:153-154.

25 Staikos, *History of the Library*, 4:412-413.

26 Staikos, 4:413.

27 Haskins, *Rise of the Universities*, 52.

28 Lovatt, "College and University Book Collections and Libraries," 1:160.

to expound on existing truths, and primarily those truths based in Christian faith, as opposed to basing discoveries on the unorthodox or novel.[29]

Probably one of the most obvious remnants of religion observable in the emergent universities of the twelfth century CE, and one which continues to this day, is the transposition of Church hierarchical and patriarchal structures onto the universities. The Roman Catholic hierarchical administrative schema of pope, cardinal, archbishop, bishop, priest, and novitiate is visible in the university schema of president, provost, dean, associate dean, faculty member, and student. Furthermore, the Catholic Church adopted this hierarchy nearly wholesale from the political administrative structure of the Late Roman Empire. The Catholic concept of the ecclesiastical diocese, for example, was taken directly from the emperor Diocletian's (reigned 284- 305 CE) reorganization of his embattled empire into civil administrative dioceses, with the Church substituting bishops for the civil title "vicarius" (i.e., vicar, a title also appropriated by the Church for denoting ecclesiastical office).[30]

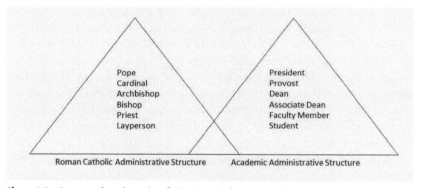

Figure 3.2 Comparative Hierarchy of Church and Higher Education Institution

This syncretism again demonstrates the close relationship and continuing dialogue between religion and secular political structures. Those modern academic libraries which confer faculty status upon (some selection of) their library workers help to keep this hoary religio-political structure alive, as they also keep alive the hierarchical

---

29   Haskins, *Rise of the Universities*, 51.

30   *Encyclopedia Britannica* (2011) s.v. "vicar," accessed May 4, 2022, https://theodora.com/encyclopedia/v/vicar.html.

and patriarchal power relationships inherent in this structure. If the academic library collection represents the cosmos in its pretensions of universality, then the crypto-ecclesiastical structure of the modern academic library shows everyone that works at the library their hierarchical position (and its attendant authority—or lack thereof) within that cosmos.

Although the names of the concepts within academic libraries and higher education have changed over the millennia, the religious or quasi-religious veneration of these concepts persisted across time and space. Evoking this historical continuity with distinctly religious language, philosopher and theologian Hastings Rashdall contended that the medieval universities resulted in the "consecration of Learning."[31] In the case of the academic library, however, the object of such continuity has not shifted from one god to another god, but from the traditional understanding of deity to the simple abstract notion of Learning itself: "[...] 'The mediaeval university,' it has been said, 'was the school of the modern spirit.'"[32] There is a notable shift from education, scholarship, and discovery as a means for the glorification of God to employing them as a way to promote the humanistic concerns that began to emerge in the Late Middle Ages, became closely associated with the Italian Renaissance, and then with the Age of Enlightenment. Although the object of veneration went through some change (from a deity to Learning), the purpose and outcome of the worship remained basically the same: to support normative social behavior and help replicate the productive forces of society. In the Middle Ages, that worship propped up feudalism; in the Early Modern period, it aided the transition from feudalism to capitalism.

The Early Modern Academic Libraries

The renaissance of the twelfth century CE was followed in the late fourteenth century/early fifteenth century CE by the Renaissance proper (hereafter referred to as the "European Renaissance"). The dominant cultural movement undergirding this period was Humanism, the beginnings of which may be seen in the late thirteenth century CE work

---

31 Hastings Rashdall, *The Universities of Europe in the Middle Ages* (Oxford: Clarendon Press 1936) 3:442.

32 Haskins, *Rise of the Universities*, 25.

of Dante Aligheri (c. 1265- 1321 CE)[33] and later, exemplified by thinkers like Francesco Petrarca (1304- 1374 CE), Leonardi Bruni (c. 1369-1444 CE), Nicholas of Cusa (1401- 1469 CE), Niccolò Machiavelli (1469-1527 CE), and Erasmus (ne Desiderius Erasmus Roterodamus, c. 1466-1536 CE). Just as the European Renaissance involved the rediscovery of the classical past, Humanism looked back to the Greek and Roman elevation of human potential and experience, a way of understanding existence that had been obscured in the long shadow of the Church. Renaissance Humanism pursued this ideal through its attempts to recover and reincorporate the spirit of the ancients into the contemporary prose, poetry, rhetoric, and art. The leaders of the movement, however, were not pagans but Christians, [34] and presumably faithful ones, although traditional religious outlooks were sometimes questioned.[35] This movement was not the rejection or negation of religion but, as Margolin wrote, "a spirit of openness and dynamism, convinced that critical intelligence and knowledge required the use of every intellectual resource."[36] In line with this new spirit, Humanism prioritized education and, despite the fact that the European Renaissance saw a "bewildering variety of literacy levels"[37] and a lack of universal free education, Graff wrote that

> What must be stressed, though, is the *extent* of the diffusion of the skills of basic reading and writing and the *expanding patterns* of their uses. That extent *should* be seen as impressive, if not astonishing, and as unprecedented, despite being persistently restricted and uneven. [...] Florentine literacy levels have long, since G. Vallani's [chronicler of Florence] time (1339), been celebrated; indeed, I believe that they have been exaggerated. Nevertheless, my demographic estimates suggest that perhaps as many as 50% of the school-aged population were in some form of education, with perhaps two-thirds of them male. Many of them gained some post-elementary schooling. Overall, adult basic literacy was as conceivably

---

33 Donald R. Kelley, *Renaissance Humanism* (Boston, MA: Twayne Publishers, 1991), 2.

34 Jean-Claude Margolin, *Humanism in Europe at the Time of the Renaissance*, trans. John L. Farthing (Durham, NC: Labyrinth Press, 1989), 41.

35 James Hankins, "Religion and the Modernity of Renaissance Humanism," in *Interpretations of Renaissance Humanism*, ed. Angelo Mazzocco (Leiden: Brill, 2006), 141.

36 Moses Hadas, *The Greek Ideal and Its Survival* (New York: Harper & Row, 1960), 119.

37 Harvey J. Graff, "On Literacy in the Renaissance: Review and Reflections," *History of Education* 12, no. 2 (1983): 72.

as high as 25-35%, with, to be sure, sharp gender, class, status, and wealth differentials.[38]

Also contributing to the increase in learning and literacy was Johannes Gutenberg's (c. 1400- 1468 CE) 1439 CE discovery of moveable type and his development of the printing press (noting that the technology had been invented centuries before by the Chinese). Bulk printing was a central component of the "general secularization, modernization, and industrialization of Western capitalist economies."[39] More people—although they were mostly still elites—were reading and more of these readers were from outside of the clergy,[40] as well as an increase in writing and publishing in the vernacular languages of various European countries. In addition, the number of literate women was slowly growing. Welch, for example, wrote that literacy among women in sixteenth century CE England was restricted to "a tiny elite, albeit an expanding one."[41] People were also reading a variety of material, with popular items among European Renaissance Italians including books meant to teach virtue, books meant to aid in salvation, and chivalric romances meant to entertain.[42]

The boost in literacy and increase in books saw a resulting increase in both the number of libraries and the size of library collections.[43] There were more privately owned libraries than in the Middle Ages, and a substantial private collection might contain as many as 800 to 900 items.[44] According to Robathan, the papal library under Nicholas V (reigned 1447-1455 CE) is said by some sources to have contained up to 9000 books at the time, although this is likely a greatly inflated number, with a more reasonable estimate being around 1200 books.[45] As noted previously,

---

38 Graff, 72.

39 W. Boyd Rayward, "Information Revolutions, the Information Society, and the Future of the History of Information Science," Library Trends 62, no. 3 (Winter 2014): 682-683.

40 Paul F. Grendler, *Books and Schools in the Italian Renaissance* (Hampshire, UK: Variorum, 1995), 453-454.

41 D'arne Welch, "Sixteenth-Century Humanism and the Education of Women," *Paedagogica Historica* 24 (1984): 244.

42 Grendler, *Books and Schools*, 453-484.

43 Kibre, "The Intellectual Interests Reflected in Libraries," 257.

44 Kibre, 258.

45 Dorothy M. Robathan, "The Catalogues of the Princely and Papal Libraries of the Italian Renaissance," *Transactions and Proceedings of the American Philological Association* 64 (1933): 142.

the number of universities increased dramatically during the European Renaissance, as did the number of their libraries. Aided by these collections, the "European universities enjoyed one of the greatest and most productive periods during the Renaissance and Reformation. They produced an enormous amount of innovative research."[46] Although the fortunes of the universities waned around the start of seventeenth century CE because of various societal calamities, the direction had been set for the rise of secularism in higher education.

The European Enlightenment began in the seventeenth century CE and inaugurated a new era of rationalism that built upon the Humanism and Scientific Revolution of the Late European Renaissance. In addition to rationalism, another term commonly associated with the Enlightenment is "emancipation."[47] Freedom was a rallying cry during the period, and, with the work of Immanuel Kant (1724- 1804 CE), the concept became closely associated with the exercise of reason.[48] In his book *Libraries and the Enlightenment*, Bivens-Tatum traces the shift of the university from being a tool for transmitting traditional knowledge to becoming a place for generating original research. He identifies the German Idealist thinkers of the later Enlightenment like Kant, Schleiermacher (1768- 1834 CE), and Schelling (1775- 1854 CE), as laying the philosophical foundations for this transformation by establishing the ideal that the university be free from the control of both religion and politics (and thus the birth of academic freedom):

> So the university was to be a place where scholars were free to study any field whatever, and their investigations were free to go wherever reason led them. The scholars were to specialize in their research and delve deeply into their subjects, for otherwise they would be unable to teach their subjects well; thus, research and teaching must be unified. Scholars were to pursue knowledge for its own sake alongside students in whom they had awakened the spirit of scientific investigation.[49]

---

46   Grendler, "The Universities of the Renaissance and Reformation," 23.

47   Louis Dupré, *The Enlightenment and the Intellectual Foundations of Modern Culture* (New Haven, CT: Yale University Press, 2004), 7.

48   Dupré, 11.

49   Wayne Bivens-Tatum, *Libraries and the Enlightenment* (Los Angeles, CA: Library Juice Press, 2012), 59.

The long winter of the Middle Ages, which had begun to thaw in the twelfth century and European Renaissance, was over.

Because of the elevation of free inquiry and emancipation and aided by these concepts' inclusion in the idea of what a university is and does, secularism became an increasingly vibrant and visible force in Western society. Writing about British Member of Parliament and historian Henry Penruddocke Windham (1736- 1819 CE), Jacob described the man as an example of an "ordinary" secular and enlightened member of society and concluded that "There were many such seekers after an aesthetic that turned away from the harshness of Protestant predestination or the Catholic Inquisition."[50] The universities and their libraries increasingly supported the self-government of thought, and they would turn out many people in the model of men like Windham. The Enlightenment also saw a continuing increase in literacy rates among women as well as publication of both educational and entertainment books aimed specifically at women[51] and a growing number of female authors who also advocated for free inquiry and emancipation as represented by Mary Wollstonecraft's classic *A Vindication of the Rights of Women* (1792).

The European Renaissance move towards Humanism and the Enlightenment's subsequent flowering of the spirits of reason and freedom did not mean that the influence of religion and the Christian Church had been entirely purged from the Early Modern university and its libraries. A large portion of Italian Renaissance collections, regardless of the type of library, remained religious works,[52] and in Moscow, like "in many other pre-modern societies, the crown and the church were major patrons of printing."[53] The reach and legacy of the Protestant Reformation and the Catholic Counter-reformation extended to the universities and academic libraries, demonstrating the enduring

---

50   Margaret C. Jacob, *The Secular Enlightenment* (Princeton, NJ: Princeton University Press, 2019), 70.

51   Maria Luisa Lopez-Vidriero, *The Polished Cornerstone of the Temple: Queenly Libraries of the Enlightenment* (London: The British Library, 2005), 7-11.

52   J. Berthoud, "The Italian Renaissance Library," *Theoria: A Journal of Social and Political Theory* 26 (1966): 71. Surprisingly though, Grendler wrote that while the Northern European universities centered their curricula around theology and the arts, the Southern European libraries focused on law and medicine. Grendler reported that the University of Bologna had "about forty professors of law and fourteen professors of medicine, plus twenty-one in arts subjects, but no theologians in the 1470's." In Grendler, "The Universities of the Renaissance and Reformation," 4-5.

53   Sergei Bogatyrev, "The Patronage of Early Printing in Moscow," *Canadian-American Slavic Studies* 51 (2017): 249.

value of recorded knowledge as religio-political capital and as an ideological weapon. The period also saw no decline in the creative use of biblioclasms in the constant struggles for political and ideological domination, with mobs of peasants burning library collections in sixteenth century CE Thuringia (Germany) and the same century's English Protestant establishment's determination to do away with all Catholic books.[54] Theology was central to the educational mission in the German universities of the sixteenth century, [55] more so than in any other European country at the time, and the German theological faculties maintained a substantial degree of supervisory power over the university. This situation resulted in some amount of censorship,[56] surely effecting the composition of university library collections. Nevertheless, such control helped to galvanize what Buzás called the "ever-present opposition within the entire teaching corps [of the universities]."[57] It is telling that an "ever-present opposition" to ecclesiastical control now existed in higher education, that it was not skulking in the shadows, and that this opposition was also present in Germany, a conglomeration of politically and religiously divided states that many historians consider having been relatively politically backwards when compared to contemporary states such like England, France, and Italy. This development demonstrates how radically the Western world had changed since the end of the Middle Ages as well as the extent of the diminishment of religion's overt power over the political sphere.

The continuation of ecclesiastical influence in the Enlightenment era universities, however, is seen in a 1648 CE screed printed in the English royalist pro-Catholic newspaper *Mercurius Pragmaticus*. The piece bemoans the Protestant Roundhead Parliament's—the governmental body being itself a conflation of church and state—control over Cambridge University and predicts its library's degradation because of a perceived imminent influx of Protestant theological texts:

> Sure it will bee a *Library* farre before that heathenish one once of *Alexandria*, or that *Antichristian* one now in *Rome*, or the more

---

54 Marc Drogin, *Biblioclasm: The Mythical Origins, Magic Powers, and Perishability of the Written Word* (Savage, MD: Rowman & Littlefield, 1989), 84-85.

55 Grendler, "The Universities of the Renaissance and Reformation," 8.

56 Ladislaus Buzás, *German Library History, 800-1945*, trans. William D. Boyd and Irmguard H. Wolfe (Jefferson, NC: McFarland & Company, 1986), 175.

57 Buzás, 175.

prophane one in *Oxford*, when all the bounty of the *Members* shall be laid out upon the *Paper-worms* of this Reformation. Truly, *two thousand pounds* sound high, among the *single-sheeted Authors*, the *Romance's* and *Gazetta's* of the famous Victories and Exploits of the godly *Quixote*; it must needs bee a rare *Library*, when it shall be said, that *Will Pryn* was brought out of *Captivity* to be chained among the *learned*, and that the Commentaries of *Austin*, and the Homilies of *Chrisosteme*, were justled out of the *Range*, to make roome for the more *glorious Revelations* of three-penny *Non-sence* in *Fast-Sermons*, and most empty *Treatises*; which may serve very well to traine up a *New-Modell* of *junior wise Arts*, to condemn all the *Ancients* to *Moths* and *Cobwebs*, till som better *generation* arise, that wil be able to understand them.[58]

In addition to outright attempts to exert ecclesiastical influence over the academic libraries, both the *idea* and the *physical mien* of the Enlightenment library remained entwined with the idea of the sacred. Francis Bacon, for instance, described Oxford's Bodleian Library as "an ark to save learning from deluge."[59]

Figure 3.3 Duke Humfrey's Library Interior 6, Bodleian Library, Oxford

---

58 From *Mercurius Pragmaticus* 1 (28 March- April 4, 1948). The £2000 in the excerpt refers to a planned resolution for the purchase of a collection Hebrew books for the collection. In quotation taken from I. Abrahams and C.E. Sayle, "The Purchase of Hebrew Books by the English Parliament in 1647," *Transactions of the Jewish Historical Society of England* 8 (1915-1917): 68.

59 In Bacon, *The Letters and the Life of Francis Bacon*. ed. James Spedding (London: Longman, 1868), 3:253.

The architecture of the Early Modern Period academic library also harkened back to the sacred origins of information institutions. The Oxford library completed in 1488 was built in a space above the Divinity School, a place that had the advantage of being "remote from secular noise."[60] In Europe, the academic libraries of the Enlightenment aimed at monumentalism.

The Library of Trinity College, Dublin, which opened in 1732 CE, was described by Craig as an immense and austere

> [...] power-house or warehouse of learning. The Dublin granite glows with no such tints of rose or lemon as one sees reflected in the waters of the Cam [i.e., from Cambridge's Wren Library] Only when, on a winter's day, seen from the top of a tram in Dawson Street across the Fellows' Garden, every pane of the old crown glass suddenly flashes with orange-fire – only at such moments does this huge building seem to relax its customary expression of measured reticence.[61]

The "Great Room" of the Library of Trinity College, Dublin measures 210 feet long and 40 feet wide.[62]

Figure 3.4 Library at Trinity College   **Figure 3.5** Radcliffe Camera in Oxford

---

60 Frances de Paravincini, *Early History of Balliol College* (London, Trubner & Company, 1891), 356-357.

61 Maurice Craig, *Dublin: 1660-1860* (Dublin: Hodges, Figgis & Co., 1952), 96.

62 Peter Freshwater, "Books and Universities," in *The Cambridge History of Libraries in Britain and Ireland*, ed. Giles Mandelbrote and K. A. Manley (Cambridge, NY: Cambridge University Press, 2006), 2:362.

Oxford's Radcliffe Camera, constructed to house a science library and opened in 1749, had a neo-classical English Palladian design featuring a great domed rotunda inspired by its architect's experience of European Renaissance and Baroque Roman churches.[63]

Although Radcliffe Camera is approximately 40 feet shy of the height of its close neighbor the University Church of St. Mary the Virgin (which is 180 feet tall, and most of that extra 40 feet is the church's towering steeple), it rivals and possibly surpasses the latter in terms of sheer beauty. Standing between the two buildings, the uninformed visitor would likely think them both to be some sort of official ecclesiastical space.

Like the European academic libraries, college libraries In the British American colonies maintained the connection to religious tradition, although they were less affected by religious conflicts on the scale of those happening in Europe (settlers tended to come to the colonies with the deliberate intention of avoiding religious conflict). In terms of the higher education in American colleges and universities, the Enlightenment appears to have penetrated only so far into the institutions, with schools being "decidedly not the type of college or university we commonly consider today. Many of them were founded as sectarian religious colleges, and their efforts at moral formation took precedence over their other educational goals."[64] In general, higher education was limited in British colonial America and in the early years of the United States in terms of curriculum;[65] Bivens-Tatum referred to the American colleges and universities of these periods as "pale imitations" of the European institutions.[66] A symptom of the anemia afflicting American higher education was the generally small size of the American library collections, and Brough wrote that the American colleges saw their collections' preservation as more important than their use.[67] This attitude sounds suspiciously like the outlook of the medieval monastery

---

63 Stephen Hebron, *Dr. Radcliffe's Library: The Story of the Radcliffe Camera in Oxford* (Oxford: Bodleian Library, 2014), 53.

64 Bivens-Tatum, *Libraries and the Enlightenment*, 68.

65 Howard Clayton, "The American College Library," *Reader in American Library History*, ed. Michael H. Harris (Washington, DC: National Card Register Company, 1971), 89.

66 Bivens-Tatum, *Libraries and the Enlightenment*, 67.

67 Kenneth Brough, "The Colonial College Library," in *Reader in American Library History*, ed. Michael H. Harris (Washington, DC: National Card Register Company, 1971), 32.

libraries presented in the previous chapter, and the religious sectarian affiliations of the American colleges and universities no doubt led to an emphasis on the development of theological collections which, as with the European libraries, predominated.[68] However, the "small library as repository first" idea likely resulted more from economic realities than from religious ones. Books were expensive and hard to procure (there were few presses in America and books many times had to be brought in from overseas), and the wooden construction of the university and library buildings made the collections particularly vulnerable to destruction by fire.[69] Interestingly enough, the American academic libraries were in one way more enlightened than their European cousins. Brough wrote that, seemingly at odds with the college administrations' thinking concerning the overriding importance of preservation, libraries like Harvard's tended to have relatively liberal borrowing policies: "Restrictive as these [lending] rules may seem today, they permitted practices which to the more conservative of that era must have appeared completely reckless. The libraries of Oxford and Cambridge still had books literally on chains."[70]

Both the American and European academic libraries of the Early Modern Period present the same fascinating contradiction: the conspicuous tension between religion and secularism. Where the sacred nature of the library had for thousands of years been taken for granted, the university and its library had become a terrain of struggle between competing ideologies that has, at times, merged. Nonetheless, during the same period that religion faced its biggest challenges, emergent capitalism both bolstered and exploited it; one might argue (dialectically!) that the opposite is true as well. The nineteenth, twentieth, and twenty-first centuries CE would see the triumph of capitalism and the realization of the academic library as crypto-temple.

The Late Modern Period and the MCAL

Beginning in the nineteenth-century CE and extending to the present day, the Late Modern Period is characterized by tremendous political, social, and technological change. The period saw the apex and

---

68 Brough, 31.

69 Louis Shores, *Origins of the American College Library* (Hambden, CT: Shoe String Press, 1966), 50.

70 Brough, "Colonial College Library," 32.

dissolution of massive colonial empires, including the British, French, German, and American. Scientific progress reached new zeniths, and secularism and science appeared to be on the verge of eclipsing religious faith. It is during the Late Modern Period that Nietzsche proclaimed the death of God and that Darwin provided evidence for, in the very least, the God concept's irrelevance. Competing ideologies vied for dominance over traditional religious systems, with capitalism being the most successful of these alternatives, both as an ideology and as a mode of production. A large degree of this success had to do with capitalism's ability to accommodate and leverage religious belief for means of its own survival and success.

Marx's most famous passage regarding religion is relevant to this circumstance: "*Religious* distress is at the same time the *expression* of real distress and the *protest* against real distress. Religion is the sigh of the oppressed creature, the heart of a heartless world, just as it is the spirit of a spiritless situation. It is the *opium* of the people."[71] Although this quotation recognizes religion as a reaction to the oppression and alienation inflicted by capitalism, Marx saw belief as supporting the system by offering an illusory happiness that distracts people from, or resigns them to, the subjugation of the economic system. In addition to encouraging religion, capitalism both coopts and sublimates it, furthering its own agenda and imperialist tendencies. Lucile M. Morsch, President of the American Library Association from 1957 to 1958, demonstrated this appropriation of religious concepts in a paper presented at an Ankara University International Series of Lectures in Librarianship during the 1960-1961 academic year. When discussing the development of the American public library, Morsch used descriptive words charged with religious meaning that allude to Christian religious concepts like proselytization and salvation while linking "a better life" to economic success and technology (emphasis added):

> American librarians have such a *faith* in education and the *power of the printed word* that as a class they can almost be said to *believe* that only books and reading are going to *save* the world. In consequence of my personal *faith* in the contribution that libraries can make to the *better life* I have used every chance I have had to persuade my own Government—through its operation of American libraries in other

---

71 Karl Marx, "Contribution to the Critique of Hegel's Philosophy of Right," in Karl Marx and Friedrich Engels, *On Religion* (New York: Schocken Books, 1964), 42.

countries, in exchange of persons programs, and its technical assistance programs in countries less highly developed economically than the United States—to put more emphasis on library programs.[72]

Morsch was referring to the American public library in her presentation, but these same terms may and have been used when describing the role of the academic library in western capitalist societies. It is also interesting that she used this imagery at a Turkish conference in a way that might be seen as proselytizing or a way to convert the "other."

The regulatory capitalism of the 1930's and 1940's was challenged by the might of neoliberalism in the 1950s, and the latter form remains the currently dominant ideological expression of late capitalism. McCarthy and Prudham defined neoliberalism as "discursive representations, and institutional practices, all propagated by highly specific class alliances and organized at multiple geographical scales,"[73] and they wrote that it is "the most powerful ideological and political project in global governance to arise in the wake of Keynesianism."[74] According to Saunders, the neoliberal ideology is "united by three broad beliefs: the benevolence of the free market, minimal state intervention and regulation of the economy, and the individual as the rational economic actor."[75] The word neoliberal has been adopted by members of the radical left as a pejorative term to describe those ideologues and institutions from both sides of the political spectrum that support free market ideals.

The term Modern Capitalist Academic Library (MCAL) refers to an academic library embedded in the social formation of an institution of neoliberal capitalism, or a social formation influenced by neoliberal capitalism (which includes nearly all social formations found worldwide). As an insidiously powerful ideological force, neoliberalism found its way into the day-to-day operations of the MCAL and continues to exert its influence from the outside through the MCAL's relationships with their parent institution and, in turn, other societal and

---

72 Lucile M. Morsch, "Foundations of the American Public Library," in *Bases of Modern Librarianship: A Study of Library Theory and Practice in Britain, Canada, Denmark, The Federal Republic of Germany and the United States*, ed. Carl M. White (Oxford: Pergamon Press, 1964), 42-43.

73 James McCarthy and Scott Prudham, "Neoliberal Nature and the Nature of Neoliberalism," *Geoforum* 35 (2004): 276.

74 McCarthy and Prudham, 275.

75 Daniel Saunders, "Neoliberal Ideology and Public Higher Education in the United States," *Journal for Critical Education Policy Studies* 8, no. 1 (2010): 44.

sociopolitical institutions such as legislatures, governing boards, etc., that comprise the superstructure sprouting from capitalism's economic base. Even if many academic library workers despise the association of their workplaces with the free market—just try polling library workers on what they think about some libraries' use of the words "customer" or "client" to refer to library users—it is difficult to deny capitalism's hold on the institution. The MCAL is, despite what terminology is settled upon for use within its operations, in neoliberalism's orbit. This confinement is ironic when one considers what Giroux describes as the contempt in which the neoliberal ideology places the traditional goals of post-Enlightenment education, particularly those relating to concepts like democracy, human liberty, and freedom from the domination of both traditional and secular religion:

> The neoliberal paradigm driving these attacks on public and higher education abhors democracy and views public and higher education as a toxic sphere that poses a threat to corporate values, power, and ideology. As democratic public spheres, colleges and universities are allegedly dedicated to teaching students to think critically, take imaginative risks, learn how to be moral witnesses, and procure the skills that enable one to connect to others in ways that strengthen the democratic polity, and this is precisely why they are under attack by the concentrated forces of neoliberalism.[76]

The ideology, Giroux concluded, has become

> [...] a fundamental organizing principle for shaping all aspects of education. At the public school level, it trains students in workplace discipline, lowers expectations, and kills the imagination; at the level of higher education, it replaces nourishing students' critical capacities with training them for careers and limiting their willingness to believe in something larger than themselves. At the level of higher education, meagerly compensated adjuncts replace tenured faculty; services are outsourced, the salaries of administrators have soared; and students are viewed as customers.[77]

76　Henry A. Giroux, *Neoliberalism's War on Higher Education*, 2nd ed. (Chicago, IL: Haymarket Books, 2014), 42.

77　Giroux, 177.

The continued dominance of neoliberalism risks further transforming higher education into a ruthlessly efficient tool of its own replication and material manifestation through the indoctrination of students into being "productive" members of society, and the viral nature of corporatization has spread to the academic library. Considering the library's role as the social, scholarly, and many times physical center of the college or university campus underscores the power of capitalism to subordinate and assimilate the "other," and hence marginalize and discriminate against them.

Because of its significant role in the reproduction of society, the genuflection of the MCAL to capitalist ideals must not be ignored. Even if the campus library's embrace of corporate operational models may be seen in many cases as happening under duress, i.e., as one more teetering domino in the corporatization of higher learning, the situation is compounded by the feedback loop existing between the MCAL and the educational system writ large. The MCAL reinforces the continuing commodification of the modern university system and that educational system's decades-long movement towards the adoption of operational paradigms based on corporate business models, a process which Slaughter and Leslie saw as emerging in post-World War II America and growing rapidly in the 1980s with that decade's increased globalization.[78] The result is universities with entrenched corporate cultures where knowledge is quantified as exchange value,[79] and the focus is on the present return on investment versus any sort of benefit to either broader society (as it includes marginalized groups) or to the future.

As stakeholders in colleges and universities, many academic library workers have not taken the institutional transformation of higher education either lightly or sitting down. But despite vocal dissension among library workers regarding this cooption, there is also a systemic buy-in amongst library workers as well as library and information science academics who either see the neoliberal transformation of the university as a positive thing, take it for granted or do not register it on their radar. This acquiescence is reflected in the academic and professional literature, even if the term neoliberalism itself is not

---

78 Sheila Slaughter and Larry L. Leslie, *Academic Capitalism: Politics, Policies, and the Entrepreneurial University* (Baltimore, MA: John Hopkins University Press, 1997), 5.

79 Eric Gould, "The University, the Marketplace, and Civil Society," in *The Business of Higher Education*, ed. John C. Knapp and David J. Siegel (Santa Barbara, CA: ABC CLIO, 2009), 1:3.

used when discussing the running of libraries like businesses or corporations. For example, in a study of the use of neoliberal terms and concepts by authors in the *Journal of Academic Librarianship* for the period of 1975-2014, Sharpe found that "Many articles used economic terms to describe reference services,"[80] reducing such interactions to transactions. Among these terms were high frequency word groups including "Market Economy," as well as new managerial terms such as "Efficiency," "Skills/Competencies," "Effectiveness," and "Quality,"[81] all of which have neoliberal connotations.

Nevertheless, the trend towards the corporatization of the MCAL should not result in the romanticization of the academic libraries that operated before the rise of neoliberalism or of those operating today that project a "traditional" model of higher education and what the academic library "should" be, doing so reinforces the "vocational awe" plaguing library work.[82] The great majority of academic libraries and library workers have actively worked to support the capitalist mode of production since the beginning of the capitalist era, regardless of the professed ideology, be it liberal, conservative, or what have you, of the library workers and their library's operational procedures. That is how capitalism works. That is, in fact, how most civic institutions, for better or for worse, work under their governing mode of socioeconomic production.

Conclusion

It is heartening to note that, dialectically, the internal workings of each of the modes of production (classical, feudal, capitalist, etc.) contain the seeds of that mode's ultimate transformation. There is evidence of this (r)evolutionary action in the rise of the early universities in the twelfth century CE and the development of increasingly secular university library collections. The late medieval and Early Modern academic libraries saw the demise of feudalism with the birth of Humanism and the nascent stirrings of capitalism. And, while the academic libraries of the former period may have at first supported the feudal mode of production and its status quo, they should be given some credit for

---

80 Krista Bowers Sharpe, "'Commonsense' Academic Reference Service: Neoliberal Discourse in LIS Article," *Library Quarterly* 89, no. 4 (2019): 310.

81 Sharpe, 305.

82 Fobazi Ettarh, "Vocational Awe and Librarianship: The Lies We Tell Ourselves, *In the Library with the Lead Pipe* (Jan. 10, 2018), https://www.inthelibrarywiththeleadpipe.org/2018/vocational-awe/.

the feudal system's downfall. Marx acknowledged both the necessity of capitalism in the historical progression towards human liberty and the benefits that it brought with it. The Late Modern Period saw capitalism's ascendancy. Nevertheless, it is the crushing inequity and alienation structurally ingrained within capitalism which necessitates change.

One can hope that, like the Late Medieval university libraries that incubated the European Renaissance, the MCAL will also be a catalyst for societal transformation. There are two possible impetuses for such a change: (1) that the absurdities of capitalism increasingly reflected in the MCAL, along with the untenability of the contradictions within these transformations, will spur a qualitative change for the academic library as well as a similar transformation in the larger society; and (2) that many academic library workers will become increasingly disillusioned with the current state of affairs in the MCAL, the system of higher education, and the larger society. A subset of these workers, the "Kynical library workers," are discussed in Chapter Seven. Although the Kynical library workers are disillusioned with the prevailing situation, they are professed and active change agents.

In summary, beginning with the twelfth century renaissance, European society went through a period of secularization that saw the influence of religion on the workings of civil society become less conspicuous. This movement towards the secular is reflected in the development of higher education and the development of the academic library as an organ of education. Higher education and the academic library would then, in effect, act as a feedback circuit to further expand and establish secularism in society. As an ideology, the impact of religion may be seen to have suffered somewhat during the societal transformations of the second millennium CE. The present chapter introduced the idea that, although the domination of religion—and that of organized religion in particular—was challenged and shaken, its influence endures. The relationship between religion and the information institution persists as the latter entity has become cloaked, transmogrified, and sublimated. While the ancient and medieval institutions essentially did not differentiate between sacred place and information institution, the end of the Middle Ages saw the beginnings of the academic library as crypto-temple and Late Modernism its mature realization. The chapters that follow detail the nature, expression, and consequences of the MCAL as crypto-temple, its place within the structure of capitalist society, and possible responses from transformative academic library workers.

Chapter 4 Serapis and the Serapeum as Metaphors

Figure 4.1 Macedonian Empire, 336-323 B.C.E. from The Historical Atlas by William R. Shepherd, 1911

There! —Behold our works! Us Greeks!—us benighted heathens! Look at and feel yourself what you are, a very small, conceited, ignorant young person, who fancies that your new religion gives you a right to despise every one else. Did Christians make all this? Did Christians build that Pharos there on the left horn—wonder of the world? Did Christians raise that mile-long mole which runs towards the land, with its two draw-bridges, connecting the two ports? Did Christians build this esplanade, or this gate of the sun above our heads?

Charles Kingsley[1]

---

1 Charles Kingsley, *Hypatia* (New York: Garland Publishing, 1975), 97-98.

The Great God Serapis

The present authors devised the term "Serapian information institution" and related terms like "Serapian library" and "Serapian MCAL" to identify information institutions that employ religious symbolism and ritual to manufacture hegemonic consent. So, who was Serapis and why attach his name to the library as crypto-temple?

The great god Serapis was a syncretic, Greco-Egyptian deity created either partially or entirely by Egypt's first Greek pharaoh, Ptolemy I Soter, who reigned 305-282 BCE.[2] One tradition holds that the then unnamed god appeared to Soter in a dream and told him to bring a certain statue, located in the city of Sinope on the Black Sea, to Alexandria, his capital in Egypt.[3] The Greek biographer Plutarch wrote that after Soter relocated the statue to Alexandria, Timotheus, "the expositor of sacred law," and "Manetho of Sebenntyus [an Egyptian priest and historian], and their associates conjectured that it was the statue of Pluto [Plutarch is referring here to the Greek god Hades], basing their conjecture on the Cerberus and the serpent [that were incorporated into the sculpture], and they convinced Ptolemy that it was the statue of none other of the gods but Serapis."[4] If the last part of the story is true, Soter's royal advisors probably did not have to expend much effort convincing him to acknowledge and adopt the new god. The pharaoh was a savvy political animal, and he saw Serapis as an opportunity to help him consolidate his rule over Egypt.

As Timotheus and Manetho noted, Serapis's representations look much like depictions of Hades, the Greek god of the underworld. Perched on top of Serapis's head, however, is a basket filled with corn.

This container, called a *modius* or *kalathos*, represents fertility and associated the new god with Osiris—Egypt's own god of the underworld—as he is represented in the form of the Apis Bull of Memphis.[5]

---

2   Even though Soter is typically credited with the introduction of Serapis, there remains some dispute as to the god's origins. Clement of Alexandria for example, credited Ptolemy II Philadelphus with its introduction. See Clement of Alexandria, *Exhortation of the Greeks*, 4. Regardless of his creator, the Serapis of Alexandria was a Ptolemaic production, and served Ptolemaic ends.

3   Tacitus, *Histories*, 4.83.

4   Plutarch, *Moralia*, 28.

5   Lauren Murphy, "Beware Greeks Bearing Gods," *Amphora* 2 (2021), 38-39.

Figure 4.2 Bust of Serapis with kalathos on his head

Figure 4.3 Illustration of Osiris and Apis Bull

The name Serapis, in fact, is thought to be a contraction of the words for Osiris and the old Memphian god Apis.[6] Among his many celestial roles, Osiris was a god of fertility and agriculture. Serapis soon assimilated with Osiris, assuming the latter's great responsibility for ensuring "the annual Nile flood and the grain supply,"[7]

Soter may have engineered the elevation of Serapis to build the legitimacy of the Ptolemaic rulers among the local Egyptian populace,[8] and the new yet familiar god served to secure Greek political and cultural legitimacy and hegemony in the newly conquered country. By combining the traditional Egyptian gods[9] with multiple Greek deities

---

6   Steven Blake Shubert, "Oriental Origins of the Alexandrian Library," *Libri* 43, no. 2 (1993): 166.

7   Judith Mckenzie, Sheila Gibson, and A.T. Reyes, "Reconstructing the Serapeum in Alexandria from the Archaeological Evidence," *Journal of Roman Studies* 94 (2004): 81.

8   Mckenzie, Gibson, and Reyes, 81.

9   There is some question as to whether Serapis was a premeditated syncretization of Osiris with the Apis Bull, but whether or not this is true, according to Sarolta A. Takács, the similarity in the names as well as the "fact that latter part of Sarapis' name could also be linked to the Greek king Apis, who died in Egypt, must have been a welcome and exploitable coincidence." In Sarolta A. Takács, *Isis and Sarapis in the Roman World* (Leiden: Brill, 1995), 28.

Figure 4.4 Pluto Serapis and Persephone Isis at the Heraklion Museum

including Hades and Zeus, Soter "discovered" a composite god that served a valuable political purpose. The god gave the Greek and native Egyptian populations of Alexandria a focal point for worship that both groups would recognize and be comfortable with. Serapis was then married to the goddess Isis, who had formerly been the wife of Osiris.

This union further cemented the political and cultural relationships between the two peoples. To top it off, Serapis was identified by the Ptolemaic pharaohs as a dynastic god to whom they traced their own origins.[10]

Soter's religio-political experiment ended up being a brilliant and highly successful maneuver. The pharaoh's innovation reaped political and cultural dividends throughout the Hellenistic and Roman periods up until the final triumph of Christianity in the late fourth century CE. Within a few centuries after the Greek invasion, the distinction between Greek colonizer and Egyptian native would begin to fade away.

---

10 Martin Bommas, "Isis, Osiris, and Serapis," in *The Oxford Handbook of Roman Egypt*, ed. Christina Riggs (Oxford: Oxford University Press, 2012), 432.

Figure 4.5 Serapeum at Saqqara

The god contributed to the "reciprocal assimilation of the value systems of the conqueror and the conquered" and helped to circumvent large occurrences of civil unrest in the Egyptian state.[11] The worship of Serapis was so successful in Alexandria and Egypt that his cult eventually spread throughout the Greco-Roman world. Temples, known as Serapea (Serapeum in singular), were constructed in Alexandria, Rome, Pergamum, and many other cities and towns surrounding the Mediterranean.

Soter's elevation of the god may be seen as an attempt to impose Greek power on a conquered nation through the clever use of religious symbolism couched in a familiar presentation, i.e., as a sort of religious Trojan Horse to stealthily insert Greek culture into Egypt. Such a tactic fits the pharaoh's general ruling strategy when considering his penchant for introducing novel and culturally variegated institutions like the Museum and the Great Library and their origins from a dialectical interplay between the "Ptolemaic thesis" and the "Greek thesis" (introduced in Chapter Two). Serapis was not a marriage of religious and secular power that operated through intimidation or violence, as was the case with the First Crusade's land grab in the twelfth century CE, where a political reality was obscured by the religious rhetoric of a pope and wrapped in the symbol of the cross. Instead, Serapis should be recognized as a potent symbol of embodied hegemony in the Gramscian sense of the word. When doing so, the god becomes a metaphor

---

11 Takács, *Isis and Sarapis*, 29.

for the manufacture of popular consent via institution through what Howson and Smith wrote was the "working together of political society with civil society; of freedom with constraint; of superstructure with structure [...]."[12] Serapis epitomizes the persuasive ideological composite figure and is a personification useful for identifying the library's symbiotic relationship with temple/crypto-temple.

Even though temple proto-libraries existed long before the Serapeum was built, the Alexandrian temple stands out as a lustrous example of the confluence of religion, state, and information institution, or the Serapian ideological plexus (SIP). Not only is the Serapeum remembered for being the first and most impressive of the ancient Serapea, but it is also legendary for having housed an impressive research library, the "daughter library" of the Great Library. Merging simple abstractions (e.g., Homeland, Knowledge, Learning), the Serapeum also incorporated religious ideology without violence for the benefit of elites, e.g., Greek and Hellenized politicians, clergy, intellectuals, and artists in positions of power and influence. So, just as the god Serapis may be seen as a symbol for hegemonic domination by means of institution, the Serapeum may be seen as symbolic of the library/crypto-temple as an instantiation of this concept into a religio-ideological tool of control.

The modern capitalist academic library's (MCAL) combination of religion and secular power is somewhat different than the merger found in Soter's new god. The MCAL's association with religion is deep-seated and well-sublimated while the god's association with secular power was novel and likely calculated. Nonetheless, the Serapian MCAL works towards the same objectives that Soter prioritized for with the introduction of Serapis himself and as materially embodied in the Serapeum. Serapis and the Serapeum preserved, as the Serapian MCAL preserves, the existing cultural-political milieus and what are perceived by most as normality, even if that normality is—like Greek domination was, and like capitalist domination remains—oppressive. Even the most "modern" academic libraries, those that have thoroughly sublimated their religious origins and symbols, remain Serapian MCALs, in a basic sense.

---

12 Richard Howson and Kylie Smith, "Hegemony and the Operation of Consensus and Coercion," in *Hegemony: Studies in Consensus and Coercion,*" ed. Richard. Howson and Kylie Smith (New York: Routledge, 2008), 10.

Since Serapis and his library are identified as guiding metaphors for the information institution qua religious institution imbedded into the cultural historical landscape and hegemonic matrix of a dominant cultural political paradigm, it is useful to continue with a description of the Serapian MCAL's namesake: the Alexandrian Serapeum. The following sections provide a brief virtual tour of Alexandria, the Serapeum, and its temple library. This tour is followed with the description of a particular Serapian MCAL for the purpose of viewing the modern institution in the light of its ancient exemplar.

Alexandria and the Serapeum

A tour of ancient Alexandria begins in the city's Greek quarter, the Bruchium, in the northeastern section of the city.

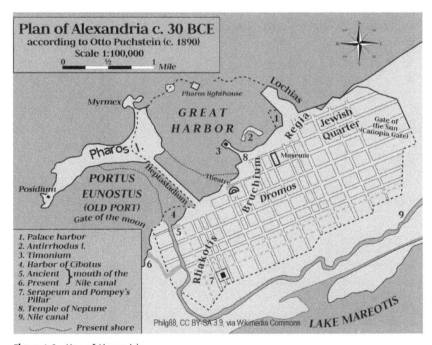

Figure 4.6 Map of Alexandria

Immediately to the north of the Greek quarter is the main point of entry into the city, the Great Harbor of Alexandria (one will notice the repeated used of the adjectival modifier "Great" when referring to landmarks in this city). The Great Harbor is deep body of water accessible

Figure 4.7 Lighthouse (Pharos) of Alexandria, 1899 illustration

by the largest of vessels,[13] providing ready access to the Mediterranean. It is guarded over by the Great Lighthouse of Pharos, the world's first true lighthouse,[14] which sits on the eastern tip of Pharos, the island from which it received its name. First century BCE Roman historian Diodorus Siculus listed the Lighthouse as one of the Seven Wonders of the World;[15] it was, according to whom you read, between 250 feet to half a kilometer tall[16] and capped with a gigantic statue of Zeus.[17]

Strolling through the Bruchium, a mid-third century BCE visitor would encounter the massive palaces of the Ptolemies.[18] During the time of the Serapeum's construction, these palaces were inhabited by Ptolemy

---

13 Strabo, *Geography*, 17.1.6.

14 Ray Jones, *The Lighthouse Encyclopedia: The Definitive Resource*, 2nd ed. (Guilford, CT: Globe Pequot Press, 2013), 119.

15 Diodorus Siculus, *Library of History*, 2.11.5.

16 Dorothy Sly, *Philo's Alexandria* (London: Routledge, 1996), 22.

17 Christopher Haas, *Alexandria in Late Antiquity: Topography and Social Conflict* (Baltimore: MD: John Hopkins University Press, 1997), 144; Dunstan Lowe, "Twisting in the Wind: Monumental Weathervanes in Classical Antiquity," *Cambridge Classical Journal* 62 (2016): 155.

18 First century BCE Greek historian Strabo of Pontus noted, "[...] the city contains most beautiful public precincts and also the royal palaces, which constitute one-fourth or even one-third of the whole circuit of the city; for just as each of the kings, from love of splendour, was wont to add some adornment to the public monuments, so also he would invest himself at his own expense with a residence, in addition to those already built [...]." In Strabo, *Geography*, 17.1.8,

III Euergetes ("The Benefactor") (reigned 246-221 BCE) and his family. Alexander's tomb, the Sema, is also located in the Bruchium and contains his mummified remains as well as those of Soter and Ptolemy II Philadelphus ("The Sister Lover") (reigned 283-246 BCE). The Museum of Alexandria sits close to the royal palaces and about 400 meters away from the Harbor.[19] This Temple of the Muses houses a community of research scholars as well as the Great Library of Alexandria. The Museum's geographic placement is an indication of the close relationships between earthly power, religious power, and the creation and control of knowledge.

The first century CE Greek geographer Strabo wrote in his *Geography* that Alexandria was "full of public and sacred structures."[20] In the city, there are indeed an impressive number of religious buildings and geography designated as sacred space. Reflecting the cosmopolitan nature of the city, these buildings are dedicated to both foreign and domestic deities: Greek, Egyptian, and those from other lands. Although the Greek gods receive pride of place in the religious life of the city—Dionysius was a particularly popular deity —[21] the traveler passes by the temples, shrines, and sanctuaries of many different cults. If she were to go farther east in the city, she would find synagogues in the vibrant Jewish quarter of the city. The many royal buildings and governmental offices that are encountered en route to the Serapeum may themselves be considered cult centers for, besides the worship of Dionysius, the "second main cult, or group of cults, centres round the royal family, and consists of the so-called 'Dynastic Cult', embracing the worship both of the Ptolemies and of Alexander."[22] Serapis is the celestial father of this regime.

In addition to the abundance of monumental architecture, art, and statuary that the traveler encounters, she passes by book stalls where vendors offer papyrus scrolls for purchase, attesting to both Greek and Egyptian bibliomania. Reynolds and Wilson noted that the Greek book trade had been vibrant among the Greeks since the fifth century

---

19 John Edwin Sandys, *A History of Classical Scholarship*, (London: IB Tauris), 1:107.

20 Strabo, *Geography*, 17.1.10.

21 P.M. Fraser, *Ptolemaic Alexandria* (Oxford: Clarendon Press, 1972), 1:204.

22 Fraser, 1:213.

BCE,[23] and Kallendorf wrote that fifth century Athens saw the creation of a "semi-circular recess in the marketplace (the orchestra) [that] had been set aside for booksellers."[24] According to Kallendorf, books were inexpensive by the fifth century, with one clue to this decrease in cost being revealed in Socrates' words to Meletus in Plato's *Apology*: [25]

> Are you so contemptuous of these men and think them so ignorant that of letters as not to know that the books of Anaxagoras of Clazomenae are full of those theories, and further, that the young men learn from me what they can buy from time to time for a drachma, at most, in the bookshops, and ridicule Socrates if he pretends that these theories are his own, especially as they are so absurd?[26]

The increase in literacy in the Mediterranean world following the introduction of the Greek alphabet had made books more accessible and desirable both physically and intellectually. The power of written language remained intact despite the increase in availability, and the continued desire for the possession of collections by state and cult signaled this power. Euergetes, for example, infamously borrowed the works of the Great Tragedians from Athens, providing 15 talents of silver as collateral, only to keep the invaluable books and forfeit the silver.[27]

Continuing their mid-third century CE tour to the Serapeum, the southbound traveler enters the Rhakotis. This is the city's Egyptian quarter and might have been built over the traces of a settlement much older than Alexandria itself. Strabo reported that it was in the Rhakotis where the Greek soldiers guarding the entrance to the Nile were stationed.[28] The Egyptian quarter would later be the home to the city's

---

23 LD Reynolds and NG Wilson, *Scribes & Scholars: A Guide to the Transmission of Greek & Latin Literature*, 2nd ed. (Oxford, Clarendon Press, 1975), 2.

24 Craig Kallendorf, "The Ancient Book," in *The Book: A Global History*, ed. Michael F. Suarez, S.J. Woudhuysen, and H.R. Woudhuysen (Oxford: Oxford University Press, 2013), 44.

25 Kallendorf, 44.

26 Plato, *Apology*, 26e. A drachma, Kallendorf wrote, was "less than a day's wage for an unskilled laborer." In Kallendorf, "The Ancient Book," 44.

27 Michael W. Handis, "Myth and History: Galen and the Alexandrian Library," in *Ancient Libraries*, ed. Jason König, Katerina Oikonomopoulou, and Greg Woolf (Cambridge, Cambridge University Press, 2013), 364.

28 Strabo, *Geography*, 17.1.10.

hippodrome, the Lageion, which would sit directly to the south of the Serapeum temple complex and exhibited wildly popular chariot races.

The Serapeum temple complex sits squarely in the center of the Egyptian quarter on the Rhakotis hill, the only natural hill in Alexandria.[29] The Greeks had the habit of constructing acropolises in their cities, and this is a particularly impressive example of one. The fourth century CE soldier and historian Roman Ammianus Marcellinus extolled the Serapeum's beauty, describing an architectural feat that stood out even in a huge city packed with fantastic sights. He wrote that the Serapeum was second in grandeur only to the Capitoline Hill of Rome:

> There are besides in the city temples pompous with lofty roofs, conspicuous among the Serapeum, which, feeble words merely belittle it, yet with almost breathing statues, and a great number of other works of art, that next to the Capitolium, with which revered Rome elevates herself to eternity, the whole world beholds nothing more magnificent.[30]

The rhetorician Aphthonius, a contemporary of Marcellinus, provided similar praise for the Alexandrian acropolis, describing the site as "beyond the power of words."[31]

The temple complex is bordered on all four sides by a thick temenos (sacred boundary) wall separating the holy landscape from the profane architecture that surrounds it and incorporates a colonnaded and covered atrium that one later observer said was gilded in gold.[32] Visitors enter through gates reached by a massive staircase of "a hundred or more steps."[33] Glazed green terracotta foundation plaques affixed to the perimeter walls address both the Greek and Egyptian populations of the city in Greek and hieroglyphics, attesting to the Serapeum's position and role as a civic and religious focal point to all of Alexandria's inhabitants: "King Ptolemy [Eurgetes], son of Ptolemy

---

29 Judith Mckenzie, Sheila Gibson, and A.T. Reyes, "Reconstructing the Serapeum in Alexandria from the Archaeological Evidence," *Journal of Roman Studies* 94 (2004): 111.

30 Ammianus Marcellinus 22.16.12, *History*, trans. J.C. Rolfe (Cambridge, MA: Harvard University Press, 1935), 2:301-303.

31 Ray Nadeau, "The Progymnasmata of Aphthonius in Translation," *Communications Monographs* 19, no. 4 (1952): 280.

32 Nadeau, 280.

33 Rufinus of Aquileia, *History of the Church*, 11.23.

[Philadelphus] and Arsinoe, the sibling Gods, [dedicated] to Serapis the temple and the sacred enclosure (temenos)."[34]

The temple complex blends together the Greek and the Egyptian, and McKenzie et al. wrote that it should be visualized as containing "Egyptian statuary and in a 'classical' setting."[35] While the actual temple building of Serapis, which sits at the northern end of the sacred enclosure and is where the god "lives," is not impressive in size when compared to the colonnaded court that encloses it,[36] it has immense religious significance for the city's inhabitants. The temple complex will eventually become of great importance to the larger Greco-Roman world. In fact, the Alexandrian Serapeum was of such significance to the ancient world that its image was represented on coins found in the second century CE, over 350 years after its construction.[37] Although in 240 BCE the Serapeum may not have been the intellectual heart of Alexandria (that would be the Museum and Great Library),[38] it remained of great interest to personages of power throughout its long history of operation: from Philadelphus to Cleopatra VII, the last Greek ruler of Egypt, and for centuries after.[39] The Serapeum remained prominent until its ultimate physical destruction in 391 CE at the hands of a Christian mob, after which Christian church buildings were built on or near the site. Orosius, a Roman Christian historian and protege of Augustine of Hippo, wrote that, by the time of his visit to Alexandria in c. 415 CE, the bookshelves in the pagan temples of the city had been

---

34 Judith Mckenzie, *The Architecture of Alexandria and Egypt: 300 BC–AD 700* (New Haven: Yale University Press 2004), 53.

35 Mckenzie, Gibson, and Reyes, "Reconstructing the Serapeum," 101.

36 McKenzie, Gibson, and Reyes wrote that "in the midst of the whole space was the temple (aedes) wrought with expensive columns and built impressively and magnificently with marble-stone on the outside. In this was an image of Serapis, so huge that its right hand was touching one wall, while its left hand touched another—a monstrous object said to have been made from all sorts of metals and woods." In Mckenzie, Gibson, and Reyes, 106.

37 Susan Handler, *Architecture on the Roman Coins of Alexandria, American Journal of Archaeology* 75, no. 1 (1971), 66. See also Mckenzie, Gibson, and Reyes, "Reconstructing the Serapeum," 86.

38 The Serapeum could have possibly risen in stature after the Great Library's final destruction. Hendrickson wrote "The Serapeum Library may have been, in some sense, the next generation of the Great Library. Once the Serapeum Library enters the historical record, it is generally construed in one of two ways, as we will see in the present section. Some authors regarded it as if it were the Great Library, or at least a continuation of the Great Library. Others regarded it not as the Great Library itself, but as a second instantiation of it." In Thomas Hendrickson, "The Serapeum: Dreams of the Daughter Library," *Classical Philology* 111, no. 4 (2016), 462.

39 Alan Rowe, *Discovery of the Famous Temple and Enclosure of Serapis at Alexandria* (Le Caire: Imprimerie De L'institute Francais, 1946), 25.

emptied, plundered "by our own men [Christians] in our time, which, indeed, is a true statement."[40]

The Temple Library of the Serapeum

The Serapeum, like all of the temples of the ancient world before and after, was a microcosmic representation of everything that exists, what Mircea Eliade would recognize as a "world-in-little."[41] Eliade said that a religious temple is an *"imago mundi"* or image of the cosmos.[42] He also referred to sacred spaces, including but not limited to temples and churches, as "centres," as places that are "sacred above all."[43] The temple as sacred center is a link between heaven and earth, it is an axis connecting the sacred and the profane worlds where "hierophanies," expressions of the divine, manifest.[44] For Eliade, the person coming into contact with the sacred reality truly lives. As with the Museum, the Serapeum was a religious institution created by a political dynasty for the purpose of supporting the interests of that dynasty. As an *imago mundi*, it replicated a vision or manifestation of reality in which the Ptolemaic rulers, through their relationship with Serapis and the gods, sat near the top. As with the Museum, the Serapeum library served as a tool for this religious authority as well as a sacred space. It was the location of intense research activity, a place where philosophers, scientists, and poets produced new knowledge in the traditions of the Peripatetics and other schools of philosophy and art that preceded them. At the same time, it reflected the Greco-Macedonian experience and supported the continuation of this reality.

As may tend to happen when entering any temple complex of the ancient world, a traveler entering the Serapeum encounters a book collection. Although the Serapeum library is not the most impressive Alexandrian library at the time of this tour—that distinction belongs to the Great Library's magnificent collection—it is most definitely an

---

40   Orosius, *Seven Books of History Against the Pagans*, 6.15.

41   Mircea Eliade, *The Forge and the Crucible: The Origins and Structures of the Academy*, 2nd ed., trans. Stephen Corrin (Chicago: University of Chicago Press, 1978), 118.

42   Mircea Eliade, *The Sacred and the Profane: The Nature of Religion*, trans. Willard R. Trask (San Diego, CA: Harcourt, 1957), 58-59.

43   Mircea Eliade, *Images and Symbols: Studies in Religious Symbolism*, trans. Philip Mairet (Princeton, NJ: Princeton University Press, 1991), 39.

44   Eliade, 39.

Figure 4.8 Statue of scribe with papyrus scroll

intellectual center as well as a religious one. Built along the wall that surrounds the temple grounds and identifies it as a sacred precinct are approximately two dozen small square rooms, and some of these cells house the library's collection of books in the form of papyrus scrolls (as well as codices in its later history).[45]

Aphthonius noted both the academic and religious nature of these cells, writing in his *Progymnasmata* ("preliminary exercises") that "Within the colonnades, enclosures were built, some having become repositories for the books available to the diligent for study, thus spurring on an entire city to the mastery of learning; others were established long ago to honor the gods."[46] Even more books may have been stored in underground passages built into the hill and accessed by a great descending staircase,[47] although this is largely conjecture, and it is not known for certain what the chambers were used for.[48]

---

45 This assertion is supported by the fact that during Roman times a furnace was added to prevent damage from Alexandrian humidity. A.J.B. Wace, "Recent Ptolemaic Finds in Egypt," *Journal of Hellenic Studies* 65 (1945), 106.

46 Nadeau, "Progymnasmata of Aphthonius," 280.

47 See Rowe, *Discovery of the Famous Temple*, 25.

48 Mckenzie, Gibson, and. Reyes, "Reconstructing the Serapeum," 97.

Regardless of exact location, packed into the temple are tens of thousands of scrolls covering works on subjects dear to the intellectuals of the age as well as possibly administrative and archival material. All this material, furthermore, is organized for retrieval and use in whatever scholarly, religious, or artistic endeavor for which they may have been required. Around 240 BCE, the Serapeum may very well have been considered a "branch library" of the Museum, what Byzantine historian John Tzetzes (lived c. 1110-1180 CE) referred to as the library outside of the palace.[49] Tzetzes said that the collection included approximately 42,800 scrolls,[50] but Fraser wrote that the Serapeum might have become the main research library of Alexandria during the Roman Imperial period upon the demise or degradation of the Great Library of Alexandria,[51] and that it "must at some time have grown to over 100,000 manuscripts in the ordinary growth of the centuries. If, as some think, here were lodged the Library of Pergamum [after it was gifted to Cleopatra VII by Julius Caesar c. 48 BCE], then it was a collection of some 300,000 scrolls."[52]

In the same instance, the Serapeum embodied the ideologies of religion and the state as well as abstract philosophical and conceptual principles such as Knowledge, the search for Truth, and Cultural Preservation. This integration of ideologies, furthermore, was tightly woven and highly complementary. Apparent contradictions such as the disconnect between religious faith and intellectual exploration may be resolved if one sees them as acting in concert to reinforce class structures; base and superstructure perpetuate each other through a feedback loop and recursive processes.

Moving From Overt to Covert: Enter the Ziggurat

Flashing forward 2300 years to the present, one encounters historical and ideological symbolism that connect the Serapian MCALs to their ancient and medieval predecessors. Thus far, the MCAL has been

---

49   John Tzetzes, "The Plautine Scholium from Caecius," trans. Ernest H. Wilkins, in Edward Alexander Parsons, The Alexandrian Library: Glory of the Hellenic World (Amsterdam: Elsevier, 1952), 108.

50   Tzetzes, "The Plautine Scholium from Caecius," trans. Ernest H. Wilkins, in Parsons, 108.

51   Fraser, Ptolemaic Alexandria, 1.335.

52   Parsons, Alexandrian Library, 349.

discussed largely *in abstracto*; it is instructive to consider a specific instance of the institution.

Hodges Library, the main library at the University of Tennessee, Knoxville, was remodeled in the 1980s to resemble an ancient ziggurat, the multi-tiered Mesopotamian temples with a shrine at their peak. The ziggurat is what Eliade called a "cosmic mountain" that links earth to heaven,[53] and its peak signals an intersection with a higher spiritual reality. In the case of the ancient ziggurats, such a connection linked the guardian deities of the Mesopotamian cultures to the peoples who worshipped these deities: the Sumerians, Akkadians, Babylonians, Assyrians, etc. With Hodges Library, this connection between people and the sacred remains, even if it is largely concealed.

Despite that the material ideological facade of Hodges Library appears secular to many casual observers, it is naive to think that the MCAL's adoption of an ancient architectural motif was done solely for aesthetic purposes. While the planners and architects may have been conscious of the history behind the building's conceptual design, it is possible that they chose the design because it is representative of libraries while not really understanding the deep meaning behind their choice; if so, this subconscious choice then possibly makes the inclusion of these motifs far more subversive and potentially insidious. The critical scholar might refer to the Hodges ziggurat as an "echo" of the past. The word echo, however, suggests something vestigial, bygone, or inoperative. An echo is a curiosity at best. Perhaps a more appropriate word is "reverberation," in the sense that a reverberation is a remnant of the past that has indelible effects on the present day.

The aesthetic effect of the Hodges designers' architectural choice for the library is a striking and compelling one. The colossal edifice projects a power that is simultaneously secular and spiritual.

It proclaims to observers that this building, as well as the sociocultural institution of the library that it encompasses, are important sources of societal capital that are also a manifest expression of the sacred, the numinous, the religious. While few people besides those who wax poetically about the meaning of the library on their lives and work (typically authors, educators, scholars, and librarians) and consciously equate the act of visiting an academic library with the act of entering

---

53 Eliade, *Sacred and the Profane*, 40.

Figure 4.9 Exterior of Hodges Library

a church to worship, the sense of sacred presence evoked by Hodges Library may well result in a similar sensation to the public.

Within the Hodges Library building are other crypto- as quasi-religious symbols and practices, as well as other ideological "tells" that more openly point to past civilizations and cultures, Mesopotamian and otherwise. Some of these symbols and practices are apparent, even to the casual observer. Others, however, are not easily decodable. One of the first things that any visitor encounters upon entering the building's second floor entrance is the substantial and imposing, even intimidating, public services/circulation desk, a piece of furniture that is over 30 feet long on its patron facing side and supports 30-inch-deep countertops.

Not only might this desk be likened to an altar—it resembles an altar or chancel table with its broad granite countertops—the desk separates library workers from patrons through both physical and persuasive ideological means.

This separation, it may be argued, symbolizes the divide between clergy and laypersons, those who have direct access and control over divine knowledge and those who seek it out. Altars and other sacred dividers performed this function openly in the past when book collections were incorporated into undisguised temples. It takes no

Figure 4.10 Hodges Desk

imaginative leap to conclude that this modern furniture works in a similar way to signify an ideologically generated and psychologically effective boundary between patron and workers, as a barrier that might be interpreted as arising from legacy religious associations.

Having encountered the service desk, visitors enter an environment of focused activity, and a place where rituals are reenacted. For instance, even though conversations are no longer discouraged on the second floor of the building due to the library's adoption of the increasingly popular "information commons" model,[54] visitors might notice that the stillness remains largely intact; it seems natural to the space.

To break the quiet, or at least to rise above hushed tones in conversation, feels to some visitors like it might invite negative attention from other library users or censure from library staff. It is as if a social convention or, using a religious term, a covenant, would be broken if one were to become too gregarious in the space.

The critical analyst might also see the Hodges service desk as separating, unofficially at least because there is no sanction against patrons

---

54 Pankl and Ryan define an "information commons" as "a collaborative working space that is technology rich and conducive to group work." In Elisabeth Pankl and Jenna Ryan, "Information Commons and Web 2.0 Technologies: Creating Rhetorical Situations and Enacting Habermasian Ideals in the Academic Library," in *Handbook of Research on Computer Mediated Communication*, ed. Sigrid Kelsey and Kirk St. Amant (Hershey, New York: Information Science Reference, 2008), 850.

Figure 4.11 Information Commons at Hodges Library

Figure 4.12 Book stacks at Hodges Library

accessing the circulating collection, the common areas of the second floor from the bookstacks qua "holy of holies."

Might the library collection, including both the circulating and non-circulating materials, signify the earthly manifestation of the supernatural? Although this conclusion seems odd, one can argue that, considering the Serapian MCAL's legacy of Humanism and secularism, the deity being worshipped is Learning and/or Knowledge as "sacred abstraction." Just as the proto-libraries of Mesopotamia and Egypt were seen as the actual physical homes of the gods for whom they were built, the MCAL might be considered the physical home of the sacred abstraction(s)—a secular god or gods that radiates forth as a meaning-laden idea. One does tend to notice an increase in the level of quiet as one ascends through floors three through six of the building, travelling through a collection of knowledge that represents the sum of human intellectual achievement.

Throughout the building, library workers administer the collection like ancient priest scribes. They act as gatekeepers and preservers of knowledge and culture, maintaining the "stream of tradition" while supporting the creation of the new. The methods that they designed and employ to organize the collection, such as the Library of Congress

Classification System, the Dewey Decimal Classification, or the Universal Decimal Classification, reflect the cosmos "in little"—an instance of *imago mundi* that betrays an ingrained worldview. In a sense, the library workers minister to the community they serve in a capacity reminiscent of, and not substantially different to, a professional member of the religious clergy from the beginning of the Christian period to the present day. As noted in the preceding chapter, the hierarchical structure of the modern university and many academic libraries was taken from the Roman Catholic Church who, in turn, had taken it from the administrative structure of the Late Roman Empire. This hierarchical and patriarchal model survives at the University of Tennessee Libraries with its dean, associate deans, faculty librarians, and library staff.

Conclusion

Looking back through the millennia, one sees the boundaries between organized religion, the state, and higher education erode and begin to disappear. Serapis was at one and the same time god and (through his dynastic associations) state. The Serapeum was simultaneously god, state, and generator and physical locus of knowledge. There was little tension between these institutions. Although the boundaries between these institutions are more formally recognized in today's MCALs and are in many instances inscribed into law, religion, state, and education continue to mesh effectively qua SIP to maintain the status quo. The Serapian MCAL is a reverberation of the ancient information institution reskinned for the late capitalist era.

The University of Tennessee Knoxville's Hodges Library is one node in a societal network of information institutions, the Serapian MCALS, all of which are explicitly tasked with maintaining the educational welfare of society and implicitly tasked with maintaining the basic integrity of existing social relations. The Serapian MCAL, like the Alexandrian Serapeum, is an *imago mundi*. It may be viewed, in fact, as two *imagines mundorum*. In the first instance, the Serapian MCAL is an *imago mundi qua idealized cosmos*, i.e., a model of the cosmos as humanity constructs it in the shadow of 6000 years of civilization. But the Serapian MCAL may also be considered as a reflection of its constitutive ideology, and it may subsequently be parsed to explore its power relations. The next chapter considers both *imagines mundorum* of the Serapian MCAL to bring light to the impact of the academic library/crypto-temple on society.

Chapter 5   Religious Ideology, Symbolism, and the Serapian MCAL

In short, not to bore the reader with the chronicle of our deciphering, when we later perfected the map definitively we were convinced that the library was truly laid out and arranged according to the image of the terraqueous orb. To the north we found ANGLIA and GERMANI, which along the west wall were connected by GALLIA, which turned then, at the extreme west, into HIBERNIA, and toward the south wall ROMA (paradise of Latin classics!) and YSPANIA.

Umberto Eco[1]

The persistence of Serapian information institutions over the course of millennia appears to support the conclusion that the relationship between religion and information institutions has been a success. It is arguably considered a success because it is deemed as profitable by and for the dominant classes of a society that benefit the most from it. Most people living under the yoke of neoliberal capitalism, however, do not have the same benefits and advantages of those in positions of wealth and power.

As a crypto-temple, the Serapian modern capitalist academic library (MCAL) at least partially conceals the iconographic, ritualistic, and ideological elements of its predecessors with varying degrees of intention and success. It is a "holy place" or, at minimum, trades upon its historical relationships with holy places and religious organizations to

---

1 Umberto Eco, *The Name of the Rose* (Boston, MA: Mariner Books, 2014), 342.

maintain a degree of ideological coherence that stretches back to the Bronze Age. The Serapian MCAL is an institution where the apparent focus of the place/idea/action assemblage has shifted away from the transparent worship of the divine without completely doing away with the basic ideological gravity of the divine and the idea that there is an external higher authority.

This chapter argues that the Serapian MCAL helps generate what Erich Fromm referred to as a "structuralized" society where although "social structures do change in the course of the historical development, they are relatively fixed at any given historical period, and society can only exist by operating within their framework."[2] Within this structuralized society, members "of the society and various classes or status groups within it have to behave in such a way as to be able to function in the sense required by the social system."[3] The present authors assume the dialectical standpoint that reality is composed of the material actions and interactions of material things and their shared relations. As described in the book's introduction, material things are not limited solely to physical objects and entities; ideas also have a material nature, and they interact with both the physical world and other ideas. Within these processes, ideology is the engine for maintaining and reproducing human reality in coherent cultural/historical forms that span time. This ideology is visible in symbols and rituals that are replicated and practiced by members of a society inhabiting all class positions. Such materially manifested ideological markers can be exceedingly powerful, defining societal norms, and structuring and even dictating the roles and actions of individuals and groups within a society.

Symbols and rituals, even when concealed, may be identified, understood, critiqued, subverted, counteracted, removed, and replaced to provide human beings with more agency. What follows is an examination of religious ideology as revealed in the Serapian MCAL, taking into consideration such material ideology's purpose and impact on society. The chapter concludes with a discussion of how such symbols and rituals' material reality constructs human existence through a process known as interpellation through ideology.

---

2   Erich Fromm, *On Disobedience: Why Freedom Means Saying "No" to Power* (New York: Harper Collins, 2010), 79.

3   Fromm, 79.

Religion, Ideology, and the Modern Capitalist Library

Religion can act as a coercive organizing force, strong-arming members of society into conformity. People, knowingly or not, perform material actions that support such conformity while they are themselves materially acted upon by the religious constructs. Religion shapes reality through the imposition of ideologies that have real world material consequences. In this sense, both gods and spirits, related concepts like magic, and the divine sanction of their earthly subalterns (e.g., clergy people, prophets, kings, and even business CEOs and politicians under capitalism) are very evident. This reality is evidenced by the substantive and observable material effects of these material concepts.

Human beings encounter material concepts every moment of their lives, and these encounters can be exceedingly weighty. They are particularly serious when they deal with issues of religion and faith. For example, the Abrahamic God or, to be precise, the consequences of the Abrahamic God-concept, is a palpable thing to the person persecuted or left disadvantaged for either believing in or disbelieving in that concept. It is also a palpable thing for everyone that lives in societies and/or cultures that draw heavily from the Abrahamic God-concept or is influenced by those societies and cultures that do. Several countries with majority Muslim populations, including Afghanistan, Saudi Arabia, and Yemen, prescribe capital punishment for the "crime" of apostasy.[4] Atheists in Saudi Arabia sometimes resort to obtaining illegal books if they desire to read something amicable to their own personal philosophy and are relegated to communicating with like-minded or sympathetic people nearly solely through social media.[5] The material ideological existence of the Abrahamic God, and that concept and associated morality's integration into the legal and legislative systems in certain nations and states, has direct consequences for individual autonomy, such as what a woman can and cannot do regarding her own body. As a result, the Abrahamic God, despite whether it exists in "actuality," is ultimately real to everyone exposed to the concept through formalization of its morality and influence on social norms.

---

4   "The Right to Apostasy in the World," Humanists International, accessed May 14, 2022, https://humanists.international/get-involved/resources/the-right-to-apostasy-in-the-world/.

5   Max Fisher, "'Fighting Reality': Life as an atheist in Saudi Arabia," *Washington Post* Nov. 21, 2012, https://www.washingtonpost.com/news/worldviews/wp/2012/11/21/fighting-reality-life-as-an-atheist-in-saudi-arabia/.

Everyone's existence has, in some way, been materially shaped by the concept of a higher power through religious ideology's incorporation into the network of relations that engulfs them.

According to the Oxford English Dictionary, ideology is a "systematic scheme of ideas, usually relating to politics, economics, or society and forming the basis of action or policy; a set of beliefs governing conduct. Also: the forming or holding of such a scheme of ideas."[6] Although this is an adequate general definition of ideology as it is commonly understood, ideology is a complex concept with different interpretations that extend beyond the deliberate development and adoption of ideas. Indeed, ideology is not limited to clearly defined and published standpoints like religious doctrine or written political platforms and includes deep structures that organize and construct human society and potentially influence material action. Religious ideology, as a result, may be consciously understood, accepted, and applied while, at the same time, it works in the background to affect how human beings live their realities. This conception of ideology as a structurally ingrained, subliminal, or para-liminal mechanism for patterning reality is referred to here as "deep belief."

Recognizing both the liminal and unconscious nature of religious ideology, nineteenth century Russian anarchist Michael Bakunin wrote that:

> Nothing is more natural than that the belief in God, the creator, regulator, judge, master, curser, savior, and benefactor of the world, should still prevail among the people, especially in the rural districts, where it is more widespread than among the proletariat of the cities. The people, unfortunately, are still very ignorant, and are kept in ignorance by the systematic efforts of all the governments, who consider this ignorance, not without good reason, as one of the essential conditions of their own power. Weighted down by their daily labor, deprived of leisure, of intellectual intercourse, of reading, in short of all the means and a good portion of the stimulants that develop thought in men, the people generally accept religious traditions without criticism and in a lump. These traditions surround them from infancy in all the situations of life, and artificially sustained in their minds by a multitude of official poisoners

---

6 *Oxford English Dictionary*, s.v. "ideology, n.," accessed March 11, 2022, https://www.oed.com/view/Entry/91016?redirectedFrom=ideology#eid.

of all sorts, priests and laymen, are transformed therein into a sort of mental and moral habit, too often more powerful even than their natural good sense.[7]

In this statement, Bakunin encapsulated the notion, one that many nineteenth century anarchists shared with the Marxists, that religion is a tool of the state for maintaining control over citizenry. He also concluded that the continued adherence to religion, and hence the state, is not rational. Instead, obedience is something accepted uncritically "in a lump;" the reality of the religious worldview is a product of repeated exposure, habit, and indoctrination. A second point that Bakunin raises is that this submission to religion is enforced by official ideologists, the "priests and laymen." Although these "official poisoners" may not be deeply cynical people that consciously use ideology to coerce while being fully aware of what they are doing, they are themselves subconsciously immersed and invested in the same ideological systems. As a result of this immersion, "the way things are" tends to appear to all involved as the natural state of reality. Twentieth century Marxist philosopher Louis Althusser's concept of the "ideological state apparatus" (ISA) provides an explanation for why "the way things are" is a reality that is both accepted and reproduced.

The Modern Capitalist Academic Library as Ideological State Apparatus

According to classical Marxist theory, ideology is false consciousness, the "ruling ideas" of the dominant class of an epoch and a distortion of reality that supports the continued domination of the oppressed classes by the dominant class.[8] More nuanced theories of ideology were later developed through the work of Marxist thinkers like V.I. Lenin, György Lukács, Antonio Gramsci, and Althusser.

The discipline of library and information science has drawn upon this wellspring of evolving ideas to consider modern information institutions' relationship to ideology. The modern library's role as an ideological means for reproducing society was considered by Michael H. Harris from critical perspectives in his 1986 paper "State, Class, and Cultural Reproduction: Toward a Theory of Library and Service in the

---

7   Michael Bakunin, *God and the State* (New York: Dover, 1970), 16.

8   Karl Marx and Friedrich Engels, *The German Ideology* (Amherst, NY: Prometheus Books, 1998), 67.

United States,"[9] a seminal article that has served as a touchstone for many LIS critical theorists that followed him. Looking at the modern library through alternative paradigms to scientific pluralism and positivism including Gramsci's theory of ideological hegemony, Harris considered the institution as a means of cultural reproduction that restricts access to the established canon of literature along class lines.[10] According to Harris, the modern library is an institution

> [...] embedded in a stratified ensemble of institutions functioning in the high cultural, region, an ensemble of institutions dedicated to the creation, transmission, and reproduction of the hegemonic ideology. Such an interpretation challenges the "apolitical" conception of the library held by library professionals, and strips the library of the ethical and political innocence attributed to it by the pluralist social theorists.[11]

The application of Althusser's idea of the ideological state apparatus (ISA) to library and information science has also been discussed in the professional LIS literature,[12] but it is worth summarizing for its relevance to this work. For Althusser, ideology had a material existence. According to him, the focal point for the production and exercise of this material ideology was located with the ISAs. He posited that the productive force of society, i.e., labor power, is reproduced through various state apparatuses that are roughly dividable into two categories: the repressive state apparatus (RSA) and the ISAs.[13] Althusser

---

9   Michael H. Harris, "State, Class, and Cultural Reproduction: Toward a Theory of Library Service in the United States, *Advances in Librarianship* 14 (1986): 211-252.

10 Harris, 241.

11 Harris, 241.

12 See Douglas Raber, "Librarians as Organic Intellectuals," *Library Quarterly* 73, no. 1 (2003): 33-53; Stephen E. Bales and Lea Susan Engel, "The Counterhegemonic Academic Librarian: A Call to Action," *Progressive Librarian* 40 (2012), 16-40; Mies Martin, "Using Cultural Studies to Rethink Library Research" (Houghton, MI: Michigan Technological University, 2013), https://www.academia.edu/7023923/Using_Cultural_Studies_To_Rethink_Library_Research; Stephen Bales, *The Dialectic of Academic Librarianship: A Critical Approach* (Sacramento, CA: Library Juice Press, 2015); Jessica Critten, "Ideology and Critical Self-reflection in Information Literacy," *Communications in Information Literacy* 9, no. 1 (2015): 145-156. Stephen Bales, "The Academic Library as Crypto-temple: A Marxian Analysis," in *Class and Librarianship: Essays at the Intersection Information, Labor and Capital*, ed. Eric Estep and Nathaniel Enright (Sacramento, CA: Library Juice, 2016); Sam Popowich, *Confronting the Democratic Discourse of Librarianship: A Marxist Approach* (Sacramento, CA: Library Juice, 2019).

13 Louis Althusser, *Lenin and Philosophy and Other Essays*, trans. Ben Brewster (New York: Monthly Review Press, 2001), 97.

held that there is a single RSA with multiple components while there are various ISAs.[14] The RSA—the formal state—includes elements like the government, military, and police and works to reproduce the socioeconomic conditions of production through either violence or the threat of violence.[15] Although the ISAs may be protected or sustained by the RSA, they do not typically use violence or threats. Instead, ISAs rely chiefly upon ideology to drive reproduction.

According to Althusser's accounting, ISAs include the following societal institutions (condensed from Althusser's original bulleted list with emphasis added by the present authors):

> [...] the *religious*: the system of the different Churches, the *educational*: the system of the different public and private Schools, the *family*, the *legal*, the *political* (the political system, including the different Parties), the *trade union* (labor organization), [and] the *communications* (press, radio and television, and other forms of media, the cultural (Literature, the Arts, sports, etc.) [...][16]

Bales argued that, while the Serapian MCAL is primarily an educational ISA (which is, according to Althusser, the dominant ISA under the capitalist mode of socioeconomic production),[17] it "also contains elements and functions of three other capitalist ISAs: the communications ISA, the cultural ISA, and the religious ISA."[18] As intimated in preceding chapters, before becoming primarily an educational ISA in the capitalist era, the information institution had for most of its existence been chiefly a religious ISA, the dominant ISA prior to the capitalist epoch and one that included educational and cultural functions under its aegis.[19] It has been only in relatively recent times that the Serapian MCAL has mystified its religious aspect. The key word here is "mystified." Religious ideology is cloaked but present in the Serapian MCAL,

---

14   Althusser, 97.

15   This is not to say that the RSA cannot be deeply internally dysfunctional. There are many examples of when these instruments of the state work against each other or for their own ends (e.g., military coups).

16   Althusser, *Lenin and Philosophy*, 96.

17   Althusser, 103.

18   Stephen Bales, *Dialectic of Academic Librarianship*, 119.

19   Althusser, *Lenin and Philosophy*, 102.

and it continues to impact individuals and groups that enter a relationship with the MCAL.

Ideology, according to Althusser, has a material existence: "Ideas have disappeared as such (insofar as they are endowed with an ideal or spiritual existence), to the precise extent that it has emerged that their existence is inscribed in the actions of practices governed by rituals defined in the last instance by an ideological apparatus."[20] Rendered somewhat crudely, one might say that ideology embodies in material actions, that material actions result in institutions that embed ideology, and that ideology imbedded in institutions results in material actions. The cycle repeats itself ad infinitum.

Placed within the context of Raymond Williams's classic work *Marxism and Literature*, the mystified, religious components of the MCAL resemble what Williams termed a "residual" culture, i.e., a legacy culture that reinforces the more dominant cultural forces found in capitalism (such as education):

> By 'residual' I mean something different from the 'archaic', though in practice these are often very difficult to distinguish. Any culture includes available elements of the past. But their place in the contemporary cultural process is profoundly variable. I would call 'archaic' that which is wholly recognized as an element of the past, to be observed, to be examined, or even on occasion to be consciously 'revived', in a deliberately specializing way. What I mean by the 'residual' is very different. The residual, by definition, has been effectively formed in the past, but it is still active in the cultural process, not only and not often at all as an element of the past, but as an effective element of the present. Thus certain experiences, meanings, and values which cannot be expressed or substantially verified in terms of the dominant culture, are nevertheless lived and practised on the basis of the residue—cultural as well as social—of some previous social and cultural institution or formation.[21]

Williams's distinction between "archaic" and "residual" is reminiscent of the present authors' differentiation between historical "echo" and "reverberation," i.e., the difference between the impotent past and the

---

20   Althusser, 115.

21   Raymond Williams, *Marxism and Literature* (Oxford: Oxford University Press, 1977), 122.

active, impactful past. Residual elements of culture continue to exert influence within modern dominant cultural systems. Levine echoed this point, stating that some cultural institutions' "ability to adapt" may (but not always) "make them all the more efficient tools of the ruling class."[22]

Althusser more or less dismissed the influence of the religious ISA, writing that the educational ISA had superseded it as the dominant ISA under capitalism.[23] Nevertheless, looking at Williams's views on culture through the prism of Althusser's work allows one to see legacy religious institutions—the Christian Church for example—as possibly maintaining their cultural/institutional presence and rudiments of their influence within institutions like the Serapian MCAL because of their ability to buttress the dominant ideological institutional mechanisms with which they are associated (i.e., the educational ISA). Although the Christian Church is no longer in the position of dominant hegemonic authority that it enjoyed for nearly a millennium under the previous socioeconomic mode of production (the feudal mode), it remains influential in secular institutions because of the survival of elements which support capitalism. Such elements include its hierarchical and patriarchal organization,[24] as well as what Schoenfeld called "liberal and inclusive-oriented' religions'" support of "submission to a higher authority."[25]

Symbol and Ritual as Material Expressions of Ideology and Tools for Control

Serapian MCALs are often named after a significant figure. The building may, for example, be dedicated to an influential leader, an important scholar, or a major donor. The University of Tennessee Hodges Library is named for John C. Hodges, former UT English professor as well as author of the popular *Harbrace Handbook*. In addition to

---

22 Gregory J. Levine, "On the Geography of Religion," *Transactions of the Institute of British Geographers* 11, no. 4 (1986): 436.

23 Althusser, *Lenin and Philosophy*, 102-103.

24 See Herbert Gintis, "The Nature of Labor Exchange and the Theory of Capitalist Production," *Review of Radical Political Economics* 8, no. 2 (1976): 38; Mary Murray, *The Law of the Father: Patriarchy in the Transition from Feudalism to Capitalism* (New York, NY: Routledge,1995); Claudia Leeb, "Marx and the Gendered Structure of Capitalism, *Philosophy and Social Criticism* 33, no. 7 (2007): 833-859.

25 Eugen Schoenfeld, "Militant and Submissive Religions: Class, Religion and Ideology," *The British Journal of Sociology* 43, no. 1 (1992): 116.

such undisguised memorials, Serapian MCALs are ideological monuments. Bakos described ideological monuments as "modern fetishes with magic powers able to set up and protect social identity;"[26] in the process, one would also assume that they perpetuate social mores. These monuments may be material memorials to ideologies, such as those standing for Cold War victories, the statues of Lenin and Stalin that peppered the Soviet Bloc countries, the multiple Gorky Parks still found across the former USSR, or the infamous statue of Saddam Hussein that stood in Bagdad's Firdos Square. However, whether they are obvious memorials or not, ideological monuments always possess a deep structure that, although obscured, aids in defining human reality. For instance, in addition to having been an image of the dictator himself, the statue of Saddam Hussein simultaneously reflected the ascendancy of the Ba'ath Party, Hussein's cult of personality, and the Iraqi milieu of state-sponsored fear. Hence, the statue's toppling is a significant response to all those things (and the similar desire to remove certain statues across universities in the US seeks the same downfall of ideals). Encountering the Hussein statue as a symbol influenced its observer to some degree, whether that influence was consciously perceived or not. When viewing the Serapian MCAL as an ideological monument, it is necessary to go beyond the institution's generally accepted air of altruism, ferret out the deep belief generated by its ideological foundations, and attempt to understand that deep belief's impact. Symbols and rituals are entry points for accomplishing this task of piercing through to the deep structure of the Serapian MCAL as ideological monument.

The following discussion deals with religious symbols and rituals and the role they play in ideology's world-building and maintenance. It is important, therefore, to consider the meanings of three terms: *sign*, *symbol*, and *ritual*. A *sign* has some concrete, consciously understood meaning; it is designed to convey certain information to an audience. A traffic sign, for instance, is designed to transmit the message "YIELD the right of way to other vehicles at the intersection" to everyone that encounters it who possesses both a command of the language and cognizance of appropriate social convention. *Symbols* have deeper meanings that vary by culture, history, and context (symbols and rituals, however, may at the same time be signs). Adopting the standpoint

---

26 Jan Bakos, "Monuments and Ideologies," *Human Affairs* 1, no. 2 (1991): 106.

that material reality is composed by and of material objects, material ideas, and their relations, the symbol may be read and interpreted as a material expression of these relations. The symbol becomes a window into understanding the deep ideological makeup of an institution. Richardson said that it "brings [meanings and relationships] together," that:

> [...] the fact that these [meanings and relationships] are brought together into a very simple, single whole, give the symbol its fascination. Who has not noticed this in his own dreams?[27] A single figure or incident will sum up a whole complicated series of patterns and relationships. The associations will be of many kinds. They will include color, names, puns, position—almost anything. And when the conscious mind begins to penetrate their significance, one often feels that there is something uncanny in the way the unconscious can join together so much into so simple a picture.[28]

Rituals are ceremonial activities that are many times but not always religious in nature. They often signal the association of an individual to a community and may represent events like becoming a member of a group or entering a shared encounter with the sacred. Rituals are, in essence, symbols in action. For example, the Christian sacrament of holy communion may symbolize things such as being a member of a group, being purified or sanctified, being a heretic, blasphemer, sacrilegious, or even being a cannibal.[29]

The symbol or ritual is a gestalt, a material whole that is more than the sum of its individual relations. And as material ideology, it has the capacity to influence and change material reality as well as be influenced and changed itself by all other material reality through dialectical action. The influencing role of symbol and ritual on society cannot be underestimated: they organize human reality and make it navigable. Anthropologist Clifford Geertz proposed two ideas concerning culture and the constitution of human experience:

---

27 The use of the male pronoun in this sentence has symbolic value; it may be seen as emblematic of a male-dominated hierarchical society. Women dream too.

28 Cyril C. Richardson, "The Foundations of Christian Symbolism," in *Religious Symbolism*, ed. F. Ernest Johnson (New York: Institute for Religious and Social Studies, 1955), 5.

29 Mari Womack, *Symbols and Meaning: A Concise Introduction* (Walnut Creek, CA: Altamira Press, 2005), 2.

> [...] the first [idea] is that culture has been seen not as complexes of concrete behaviour patterns—customs, usage, traditions, habit, clusters—as has by and large been the case up to now, but as a set of control mechanisms—plans, recipes, rules, instructions (what computer engineers call "programs")—for the governing of behavior. The second idea is that man is precisely the animal most desperately dependent upon such extragenetic, outside-the-skin control mechanisms, such cultural programs for ordering his behavior.[30]

According to Geertz, the bases of culture patterns are "organized systems of significant symbols" without which "man's behavior would be virtually ungovernable, a mere chaos of pointless acts and exploding emotions, his experience virtually shapeless."[31]

The meanings of symbols and rituals are mutable and perspectival. But even though the meanings of symbols and rituals are complex entities that are many times rooted in the subconscious mind, they may be identified, examined, parsed, and critiqued to comprehend their significance within systems. While symbols are defined by their multi-valence (i.e., a symbol may signify multiple things at the same time), Victor Turner developed the idea of the positional meaning of individual symbols within larger systems of symbols. Positional meaning holds that the meaning or meanings of a symbol (or ritual as symbol) are influenced by its relationship to other symbols within an entire system of symbols.[32] In relative isolation, a stray religious symbol may mean little or be explained in multiple different ways. But when considered within a constellation of related symbols, the observer becomes more capable of assigning them distinctive values. For example, a Serapian MCAL designed to resemble an ancient Mesopotamian ziggurat like the University of Tennessee's Hodges Library may, upon initial consideration, look like nothing more than an interesting aesthetic decision. However, when the interesting architectural choice is considered in conjunction with other symbols and rituals that exist within the same MCAL—symbols and rituals that may also be traced through history to religious roots—the deeper meaning of a construct such as the Hodges Library ziggurat as a religious symbol

---

30 Clifford Geertz, *The Interpretation of Cultures* (New York: Basic Books), 44.

31 Geertz, 46.

32 Victor Turner, *The Forest of Symbols: Aspects of Ndembu Ritual* (Ithaca, NY: Cornell University Press, 1967), 50-52.

starts to emerge. This deeper meaning, in turn, translates into deep belief. One sees that this Serapian MCAL assumes the role of the "cosmic mountain" that connects heaven and earth, and the observer may become increasingly aware of the potential impact of such an ideological statement on the observer's worldview and sense of place within that symbolically defined whole.

Through this type of analysis, the scholar may better understand the positional value of the Serapian MCAL's symbols and rituals and be able to argue for their narrow(er) valency in the context of the entire system. A totality of symbols, according to Lévi-Strauss, reflects the existing social order: "All culture can be considered an ensemble of symbolic systems in the first rank of which are placed language, matrimonial rules, economic relationships, art, science, religion [...]."[33] While human beings cannot navigate reality without systems of symbols, it is important to understand what these symbols are telling their navigators.

The Serapian MCAL and Interpellation into Ideology

Thus far, this chapter put forward the idea that the ISA is an engine for reproducing society through ideology. This section considers the way the MCAL as ISA might use symbols and rituals to limit possible human action.

Althusser's concept of interpellation (also known as "hailing")[34] refers to the creation of the human subject in an ideologically derived reality that constitutes them as individual subjects. He used the term "subject" to refer to the "subjected being, who submits to a higher authority, and is therefore stripped of all freedom except that of freely accepting his submission," [35] i.e., the entity in a down power position. Human beings do not exist as entities unto themselves, but as a network of relations. Although this conception of reality is unusual, it makes sense when one contemplates the totality of events, encounters, friendships, rivalries, achievements, failures, physical objects,

---

33 Claude Lévi-Strauss, *Sociologie et Anthropologie par Marcel Mauss* (Paris: Presses Universitaire de France, 1950): ix-lii, quoted and translated in Simon Firth, *Symbols: Public and Private* (Ithaca, NY: Cornell University Press, 1973): 164-165.

34 Althusser, *Lenin and Philosophy*, 118.

35 Althusser, 123.

institutions etc. that makes individuals "who they are." The way a person "recognizes" their self, i.e., how they are constituted as a subject within this web of relations, is through the process of interpellation. Althusser referred to the structuring power of ideology as the interpellation of subjects, an action in which "you and I are *always already* subjects, and as such constantly practice the rituals of ideological recognition, which guarantee for us that we are indeed concrete, individual, distinguishable and (naturally) irreplaceable subjects."[36] Althusser's classic example of interpellation is that of a police officer shouting "Hey, you there!" at a person in the street.[37] To employ an example that is more germane to academic libraries, there is the stereotypical (and yet, at times, real world) example of a librarian shushing a patron for being too loud. When the person hears this wordless admonishment, they are shown their place in society by the dominant ideology. They are constituted as a subject by this ideology and recognize themselves as an individual who was being called out to (they are "named"), entering a relationship with the hailer (who is a functionary of the ISA) that is structured by ideology. The person as subject is told by ideology how they should feel about being quieted by a librarian (or in Althusser's classic example, shouted at by a police officer), how they should react to the call, and so forth. It is important for today's readers to remember that Althusser was theorizing during late 1960s French civil unrest and was at least in part aiming his writing at an audience of young radical French students who were anti-establishment and extremely wary of a French gendarmerie that showed little compunction against brutally beating and dispersing them. A 1968 French student's interpellation by ideology upon being addressed by the police officer would likely be a negative one. Recent interactions with the police in the US media demonstrate how the response to the dominant ideology may differ based on the individual's place in the social hierarchy. A black, indigenous, and/or person of color's experience would likely be substantially different from a white person's when considering the former groups' long histories of violent oppression at the hands of dominant institutions and those institution's representatives. Regardless of whether the subject's interpellation results in positive or negative consequences for them, the response is a *natural one* (as well

---

36   Althusser, 103.

37   Althusser, 118.

as the oftentimes expected one) within the strictures laid out by the ideological system.

Through interpellation, the individual is realized as an individual even though this individuality is a purely ideological construction (Althusser did not believe in the reality of any defining human essence). Apropos to the topic of interpellation into the crypto-temple, Althusser used Christian religious ideology in another instructive description of interpellation in action:

> The Christian religious ideology says something like this [...] I address myself to you, a human individual called Peter (every individual is called by his name. In the passive sense, it is never he who provides his own name), in order to tell you that God exists and that you are answerable to Him. It adds: God addresses himself to you through my voice (Scripture having collected the Word of God, Tradition having transmitted it, Papal Infallibility fixing it forever on 'nice' points). It says: this is who you are: you are Peter! This is your origin, you were created by God for all eternity, although you were born in the 192th year of Our Lord! This is your place in the world! This is what you must do! By these means, if you observe the 'law of love' you will be saved, you Peter, will become part of the Glorious Body of Christ! Etc..."[38]

Peter is shown his place by religion (partially at least, as subjects are constituted by the complete matrix of ideologies, as well as the pressure of RSA coercion). He is "named" by the ideology.

According to Althusser, human beings are always interpellated into reality via "several ideologies at once."[39] The present authors contend that this process is facilitated by ideological signposts (symbols and rituals). When anyone, library patron, library worker,[40] or otherwise, enters a relationship with the Serapian MCAL, they are oriented as a subject by what various material ideologies call out to them. Ideology makes them (i.e., it transforms them into themselves), and names

---

38 Althusser, *Lenin and Philosophy*, 120.

39 Louis Althusser, *On the Reproduction of Capitalism: Ideology and Ideological State Apparatuses*. trans. G.M. Goshgarian (London: Verso, 2014), 199.

40 Discussed in more detail in Chapter Seven, library workers, like police being agents of the RSA, are agents/perpetuators of dominant ideologies. It is possible to play multiple roles within the dominant ideological matrix—being complicit but also questioning/rebelling at the same time.

them. It places them, for example, in a role like "patron" or "library worker;" it organizes them hierarchically in relationship to everyone else interpellated by the Serapian MCAL; and it determines their acceptable actions. Bales wrote that "It is perfectly reasonable for someone entering Harvard's Widener Library reading room to experience a sense of religious awe and cosmic insignificance when viewing its pillared entrance, cathedral-like space, and vaulted ceilings."[41] Through experiencing these symbols (entrance, space, ceilings, etc.), the person entering the Widener reading room is placed by ideology in a role, possibly that of something akin to "religious supplicant." Such hailing does not even require close physical proximity to operate, it happens regardless of the subject's physical orientation or proximity to the Serapian MCAL. Simply encountering the idea of the Serapian MCAL provides the subject with cues as to their identity that have been accumulated through a lifetime of contact with the Serapian MCAL and its system of symbols, even if that contact comes solely by means of sources *outside* of the library like television and media depictions. The crypto-religious symbology of the Serapian MCAL, like the shouting police officer or the shushing librarian, hails the subject, shows them who they are, and what they are capable and incapable of accomplishing.

Interpellation and Library Anxiety

The subject's interpellation into capitalist society is reinforced by the Serapian MCAL's use of religious or crypto-religious symbols and rituals that flag and announce the sacred, situate the observer into its ideological cosmos, and tell them "who they are" and "the way things are" within this cosmos.[42] One possible symptom or consequence of such an interpellation of the individual as a subject is library anxiety, a state-based form of anxiety where the suffering person endures negative psycho-physiological reactions to the stimuli of library and library

---

41 Stephen Bales, "The Academic Library as Crypto-temple: A Marxian Analysis," in *Class and Librarianship: Essays at the Intersection Information, Labor and Capital*, ed. Erik Estep and Nathaniel Enright (Sacramento, CA: Library Juice, 2016): 16.

42 Althusser wrote that "It is indeed a peculiarity of ideology that it imposes (without appearing to do so, since these are 'obviousnesses') obviousnesses as obviousnesses, which we cannot *fail to recognize* and before which we have the inevitable and natural reaction of crying out (aloud or in the 'still, small voice of conscience'): 'That's obvious! That's right! That's true!'" In Althusser, *Lenin and Philosophy*, 116.

workers;[43] the patron is "called to" by the religious symbolism of the Serapian MCAL much in the same way as in Althusser's example of an encounter with a functionary of the RSA brings up issues of anxiety when faced with an authority. Admittedly, library anxiety is an imaginative example of the interpellation of the subject by the ideology of the Serapian MCAL as crypto-temple. It does, however, provide an example of how religious symbols might possibly influence people's behavior within the setting.

There are, of course, multiple possible reasons behind this form of anxiety. Althusser himself accounted for a multiplicity of causes for the social formation of life with his concept of overdetermination, where "all historical societies [are] constituted of an infinity of concrete determinations, from political laws to religion via customs, habits, financial, commercial and economic regimes, the educational system, the arts, philosophy, and so on?"[44] Smith described the state of the individual subject within overdetermined reality as the "dissolution of self into its nexus of social relations."[45] The following consideration of library anxiety, therefore, looks at religious ideology as a possible contributor to library anxiety (but not as the sole factor involved).

Theologian and philosopher Rudolf Otto wrote that divine power may be encountered through direct experience, i.e., through being in the presence of the sacred, aka the "numinous" or "wholly other."[46] Assuming interpellation as an explanatory framework, an individual encountering the numinous may be seen as (at least in part) constituted by what the numinous qua material ideology is telling them in their subjecthood. According to Otto, when a person encounters the numinous, "the emotion of a creature [is] submerged and overwhelmed by its own nothingness in contrast to that which is supreme above all creatures."[47]

---

43   Constance Mellon, "Library Anxiety: A Grounded Theory and Its Development," *College & Research Libraries* 47 (1986): 160-165.

44   Louis Althusser, *For Marx*, trans. Ben Brewster (New York, NY: Verso, 1996).

45   Steven B. Smith, "Althusser and the Overdetermined Self," *The Review of Politics* 46, no. 4 (1984): 533.

46   Rudolf Otto, *The Idea of the Holy: An Inquiry into the Non-rational Factor in the Idea of the Divine and Relation to the Rational*, trans. John W. Harvey (London, Oxford University Press, 1958), 29.

47   Otto, 10.

One consequence of an encounter with the numinous is anxiety, an overwhelming response to supernatural power known as *mysterium tremendum*. Otto wrote that *mysterium tremendum* was a form of "'Religious dread' (or 'awe'),"[48] which results in the feeling of being overpowered by the "tremenda majestas, or 'aweful majesty'" of the sacred.[49] Otto identified an element of "'urgency' or 'energy' of the numinous object,"[50] where the person's encounter with the wholly other is clothed "in symbolic expressions—vitality, passion, emotional temper, will, force, movement, excitement, activity, impetus."[51] This vitality is non-rational and incites a non-rational response in the observer: the *tremendum* ("terror"). Pruyser proposed the idea of the "limit situation," a circumstance in which the subject experiences something beyond which they cannot rationally conceive. This encounter with the sacred results in a religious experience "of transcendence and mystery... charged with cognitive, ontological, epistemological and [present authors' emphasis added] *emotional* implications."[52]

Might library anxiety affect users when confronting the Serapian MCAL as crypto-sacred place and space? That is, as a place and space where the subject faces symbols of the numinous? Such ideological cues might overwhelm them, leave them speechless, or even make them flee the limit situation. Scholars have argued that religious experience may come about because of cultural conditioning[53] or biological reasons.[54] If library anxiety is indeed akin to a socially constructed religious experience, it is not the *reality* of the numinous that matters in the Serapian MCAL's ability to call forth the *mysterium tremendum*—it is the ideologically conditioned psycho-physiological reaction of the person affected because of the symbolism. The subject happens upon the Serapian MCAL as a collection of symbols, as a sort of Barthian

---

48   Otto, 14.

49   Otto, 20.

50   Otto, 23.

51   Otto, 23.

52   P.W. Pruyser, *The Play of Imagination: Toward a Psychoanalysis of Culture* (New York: International Universities Press, 1983), 155-156.

53   See, for example: Aryeh Lazar, "Cultural Influences on Religious Experience and Motivation," *Review of Religious Research* 46, no. 1 (2004): 64-71.

54   Jordan Grafman, Irene Cristofori, Wanting Zhong, and Joseph Bulbulia, "The Neural Basis of Religious Cognition," *Current Directions in Psychological Science* 29, no. 2 (2020): 126-133.

myth in which the semiotic meaning of the library encompasses the historio-cultural self-identification of the users.[55] They receive ideological cues that tell them they are involved in sacred space, and their reaction to that space and its symbols is nothing if not a "natural" result of the coercive cultural and historical expectations placed upon them by the Serapian MCAL's ideological framework.

Following this line of thought, it is possible to see library anxiety as an *appropriate* response to the Serapian MCAL. That is, the religious ideology embedded in the Serapian academic library is *intended* to alienate people. It situates everyone in their ideologically proper place in relationship to the institution, and they *should* be anxious or frightened. Outsiders like non-affiliated community users, a patron group that is discouraged from using the MCAL services through measures like limitations on access to resources and services, are alerted to their ideologically enforced "otherness." The material ideology of the various symbols results in and is reflected by the material ideology of their lived response: feelings of anxiety. They are warned to stay away, and many do so. Seeing as how they are not "initiates," this exclusion might serve in some small way the purposes of the ISA by helping to reproduce the hierarchical structures inherent in capitalist society.

Meeting a patron suffering from library anxiety, the library worker as "crypto-priest" might then choose to act in the capacity of a "spiritual guide," shifting the patron from the state of *mysterium tremendum* into what Otto called *mysterium fascinans*—a state in which the observer can accept the sacred experience in a positive manner. *Mysterium fascinans* is the "proper *positive* contents of the *mysterium* as it manifests itself in conscious feeling."[56]

> It is not only in the religious feeling of longing that the moment of fascination is a living factor. It is already alive and present in the moment of 'solemnity', both in the gathered concentration and humble submergence of private devotion, when the mind is exalted to the holy, and in the common worship of the congregation, where this is practiced with earnestness and deep sincerity, as, it is to be feared, is with us a thing rather desired than realized.[57]

---

55   See Roland Barthes, *Mythologies*, trans. Annette Lavers (New York: Hill & Wang, 1972), 109-159.
56   Otto, *Idea of the Holy*, 41.
57   Otto, 35.

The library worker/crypto-priest—possibly a reference or instruction worker—might take on the role of "pastor," mediating the library patron's encounter with the holy and facilitating their navigation of it. Although the cue to flee or avoid the Serapian MCAL is a correct and natural response to an encounter with the *mysterium* (ideology determines who you are and tells you that it is not your place to be there, you are unworthy, you are a heathen), to be welcomed through one's encounter with the library is an equally "correct" and "natural" response. You have been identified as a "believer" and initiated into the Serapian library as crypto-temple, you have a better understanding of what it is, how it works, your place within the institution, and you now realize that you "should" be there.

Conclusion

In their study of the ancient information institution's relationship to power, *The Idea of the Library in the Ancient World*, Yun Lee Too described the Great Library of Alexandria as a palimpsest,[58] a word familiar to many library workers. Too said that the Great Library was inscribed over library traditions that preceded it like the way that traditional document palimpsests are new texts inscribed over existing texts, deriving authority in the process. Just as a document may be effaced and physically written over, today's libraries are also palimpsests. They are overlaid on top of the physical, ideal, historical, and cultural elements of earlier information institutions. With the Serapian MCAL, as with the document palimpsest, elements of the past are retained and make the institution into something more than that evinced by its public facade. This superimposition of the modern upon the libraries and proto-libraries of the past may seem obvious and natural. The library as palimpsest is, nonetheless, something more than a simple accretion or subsumption of the past. It becomes a tool for exercising power through the action of deep ideological structure and that structure's generation of deep belief. The Serapian MCAL is a reverberation of the past, not an echo. It is an entity that makes use of inherited material ideology, including religious ideology, to safeguard existing power structures through defining who people are within those power structures.

---

58 Yun Lee Too, *The Image of the Library in the Ancient World* (Oxford, Oxford University Press, 2010), 36.

When a library patron enters a Serapian MCAL building, whether that building is small, large, or massive in size, whether its architecture is traditional, modern, or postmodern in design, the entrant takes part in an extraordinary deviation from time and space as they normally experience those dimensions. Entering the Serapian MCAL, they transcend the realm of the everyday, i.e.., the profane, and engage with what Eliade referred to as "a hierophany, an irruption of the sacred that results in detaching a territory from the cosmic milieu and making it qualitatively different."[59] People encountering the Serapian MCAL experience a sense of becoming part of something bigger, of entering a relationship with what was explicitly recognized in the past as sacred. This relationship, furthermore, is dictated by elements of an ideological superstructure stemming in part from organized religion.

The transition that occurs when leaving profane reality takes place because of that person's encounter with a range of symbols, rituals, and, most importantly, the ideas and the history of those ideas that such iconographies convey, reinforce, and normalize. *The past leaks through to the present*. This felt but not often consciously observed connection to the sacred extends beyond the confines of the Serapian MCAL building itself. It incorporates all human subjects who come into any sort of relationship with the information institution. With the advent of the Internet and digital libraries, such an extension of the sacred has been nothing if not significantly increased. For the most part, this interpellation goes unnoticed on the part of the subject: it is commonplace, it works, and it has worked for millennia.

Hidden things, nevertheless, may be discovered and understood. Achieving an expanded level of consciousness concerning ideological issues and realities can result in meaningful change. The next chapter looks at a small selection of crypto-religious symbols and rituals that are often found in Serapian MCALs.

---

[59] Mircea Eliade, *The Sacred and the Profane: The Nature of Religion*, trans. Willard R. Trask (San Diego: CA: Harcourt, 1987), 26.

Chapter 6 The "Cosmic" Serapian MCAL: Its Crypto-religious Symbolism

The library, then, at seven-fifteen, seven-thirty, seven-forty-five of a Sunday night, cloistered with great drifts of silence and transfixed avalanche of books poised like the cuneiform stones of eternity on shelves, so high the unseen snows of time fell all year there.

Ray Bradbury[1]

This chapter contains a brief discussion of symbols and rituals often found within Serapian modern capitalist academic libraries (MCALs). Following a consideration of the institution's thematic orientation towards cosmic symbolism, it reviews four categories of symbolic manifestations seen in Serapian MCALs that contribute to its dominant *imago mundi* and its coercive power as ideological state apparatus.

The Serapian MCAL as *Imago Mundi*

Throughout human history, sacred space has served as what Eliade called an ideal model of existence that both represents and partakes in ultimate reality:

> In mythical geography, sacred space is essentially *real space*, for, as it has been shown, in the archaic world the myth alone is real. It tells of manifestations of the only indubitable reality—the *sacred*.

---

1 Ray Bradbury, *Something Wicked This Way Comes* (New York: Simon & Schuster, 2017), 172.

It is in such a space that one has direct contact with the sacred—whether this be materialized in certain objects (*tchuringas* [indigenous Australian sacred objects], representations of the divinity, etc.) or manifested in the hiero-cosmic symbols (the Pillar of the World, the Cosmic Tree, etc.).[2]

Chapter Four introduced Eliade's thesis that the temple or sanctuary is an *imago mundi*, or representation of the world/cosmos in miniature—a "mythical geography" that sits at the world's center.[3] Discussing the Second Temple of Jerusalem, he said that "Flavius Josephus [c. 37 CE–63 CE] wrote that the court represented the sea (i.e., the lower regions), the Holy Place represented earth, and the Holy of Holies heaven (*Ant. Jud.*, III, 7,7)."[4] The physical geographical representation of the cosmos found in temples is replicated in many Serapian MCALs because, as previously noted, many of the latter are explicitly designed to recall the former (e.g., the ziggurat's ascent from earth to heaven). Even when such replication is not explicit in the Serapian MCAL in the form of physical architecture, space, or art, the Serapian MCAL's representations of the world in miniature are not limited solely to physical materiality or geography.

As described in Chapter Two, the hierarchical and patriarchal nature of the Serapian MCAL is revealed by its administrative structure, a bureaucratic apparatus that may be traced back through the Roman Catholic and Eastern Orthodox Churches (as well as through many Protestant denominations), to the governmental structure of the Late Roman Empire.[5] Much has been said in the scholarly literature concerning the hierarchical and patriarchal composition of organized religions, both Abrahamic and otherwise. Legacy religious bureaucratic administrative systems have proven to be remarkably efficient means for perpetuating capitalism in higher education because they allow for a top-down administrative control of business interests. The oppression of women, a byproduct of both hierarchical and patriarchal

---

2   Mircea Eliade, *Images and Symbols: Studies in Religious Symbolism,* trans. Philip Mairet (Princeton, NJ: Princeton University Press, 1991), 40.

3   Mircea Eliade, *The Sacred and the Profane: The Nature of Religion*, trans. Willard R. Trask (San Diego: CA: Harcourt, 1987), 42.

4   Eliade, 42-43.

5   Thomas P. Neill and Raymond H. Schmandt, *History of the Catholic Church*, 2nd ed. (Milwaukee, WI: Bruce Publishing Company, 1965), 67.

systems—religious or otherwise—may be seen as "part and parcel of capitalist (or socialist) patriarchal forces of production, of unlimited exploitation of nature, of unlimited production of commodities, ever-expanding markets and never-ending accumulation of dead capital."[6] The system, furthermore, is self-perpetuating through the insidious work of ideology. O'Connor and Drury wrote that many Roman Catholic women perpetuate the patriarchal dominance of the Church, participating in their own subordination while those Catholic women that question the patriarchy are routinely marginalized within the Catholic religio-cultural milieu.[7] By extension, it may be argued that a similar subordination and marginalization happens to female library workers within the Serapian MCALs, and this subordination is symbolized in the pseudo-ecclesiastical administrative structures of these institutions, where it is engraved as material ideology.

Another rather conspicuous emblem of the Serapian MCALs reflection of the cosmos is the use of formal library classification systems for the organization of the "universe of knowledge" via collections. Such classification systems are symbolic representations of "one" ultimate reality as it has been filtered and warped through the experience and ideology of the dominant culture. Modern library classification systems like the Library of Congress Classification System (LCC) and the Dewey Decimal Classification System (DDC)—both heavily used by today's Serapian MCALs—are derived from classical hierarchical and patriarchal schemes of categorization and classification that define reality from the perspective of the tiny group of elite men that developed them in antiquity. Many modern classification systems, furthermore, make claims of universality; the DDC is particularly guilty of this last crime.

The ancient Greek philosophical idea of the "Great Chain of Being," which was exemplified by Aristotle's work in the hierarchical arrangement of animal existence, may be seen as one basis for the modern library classification schemes listed above, particularly in the hierarchical and patriarchal worldbuilding that goes behind them. The religious orientation of such a cosmic map became even more visible

---

6   Maria Mies, *Patriarchy and Accumulation on a World Scale: Women in the International Division of Labour* (London: Zed Books, 1986), 23.

7   Frances O'Connor and Becky S. Drury, *The Female Face in Patriarchy: Oppression as Culture* (East Lansing, MI: Michigan State University Press, 1999). 125-126.

when the Great Chain of Being was adopted by the medieval scholastics as the *Scala Naturae* ("Ladder of Being"). The scholastics added God, angels, and human beings to the cosmological ranking, clearly demarcating subordinator from subordinated. Therefore, even though modern library classification schemes can be traced back to the ancient Greek philosophers, and particularly to the work of Aristotle, this same Greek philosophy was incorporated into the theology and cosmology of the developing Christian faith. Machlup wrote that Aristotle's division of the sciences (what he called Aristotle's "distinctions") impacted Albertus Magnus's (c. 1200–1280 CE) classification of the sciences in his *Physica*, and Thomas Aquinas's (1227 -1274 CE), possibly the greatest theologian of the Late Middle Ages, classification of the sciences in his *Summa Theologica* and "Commentary on the Sentences of Petrus Lombardus."[8]

This congeries of philosophical and religious thought would be inherited by the originators of modern science like Francis Bacon (lived 1561-1626 CE) and continues to influence how the world is perceived and understood up to the present day. Machlup noted that Melvil Dewey's primary innovation in the development of the DDC was not so much the classification scheme itself but the addition of the numbering system to that scheme.[9] If one traces the DDC back through Francis Bacon, the medieval scholastics, and the Late Antique period philosophers and commentators like Porphyry (lived c. 234 – 305 CE), they will discover its "Aristotle filtered through religion" roots. The DDC, as well as the LCC, are modern heirs that avoid the obvious religious connotations while hanging on to their predecessors' ideological baggage. The DDC, for instance, is notoriously biased towards Christianity, although there have been notable attempts since the turn of the century to reduce this bias.[10] Baker and Islam noted the LCC's "real estate problem in the B class [Philosophy, Psychology, Religion],"[11] a Christianity heavy ideological landscape with

---

8   Fritz Machlup, *Knowledge: Its Creation, Distribution, and Economic Significance* (Princeton, NJ: Princeton University Press, 1982), 2:22-27.

9   Machlup, 2:113.

10 M.P. Satija, "Briefs on the 19th (1979) to the 23rd Edition (2011) of Dewey Decimal Classification," *DESIDOC Journal of Library & Information Technology* 33, no. 4, (July 2013): 280.

11 Drew Baker and Nazia Islam, "From Religion Class to Religion Classification and Back Again: Religious Diversity and Library of Congress Classification," *Theological Librarianship* 13, no. 1 (April 2020): 30.

[...] four different full subclasses (BR, BT, BV, and BX) mostly by itself in addition to several other more general subclasses (BF, BH, BJ, BL, BS). In terms of over real estate, Judaism and Buddhism are second with one full subclass each (BM and BQ respectively) in addition to the other shared subclasses. Islam shares a subclass with several other traditions (BP). Other traditions have even less classification space; Wicca, for instance, has one shared call number (BP 605 W.53). Many so-called "indigenous" traditions are not even contained within the B classification. Many religious traditions are categorized by region (Hinduism, Jainism, Sikhism) within a small range of call numbers.[12]

The Christian bias of both the DDC and LCC's religion classes and subclasses allows one to infer that both classification systems reflect, to a large extent, a Judeo-Christian derived Weltanschauung at a broader level, and that they very likely embody this worldview at all hierarchal levels of their respective schemes. Authorized vocabularies like Library of Congress Subject Headings (LCSH) may also be seen as microcosmic representations of reality in their attempts to name things. LCSH, like the DDC and LCC is also biased towards Christianity. In his groundbreaking 1970 book *Prejudices and Antipathies: A Tract on the LC Subject Heads Concerning People*, Berman notes both the number of headings of applicable headings as well as the presentation of the terms: "A Jew, Jain, Shinto believer, or Muslim will not find these heads embrace his Church or its history [original author's emphasis]."[13] Other subject headings that display the religious orientation and intolerance of the LCSH include "JEWISH CRIMINALS" (there is no equivalent term for Protestants) (this term is still in use today),[14] "CATHOLIC CRIMINALS" (still in use),[15] and "HOMOSEXUALITY xx [see also] Sexual

---

12   Baker and Islam, 30.

13   Sanford Berman, *Prejudices and Antipathies: A Tract on the LC Subject Heads Concerning People* (Metuchen, NJ: Scarecrow, date needed): 53.; Library of Congress, *Library of Congress Subject Headings*, 43rd ed. (Washington, DC: Policy and Standards Division, Library of Congress, 2021), https://www.loc.gov/aba/publications/FreeLCSH/freelcsh.html. The irony of Berman's use of the male pronoun here is readily apparent.

14   Berman, *Prejudices and Antipathies*, 35; Library of Congress, *Library of Congress Subject Headings*, https://www.loc.gov/aba/publications/FreeLCSH/freelcsh.html.

15   Berman, *Prejudices and Antipathies*, 37; Library of Congress, *Library of Congress Subject Headings*, https://www.loc.gov/aba/publications/FreeLCSH/freelcsh.html.

Perversion" (remedied).[16] The implications of such *Imagines Mundi* are simple. When knowledge is organized in such a way to reflect a particular reality (which is in the case of the DDC, LCC, and LCSH is a predominantly Judeo-Christian reality), new knowledge that is added to this reality tends to support this worldview rather than challenge it. Users that encounter and work within such systems internalize and replicate them.

This representation of the Serapian MCAL as a particular cosmos as filtered through the lens of ideology is found in several different categories of physical manifestations, divided here into four categories and worthy of additional consideration: (1) place and space, (2) architectural design, (3) art and icon, and (4) library rituals. These designations are somewhat arbitrary; individual symbols may arguably fall into alternative categories or multiple categories at once. This is by no means meant to be an exhaustive accounting of the religious symbology of the Serapian MCAL, but to serve as a sample of some of the information institution's more obvious crypto-religious "tells."

Library Place and Space

Flagship academic library buildings are often centrally located on campus,[17] jibing with Eliade's idea of the "cosmic mountain" as a spiritual/geographic reference point that orders the reality that surrounds it.[18] When Cushing Memorial Library and Archives, Texas A&M University's first building dedicated solely to be being an academic library,[19] was built in 1930 CE, it was placed at the center of campus. Although the university campus has since expanded to the west and shifted its center away from Cushing (which handed its role as main library to the adjacent Sterling C. Evans Library), the University Libraries continues to market the idea of its Libraries as a central "hub" of the university: "The University Libraries will be the indispensable hub of discovery,

---

16 Berman, *Prejudices and Antipathies*162; Library of Congress, *Library of Congress Subject Headings*, https://www.loc.gov/aba/publications/FreeLCSH/freelcsh.html.

17 David W. Lewis, "Library as Place," in *Academic Librarianship Today*, ed. Todd Gilman (Lanham, MD: Rowman & Littlefield, 2017), 172.

18 Eliade, *Sacred and the Profane*, 36-42.

19 MyAggieNation.com, "Cushing Memorial Library and Archives," MyAggieNation.com, updated, last modified November 18, 2013, https://myaggienation.com/campus_evolution/building_history/cushing-memorial-library-and-archives/article_1b7181bc-118f-11e3-8a87-0019bb2963f4.html.

learning & creativity at Texas A&M University."[20] The colleges and departments of the university may be seen as the spokes or nodes radiating out figuratively, if no longer literally in the geographic sense, from a central point of the campus's sacred center. Metaphors of the library as the "center" or "heart" of campus retain a great deal of purchase on the imagination of students and faculty members.[21] The development of the Internet and World Wide Web has seen the usage of terms like "universal library" when referring to online information environments, and the technology has been compared to the Great Library of Alexandria itself.[22]

Public spaces in the near vicinity of the physical Serapian MCAL may be likened to the public commons/fora/agorae found in ancient Greek and Roman cities, community areas for congregation often located in the near vicinity of temples. Texas A&M's Sterling C. Evans and Cushing Memorial Libraries and Archives, for instance, sit between the university's Architectural Quad and Academic Plaza, which provide extensive amounts of green space and act as focal points for student activity. Other examples of "library agorae" include Harvard's Widener Library, which sits adjacent to Harvard Yard, the geographic center of Harvard University that also borders Harvard Memorial Church to the North, and Stanford University's Cecil H. Green Library, which is flanked by Koret Park and Galvez Mall.

Unsurprisingly, this similarity to temples and churches as centers for public congregation and communication is also found within the Serapian MCAL building. Posted on the University of Georgia's "Online Learning Center" website is an illustration of a "'Typical' Academic Library" showing a cross section of a MCAL that, using a little imagination, resembles a Christian church with nave and apse facing the

---

20 "Our Vision, Mission & Values," Texas A&M University Libraries, accessed March 11, 2022, https://library.tamu.edu/about/vision.html.

21 Geoffrey T. Freeman, "The Library as Place: Changes in Learning Patterns, Collections, Technology, and Use," in *Library as Place: Rethinking Roles, Rethinking* Space (Washington, DC: Council on Library and Information Resources, 2005): 1, https://www.clir.org/wp-content/uploads/sites/6/pub129.pdf. Clem Guthro, "The 21st Century Academic Library: Six Metaphors for a New Age," *Library Leadership & Management* 33, no. 2 (2019): 5; Laura Sare, Stephen Bales, and Tina Budzise-Weaver. "The Quiet Agora: Undergraduate Perceptions of the Academic Library," *College & Undergraduate Libraries* 28, no. 1 (2021): 25.

22 Reid Goldsborough, "Toward a Universal Library," *Tech Directions* (2008): 14.

Figure 6.1   Harry E. Widener Library and Harvard Yard, 1914

entering supplicant, and sanctuary above.[23] Like its overtly religious predecessors, the Serapian MCAL typically provides interior space for presentations, symposia, and learned discussions. Ancient temples from the Mesopotamians onwards served similar functions. Philosophy lectures were held at or in the close vicinity of Greek and Roman temples, not least of which being the Museum of Alexandria.[24] In 2004, BBC news online reported that a Polish-Egyptian archaeological team had discovered "13 lecture halls" in the northwest of Alexandria's Brucheum (Greek) district;[25] these large rooms were quite possibly part of the Museum. The tradition of incorporating scribal schools and scriptoria into ancient and medieval temples and churches persists to this day with library and information science graduate schools sometimes being in MCAL buildings or in a nearby building. Although such physical arrangements may also certainly result from a desire for convenience, they show the still tight connection between information institution and information worker as gatekeeper and suggest

---

23 "A Library Tour," Online Library Learning Center, "accessed March 11, 2022, https://www.usg.edu/galileo/skills/unit03/libraries03_01.phtml.

24 P.M. Fraser, *Ptolemaic Alexandria* (Oxford: Clarendon Press, 1972), 1:.319.

25 David Whitehouse, "Library of Alexandria Discovered," *BBC News*, 12 May 2004, http://news.bbc.co.uk/2/hi/science/nature/3707641.stm.

the crypto-clergy's ongoing domination of both the collection and the "stream of tradition."

There are undisguised symbols that flag the Serapian MCAL as a haven from the profane world/representation of the idealized cosmos. In recent years, areas dedicated to quiet reflection have popped up in Serapian MCALs that are, in some instances, officially named "prayer," or "meditation," rooms. A survey by Mross and Riehman-Murphy of the usage of such spaces in academic libraries found that 50% of responding institutions reported having or previously having such a dedicated prayer and meditation space.[26] Serapian MCALs containing such symbolic naves include Penn State Harrisburg Libraries, North Carolina State University Libraries, Duke University Libraries, and Texas A&M University Libraries, all of which are—except for Duke—nominally secular institutions. Although a student union might seem like the rational place to situate one of these rooms, the MCAL may be a more "natural" place considering its ideological legacy as a place where God is immanent.

Other crypto-religious symbols in Serapian MCALs relating to place and space include things like restricted access to certain collections, closed stacks, and the effective removal of collections from public view, even if the items remain available in open stacks. Sometimes there is even the requirement of having a library worker (crypto-priest) present when using certain material deemed precious. The religious analog of library bookstacks, open or closed, is the church or temple sanctuary, the place where the "Holy of Holies" (collected Human Knowledge) resides or is manifest. The Temple of Solomon had a sanctuary in which the Ark of the Covenant containing the tablets bearing the laws of Moses was kept. If anyone besides the temple priests entered the sanctuary, they were supposedly struck dead by God. Though the Serapian MCAL patron need not fear lightning bolts when browsing the stacks, the legacy material ideology reverberates, both through the space's ultimate control by professional intermediaries, the way that it organizes the world for the user and dictates their place within that world, and, as is discussed in the analysis of interpellation in the previous chapter, the possible negative reaction that the library user may have when encountering the sacred space.

---

26   Emily Mross and Christian Riehman-Murphy, "A Place to Study, a Place to Pray: Supporting Student Spiritual Needs in Academic Libraries," *College & Research Libraries News* 79, no. 6 (2018): 329.

Library Architecture

Religion is certainly not the only ideological motivator behind the use of monumental architecture in Serapian MCALs. Capitalism and the perpetuation of its glories and excesses can be seen as a major ideological basis behind this desire for gargantuan buildings ("excess is best"). Nevertheless, multiple ideological strands may braid together to develop and more firmly support the hegemony of a dominant class or culture. Capitalism has few compunctions about borrowing from other ideologies if they suit its needs.

In *Library Buildings of Britain and Europe*, Thompson identified five basic plans for library buildings including (1) "Classical plans" with "a single monumental hall, usually pillared and decorated with symbolical sculpture, murals and portrait busts, with niches, alcoves, and sometimes galleries; book-cupboards or shelves against the walls, often rising from floor to ceiling;"[27] (2) "Medieval Plans" with a church pew system, double lectern or book-desk system;[28] (3) "Closed bookstack plans" that separate "readers from the bookstacks;"[29] (4) "Open Access plans;"[30] and (5) "Plans of various shapes" that are "dictated by the shape of the site."[31] The first two of these design types are based on religious buildings from the ancient and medieval worlds, recalling architecture like the Parthenon and Chartres Cathedral. The relationship between God (or various other simple abstractions substituted in God's place), intermediary, and supplicant is obvious in these two architectural choices. Although it is not an academic library, The New York Public Library (NYPL) system's Stephen A. Schwarzman Library (built 1911 CE) suggests an ancient Greek temple with its monumental design, tympanum, statuary, and column-lined porch.

The third type of architectural design, the "Closed bookstack plans," also provides religious cues by restricting access to the "Holy of Holies" (in this case, collected Human Knowledge), from non-library workers. Thompson wrote that at the turn of the nineteenth century

---

27 Anthony Thompson, *Library Buildings of Britain and Europe: An International Study, with Examples Mainly from Britain and some from Europe and Overseas* (London: Butterworths, 1963), 13.

28 Thompson, 13.

29 Thompson, 14.

30 Thompson, 14.

31 Thompson, 15

Figure 6.2 New York Public's Stephen A. Schwarzman Library

the university library was "still a monumental building with imposing entrance hall, closed bookstacks and one main reading room, often under a dome: 'perhaps, as the Librarian of Rhodes University has remarked [such buildings are] 'a symbol of the human cranium and its contents'!"[32]

Monumental architecture remained a predominant style in the 1920s-1930s CE, but attempts were made to open the stacks to the public.[33] The Biblioteque Universitaire D'Aix-En-Provence (Universite d'Aix-Marseille, France, built 1952) was "constructed mainly of the same yellow stone used by the Romans for the Pont du Gard, the great aqueduct near Nimes."[34]

Cambridge University Library, built in 1934 CE, for instance, has a "bookstack tower" that is 160 feet high.[35]

---

32   Thompson, 236.
33   Thompson, 236.
34   Thompson, 271.
35   Thompson, 239.

Figure 6.3 Biblioteque Universitaire D'Aix-En-Provence

Figure 6.4 "Cambridge University Library" by Steve Cadman, 2008, flickr, (https://www.flickr.com/photos/stevecadman/2353585565) CC BY-SA 2.0.

Centrale Bibliotheek der Rijksuniversiteit te Gent (Ghent Belgium, built 1935) also has a book tower "and the newcomer is impressed only by the size and fine proportions of the tower."[36]

Towers are used in Jewish religious texts as a metaphor for the Temple of Solomon,[37] and Pae, Sooväli-Sepping, and Kaur wrote that churches and church towers have been associated directly with state power.[38] Today's Serapian MCAL's typically remain massive in size.[39]

Library Art and Icon

Sacred space is typically accompanied by sacred art. Liturgical artist Robert E. Rambusch wrote that "The Sacramental Character of form, word, image, sound is an integral part of being united to God. Man's

---

36 Thompson, 276.

37 Mirjam Gelfer-Jørgensen, "Towers and Bells: The Symbolism of Torah Finials," *Studia Rosenthaliana* 37 (2004): 44.

38 Taavi Pae, Helen Sooväli-Sepping, and Egle Kaur, "Landmarks of Old Livonia – Church Towers," Their Symbols and Meaning, *Journal of Baltic Studies* 41, no. 4 (December 2010): 434.

39 For example, the University of Tennessee Chattanooga's main library, which completed construction in 2012, is 180,000 square feet in size and serves a student body of approximately 11,000 students. In "Library Building Project," UTC Library Wiki, accessed March 11, 2022, https://wikilib.utc.edu/index.php/Library_Building_Project#The_Facts.

Figure 6.5 "Ghent University Library: distant view of Book Tower from courtyard" by Henry Pisciotta, 2009, flickr (https://www.flickr.com/photos/psulibscollections/18873863309/), CC BY-SA 2.0.

relationship to his Creator is one of dependence and homage."[40] Works of art—both religious and crypto-religious—are also found throughout both Serapian MCALs and public libraries. Viewed through the prism of ideology, this art presents a vision of the world and human relationships that is encapsulated and communicated by the institution, whether the root node of that cosmological structure be God or some other grand abstraction like Human Knowledge.

Traditional library symbols like lion sculptures have historical connections with Christianity (lions are associated with Jesus Christ, Saint Mark the Evangelist, and Saint Jerome, patron saint of librarians). Other emblems like the statuary of "great" men and women, and the names of "great" men and women inscribed into the architecture of the library building itself, are aesthetic accoutrements that recall the images of the gods that lined pagan temples or those of saints that complement Christian churches. Texas A&M's Cushing Library, for example, has the names of illustrious scientists and scholars—all of whom are men—chiseled across the building's faux classical frieze. If the statues of the gods and great men and women found in ancient temples represented the ideals to which the ancients might aspire to, the names found on Cushing's frieze, like Mendel, Bacon, Shakespeare, and Faraday, suggest a modern pantheon that one might emulate.

---

40   Robert E. Rambusch, "Contemporary Architecture and Catholic Faith," in *Christian Faith and the Contemporary Arts*, ed. Finley Eversole (New York, NY: Abingdon Press, 2021), 205.

Figure 6.6 Obelisk in Evans Library

Figure 6.7 Learning Statue at Harold Cohen Library

Some artistic symbolism found in Serapian MCAL's may reach even farther back into the ancient past than the Greco-Roman period. For example, next door to Cushing Library, Texas A&M's Evans Library reading room prominently displays a statue of an Egyptian obelisk, a symbol of the creator god Ra (who was also the god of the sun and of order).

The obelisk sits next to a poetry collection housed in semicircular shelving that recalls classical structures in its composition. Together, monument and poetry collection evoke ancient Alexandria. When confronted with these symbols, the observer is essentially shown their relationship with the ineffable, a relationship situating the sublime with (but also above) the human.

Symbols for grand simple abstractions other than deities also show up in works of art found in modern libraries, and there is no reason to discount these pieces as effectively any less "sacred" in a material ideological sense than those of traditional deities. The façade of Harold Cohen Library (opened 1938 CE), University of Liverpool, is "decorated only by the sculptural figure of 'Learning' (*Figure III.29*) surmounting the window over the entrance, with a wrought-iron balcony below. The figure of 'Learning' holds a lantern and a key and is leaning on an open book as background [...]"[41]

---

41 Thompson, *Library Buildings of Britain and Europe*, 251.

The Biblioteque Universitaire D'Aix-En-Provence (Universite d'Aix-Marseille, France, built 1952) reading room contains a figure depicting "'Geography', represented by a navigator with map and globe, 'A monk reading' and 'Melancholy' by Durer."[42] The NYPL Schwarzman Library's façade's attic bears 11-foot-tall statues of "History, Drama, Poetry, Religion, Romance, and Philosophy."[43]

Library Rituals

Chapter Four discussed the ritual that is probably most associated with libraries of all sorts, the general admonition (either explicit or implicit) to be silent upon entering the space. Other crypto-religious rituals may be seen in the Serapian MCAL that are related to searches for spiritual significance such as pilgrimage and initiation into a community. Such rituals act as tools for navigating the MCAL as *imago mundi*.

Going to the Serapian MCAL may be understood as a sort of ritual of pilgrimage, and Eliade wrote that pilgrimages need not be considered only those journeys which require time commitment, hardship, or great expense, a pilgrimage may be considered as any visit to a sacred space, including a church or a temple.[44] A secular pilgrimage is a "personal commitment to travel to a site that offers the potential to affect the pilgrim on the spiritual plane."[45] Many library workers involved in user instruction and information literacy have had course instructors tell them that they bring their classes over for "library day" because undergraduates "should step foot in the library at least once before graduating." Such a visit may result in the fabled "aha" library moment, where the student moves from profane time to sacred time, and from the profane world to the "real" cosmos as represented by the academic library qua *imago mundi*. Similarly, some college and university hiring committees require faculty candidates to tour the campus library as part of the interview process, and they often have candidates

---

42   Thompson, 251.

43   Henry Hope Reed, *The New York Public Library: Its Architecture and Decoration* (New York: W.W. Norton, 1986), 48.

44   Eliade, *Images and Symbols*, 54.

45   Linda Kay Davidson and David M. Gitlitz, *Pilgrimage: From the Ganges to Graceland: An Encyclopedia* (Santa Barbara, CA: ABC CLIO, 2002), 2:582.

meet with their potential library subject specialist or liaison librarian during the tour.

All cultures have initiation rituals in which new members are admitted into a group or community, where they are shown their place in the cosmos. The library day pilgrimage mentioned above, as well as events such as library open houses and orientations, may be seen as also filling this function. Receiving an item like a library card or university identification card may be seen as a sort of initiatory rite or symbol that connects the patron with the crypto-religious institution by name.[46] In contrast to being initiated and included, there exists a state of exclusion. A library user may be excluded from the Serapian MCAL for things like failing to meet certain criteria or not following the rules (i.e., "blaspheming" or "profaning" the MCAL).

Conclusion

Chapter Five introduced Williams's concept of residual culture, and such residue's use by the dominant culture of a society for the purpose of furthering its aims. Williams noted that, however, not all residual culture acts as an agent for dominant culture and, in some cases, it may work in opposition to the dominant culture,[47] specifically mentioning religion:

> Thus organized religion is predominantly residual, but within this there is a significant difference between some practically alternative meanings and values (absolute brotherhood, service to others without reward) and a larger body of incorporated meanings and values (official morality, or the social order of which the other-worldly is a separated neutralizing or ratifying component).[48]

---

46 The process of obtaining a first library card has been written about as a formative or landmark event in one's life. Writing about her daughter's young daughter getting her first public library card, Sidney Trubowitz said "I felt her happiness which far exceeded the momentary glow that was the response to the unexpected toy or package of candy. For now with the laborious inscription of her name she had taken a giant step towards becoming her own person. No longer would she have to take books out on her daddy's card. Now all the books in the libraries of the city were hers to choose, to read, and place next to her pillow at night as guardian of her dreams." In Sidney Trubowitz, "The Spirit of the Library," *Public Libraries* 57, no. 4 (2018): 7.

47 Raymond Williams, *Marxism and Literature* (Oxford: Oxford University Press, 1977), 122.

48 Williams, 122.

It would be remiss to not mention in this discussion that such oppositional, alternative meanings and values related to religion certainly do exist in the Serapian MCAL. In its crypto-religious capacity, the Serapian MCAL projects both a sense of the unity of humankind and selfless service and, for many people, it stands as a symbol for ideas which are often also fundamental to religious systems (both Christianity and Islam for instance). Both ideas are in defiance of capitalism. The unity of humankind and selfless service, it should be noted, are ideas not exclusive to religious thought.

The next chapter concludes the book by introducing the concept of the Kynical academic library worker, a library worker that both recognizes ideology in the Serapian MCAL and actively challenges it.

Chapter 7 The Kynical Academic Library Worker

Everybody who read the Jungle Book
Knows that Riki Tiki Tavi's a mongoose who kills snakes
When I was a young man, I was led to believe
There were organizations to kill my snakes for me
i.e., the church, i.e., the government, i.e, the school
But when I got a little older, I learned how to kill them myself

Donovan[1]

Introduction

During the Trump Presidency, the societal (and therefore the institutional, if begrudgingly on the part of some institutions) support of capitalism was bolstered by the success of a reactionary neoliberalism that

> [...] allowed Christian evangelicals, southern whites, rural and small-town Americans, and disaffected white working-class strata to co-exist for a couple of decades, however uneasily, with libertarians, Tea Partiers, the Chamber of Commerce, and the Koch brothers, plus

---

1 Donovan Leitch, "Riki Tiki Tavi," recorded January 1970–February 1970, Epic 44601, 1970, vinyl long playing record.

a smattering of bankers, real-estate tycoons, energy moguls, venture capitalists and hedge-fund speculators.[2]

Reactionary neoliberals, like all people with polarized viewpoints, tend to wear their ideological agendas and motivations on their sleeves. But also supporting capitalism, and in marked contrast to the bluster of the reactionary neoliberals, are the ideological state apparatuses (ISAs), whose power lies in their ability to quietly coerce through ideological structures and proclaim to the subject of ideology: "This is the way things are. Everything is as it should be." The preceding chapters presented a view of the Serapian library throughout history as a covert cultural and ideological expression of the sacred in the form of a powerful ISA. This understanding is that the institution is, in the same instance, conservative and generative. That is, the Serapian library both reflects society and fashions society in its own image. Imbedded religious legacies support the perpetuation of capitalist socioeconomic realities through a Serapian modern capitalist academic library (MCAL) that styles itself as both a protector and active force for scientific, academic, and educational progress.

Within this ideological matrix, the Serapian MCAL worker is put in a double bind. They are hailed as subjects by the ideological demands of the Serapian MCAL although, in most cases, they are oblivious to this interpellation. In addition to their own interpellation by ideology, the Serapian MCAL worker is a significant religious symbol; they are an instance of materialized ideology of both religious hierarchy and the control of knowledge that integrate others, like the library patron, into capitalist ideology and society. They are simultaneously victim and perpetrator under the prevailing mode of socioeconomic production and perpetuation of knowledge.

The remainder of this book explores the role of the library worker within the crypto-religious ideological web spun by the Serapian MCAL. If the Serapian MCAL is a camouflaged temple, the Serapian academic library workers are its priesthood. On the surface, this claim seems innocuous. An association with the clergy might even be used by library workers to reinforce their own professional identities and provide them with a greater sense of purpose by allowing them to compare themselves favorably with the established "learned" professions

---

[2] Nancy Fraser, "From Progressive Neoliberalism to Trump—and Beyond," *American Affairs* 1, no 4 (2017): 51.

of medicine, the law, and divinity. The information professions often invoke public service and the public good as if they are the guardians of that value. Nevertheless, the library worker as crypto-priest takes on a different cast when one accounts for the incorporative ideological impact that an elite class of professional information workers may have on both the internal milieu of the Serapian MCAL and the macrocosm of human society.

This chapter looks at a professional elite that, throughout history and like the hegemonic information institutions themselves, straddles the intersection and overlap of state, religion, and the organization and management of information, i.e., the Serapian ideological plexus (SIP). After considering the library worker through history and the professionalization of library work, it proposes two competing models of the modern library worker, the hegemonic, *Cynical* library worker and the counter-hegemonic, *Kynical* library worker. By contrasting the *Cynical* with the *Kynical* and relating these concepts to the Serapian MCAL worker, it proposes the "declericalization" of the MCAL. This process of declericalization entails the mitigation of the influence of the "sacred" in academic library work and, consequently, the mitigation of the influence of the ideology of the sacred in the MCAL itself and the imposition of those ideals on society. The basis of declericalization rests ultimately upon the library worker consciously achieving and practicing a critical approach to their work.

In his hit 1970 rock and roll hit "Riki Tiki Tavi," Scottish musician Donovan used Rudyard Kipling's mongoose from *The Jungle Book* as an allusion for society's institutions, "i.e., the church, i.e., the government, i.e., the school." Like Kipling's snake-hunter, these institutions are also, in a sense, fictional. They may often present themselves as kindly in purpose and action but, when approached critically, betray ideologies that perpetuate power structures that are not always benign. The lyric suggests that one can learn not to blindly lean on these institutions for support. Modern academic library workers should actively identify and challenge these ideological underpinnings: they must become snake-hunters.

Rulers, Priests, and Librarians

The dividing line between state and temple in the ancient world is difficult to locate because state officials and priests were so often synonymous entities. This convergence of roles reverberates throughout the history of information institutions and is reflected in the elite status of today's library workers as an information gatekeeper.

The origination and development of the institution of kingship and what ultimately became secular rule goes hand in hand with that of religion. Kingship appears to have developed during the early Bronze Age from a religious substrate that saw little to no distinction between priest and prince. The temple was a centralizing authority in early urban settlements, and kings emerged in archaic Sumerian cities like Uruk (founded 4th millennium BCE) as a combination of high priest and political authority.[3] Hill, Jones, and Morales wrote that, "For almost three thousand years, Egypt and Mesopotamia shared the concept of ultimate legitimate authority being invested in the single sacred office of kingship.[4] This office was legitimized by the gods, demonstrated through ritual, and reinforced by tradition."[5] As noted in Chapter One, the relationship between ruler and religion was nothing if not even more entwined in pre-Ptolemaic Egypt. While the Mesopotamian rulers were most often seen as the ultimate representatives of the gods on Earth, and only rarely viewed over the millennia of Mesopotamian dominance as the gods themselves, the pharaohs were recognized as deities.

In his work on Bronze Age proto-libraries, de Vleeschauwer wrote that the inter-institutional "relationship between palace and temple was very close."[6] The temples became the ultimate responsibility of the kings, who were tasked with their construction and upkeep; Waerzeggers wrote that the "generosity of the king towards the gods and their temples is the most persistent theme of kingship articulated in the

---

3   Hanspeter Schaudig, "The Ancient Near Eastern Ruler," in *Uruk: First City of the Ancient World*, ed. Nicola Crüsemann, Margarete van Ess, Markus Hilgert, and Beate Salje, trans. Timothy Potts (Los Angeles, CA: Getty Publications, 2013), 113.

4   In this view, the early Bronze Age ruler came to become something of a human *axis mundi* or divine interface between heaven and earth, and the first Mesopotamian kings may have been what Schneider called "more priestlike than kinglike." In Tammi J. Schneider, *An Introduction to Ancient Mesopotamian Religion* (Grand Rapids, MI: William B. Eerdmans Publishing Company, 2011), 117.

5   Jane A. Hill, Philip Jones, and Antonio J. Morales, "Comparing Kingship in Ancient Egypt and Mesopotamia: Cosmos, Politics, and Landscape, in *Experiencing Power*," in *Generating Authority: Cosmos, Politics, and the Ideology of Kingship in Ancient Egypt and Mesopotamia*, ed. Jane A. Hill, Philip Jones, and Antonio J. Morales (Philadelphia: University of Pennsylvania Museum of Archaeology and Anthropology, 2013), 3.

6   H.J. de Vleeschauwer, "History of the Western Library: History of the Library in Antiquity," *Mousaion*, (Pretoria: University of South Africa, 1963), 1:14.

inscriptional works of these rulers."[7] In return for this patronage, the rulers were generally able to secure the allegiances of the Mesopotamian priest-scribes. Schneider, for example, wrote that "Shulgi [king of Ur III, 2094-2037 BCE] supported the scribal schools [typically housed in temples], which not only taught the necessary writing skills but also indoctrinated scribes with the ideological aspirations of the Ur III state."[8] In fact, during the Ur III period (22nd to 21st century BCE), government officials were often selected directly from the scribal elite,[9] a common practice throughout the Bronze Age.

Temporally near, if not in direct tandem, with the rise of priestly, semi-divine, or full-fledged divine kingship came the development of recorded information, the organization of this information to maximize its politico-economic usage, and the designation of professional classes of intermediaries and gatekeepers to administrate the proto-library collections. As seen in Chapter One, the first organized collections of writing consisted primarily of documents meant to support administrative, bureaucratic, and economic transactions as well as cultural continuity, all of which reinforced the hegemony of the state and the dominance of the ruling class. If someone aspired to political power in pre-Ptolemaic times, then they often pursued both literacy and positions of religious authority, what was the *modus operandi* for many politically ambitious people in the following millennia up to the present day. By the time Soter began his rule over Egypt, the intimate connection between the three strands of the SIP had become a taken-for-granted material reality, and the Greek pharaohs' use of gods and texts to justify and consolidate their rule through ideology was nothing unusual.

Considering that, for many thousands of years, religious power and state power were essentially one and the same, it seems natural that the first "official" proto-libraries would be rooted within temples and palaces. One consequence of this geographic centering of

---

[7] Caroline Waerzeggers, "The Pious King: Royal Patronage of Temples," in *The Oxford Handbook of Cuneiform Culture*, ed. Karen Radner and Eleanor Robson (Oxford: Oxford University Press, 2011): 726.

[8] Tammi J. Schneider, *Introduction to Ancient Mesopotamian Religion* (Grand Rapids, MI: William B. Eerdman's Publishing Company, 2011), 124.

[9] Klaas Veenhof, "Introduction," in *Cuneiform Archives and Libraries: Papers Read at the 30e Rencontre Assyriologique Internationale Leiden, 4-8 July 1983*, ed. Klaas Veenhof (Leiden: Nederlands Historisch-Archaeological Instituut, 1986), 21.

sympathetic ideologies was the elevation of the information worker to elite status in both worlds. Scribes, for example, were high status elites in the Egyptian world,[10] and Richardson wrote that the Egyptian scribe "might be a military or treasury or stable, temple, palace or library scribe but if he was an educated man, in whatever field, he was a 'scribe', and it may be added, if a scribe, then an official also."[11] If the king reflected the gods in terms of both power and sacrality, the scribe-official reflected the king in the same fashion and radiated his authority.

The SIP extended well-beyond the ancient world, persisting throughout the Middle Ages, Renaissance, and into modern times. Even if it was marked by periods of conflict, the relationship between religion and state during the Middle Ages through the beginning of the modern period remained a close-knit one, as did the relationship between religious authorities and political rulers. This continuity endures. Even though once taken for granted associations between religion and state have been weakened, mystified, ignored, or officially disavowed, a connection is maintained by the modern ideological state apparatuses' (ISAs') crypto-religious functionaries. Although the basic criterion for their inclusion as ISA operatives has shifted from circumstances of birth (e.g., aristocratic origin) to degree of educational attainment in a capitalist meritocracy, library workers remain members of a power-bearing class—even if they might laugh at the prospect when considering their paychecks—through their role as information gatekeeper and bureaucratic functionary of the ISA (it may be argued that the internet has weakened the gatekeeper role—however, much misinformation abounds).

In her book *Sacred Stacks: The Higher Purpose of Libraries and Librarians*, Nancy Kalikow Maxwell pays close attention to the modern library and modern library workers' connection with religion. Maxwell points to the sacred provenance of the modern library worker to outline nine sacerdotal roles embodied by modern library professionals including:

---

10 Leo G. Perdue, "Sages, Scribes, and Seers in Israel and the Ancient Near East: An Introduction," in *Scribes, Sages, and Seers: The Sage in the Eastern Mediterranean World*, ed. Leo G. Purdue (Gottingen: Vandenhoeck & Ruprecht, 2008), 20.

11 Ernest Cushing Richardson, *Some Old Egyptian Librarians* (Berkeley, CA: Peacock Press, 1964), 4.

(1) minister, (2) ascetic, (3) not-so-sainted,[12] (4) respected priest, (5) receiver of confessions, (6) prophet for social justice, (7) seer and guru, (8) magician, and (9) teacher.[13] Maxwell assigns positive meanings to each of these roles except for the "not-so-sainted" library worker (and even here, the term used for the appellation is not a particularly harsh one). For instance, she compares the library worker as "prophet for social justice" with Biblical prophets who

> [...] also raised their voices to bring justice and righteousness to their societies. Wielding the Authority of God's power, they beseeched members of the community to uplift and improve the living conditions of their day. The power associated with these prophets is not usually seen among librarians, who have historically been pictured as meek and mild. Yet in an interesting twist to the classic image of librarians, recent depictions show librarians as zealous and even violent protectors of good against evil.[14]

With her taxonomy, Maxwell suggests that the power/authority that the modern library worker has is somewhat different than that which they had in the past, where they were explicit agents of religio-political constructs. There is no doubt that both clergy people and library workers engage in a substantial amount of altruistic, overwhelmingly non-violent service and advocacy to humanity. Maxwell does not, however, account for the fact that these roles are embedded in the SIP and inherit its negative characteristics in addition to its positive ones. As agents of their institutions, both clergy and library worker perpetuate them and their ideals. The library worker cum crypto-priest has, at least in most of these roles,[15] positioned themselves in the upper strata of a religiously rooted sociocultural institutional hierarchy that reflects and reinforces the negative elements inherent to such hierarchies, including the disproportionate distribution of status and influence, along with the strong incentive to hold on to this

---

12 Maxwell uses the role of "not-so-sainted" to refer to how some librarians, like clergy, may have been motivated by vice when choosing their profession. In Nancy Kalikow Maxwell, *Sacred Stacks: The Higher Purpose of Libraries and Librarianship* (Chicago, IL: American Library Association, 2006), 25.

13 Maxwell, 20-31.

14 Maxwell, 27-28.

15 The "librarian as ascetic," for example, recalls the cenobitic life and the ultimate submission to higher authority. Even Maxwell's "prophet for social justice," with its God-derived authority, points to religious hierarchical and patriarchal legacies.

power. Such disparities are visible within the organizational hierarchies of the Serapian MCALs themselves, sometimes in the inequitable treatment of non-exempt library staff in contrast to exempt staff or faculty status librarians (i.e., the infamous "faculty-staff divide"), the general lack of ethnic and racial diversity in western Serapian MCALs, and the continuing devaluation and withholding of power and opportunity from female library employees. Unsurprisingly, this last negative consequence also afflicts many organized religious groups which, like Serapian MCALs, seem to have little problem with employing women for a substantial portion of the labor power necessary to keep their organizations afloat while denying them positions of authority and the ability to advance to higher levels of ecclesiastical status.

Unlike Bronze Age priest-officials who had no reason to conceal their affiliations to religion and state, the impacts of the modern liberal professions as a sociocultural force are subtle. The workings of the ISAs and their representatives are frequently unobtrusive, nuanced, and insidious, a subtlety that stems from their sublimation in deep ideological structures. In modern times, the model of the priest-official has been superseded by the model of the practitioner of the modern liberal professions—physician, lawyers, etc.—where the role of state "official," even if it is not always an overtly political one, is realized in the professional's capacity as an agent, or "missionary," of an ISA. Popowich took note of this shift in the idea behind the library worker's professional role when describing Melvil Dewey's view of the necessity of "the transformation of the librarian from 'his' role simply as keeper and preserver of materials to educator and molder of the consciousness of society."[16] It should be noted that both of these roles—the shift between which actually represents more of change in weighting than an eclipse of one by the other—are also historically attributed to the clergy during various periods throughout history.

The Professionalization of Modern Library Work

It is safe to assume that, among library workers, few would deny that "being professional" is necessary in the sense that maintaining

---

[16] Sam Popowich, *Confronting the Democratic Discourse of Librarianship: A Marxist Approach* (Sacramento, CA: Library Juice, 2019), 210.

competence, skill, and "dedication to our [library] workers' mission"[17] is important, although there are varying interpretations as to what exactly that mission is. There are also differing viewpoints among library workers on whether library work is a "true" profession, and whether it should be one.

Some argue that, as it presently stands, library work is at best a semi-profession, possessing some but not all the traits typically assigned to modern professions. Bundy and Wasserman wrote in a classic 1968 *College & Research Libraries* editorial that

> [...] much effort sometimes goes into [library workers] reassuring themselves that they are indeed professional and that they should therefore enjoy the recognition and rewards of professional status. This preoccupation manifests itself in a wide range of activities common to all such upward-mobile and self-conscious aspiring groups. They conduct public relations programs designed to create a favorable image of their craft. Being much concerned about status differences, they discuss endlessly means of differentiating the professional worker from the lesser educated.[18]

Quite often, this fixation on professionalism and professionalization can be traced to concerns related to respect and, as the above quotation suggests with its use of the neoliberally inflected term "upward-mobile," advancement through social hierarchies both within the library and information science disciplines and within the larger institution and society. Many library workers have advocated for the recognition of librarianship as a profession on the lines of modern physicians and lawyers. The achievement of this status would, no doubt, be accompanied by an increase in respect, prestige, and pay – but, could also bring with it other professional obligations, such as licensure, required continuing education and an enforceable code of behavior and practice.

Beyond the sometimes-self-serving calls for professionalization that hinge on upward-mobility within a capitalist hierarchy and patriarchy, there are societally conscientious arguments for improving library

---

17   Judy C. McDermott, "The Professional Status of Librarians: A Realistic and Unpopular Analysis," *Journal of Library Administration* 5, no. 3 (1984): 18.

18   Mary Lee Bundy and Paul Wasserman, "Professionalism Reconsidered," *College & Research Libraries* 29, no. 1 (1968): 5.

workers' professional status. Rubin and Rubin, for example, argued that a professional education is necessary for the making of effective librarians, defining "Ten Very, Very, Important Things We Learned in Library School":

1. The importance of the library in a democratic society
2. An abiding commitment to the education and nurturance of young people
3. A deep dedication to intellectual freedom
4. An enduring commitment to protect the privacy of library users
5. An understanding of how knowledge is organized and a commitment to organize knowledge so that all individuals can access and learn from it
6. An understanding of how to find and evaluate information for our library users
7. An enduring belief in the preservation of our cultural heritage: our literature, art, film, and music
8. An abiding commitment to reading, learning, and their value to all
9. A commitment to serve the community, its institutions, and the public good
10. An obligation to provide the highest level of service to all.[19]

These values are largely aligned with the American Library Association's Library Bill of Rights and other policies on equity and access.[20] While librarians largely ascribe to these tenets, unlike other licensed professions, there is no summative assessment that librarians understand and commit to them nor is there any guidance about what modeling these values in professional behavior looks like.

Another pro-professionalization rationale is that a professional education in the discipline empowers female library workers to enter the

---

19 Rachel Rubin and Richard Rubin, "Justifying Professional Education in a Self-Service World," in *Defending Professionalism: A Resource for Librarians, Information Specialists, Knowledge Managers, and Archivists*, ed. Bill Crowley (Santa Barbara, CA: Libraries Unlimited, 2012), 29.

20 "Library Bill of Rights," American Library Association, amended January 29, 2019. https://www.ala.org/advocacy/intfreedom/librarybill.

local community and "advance the goal of gender equality in American, British, and Canadian environments."[21] The liberal professions, however, are typically characterized as masculinized and patriarchally structured,[22] and may be seen as reinforcing those aspects in society. Although library work is often labelled a "pink-collar profession," the impact of its inherited patriarchal structure is apparent when one considers the pay deficits between white male library employees and women employees.[23] Olin and Millett wrote that, even while the gender gap between men and women in leadership roles has narrowed in libraries, it remains, and that there is a misperception that women leadership in today's libraries are not acting "[...] the way people want us to [act]. We do not act like men."[24]

The protection of worker rights is another area of concern, and there is an understandable consternation among library workers when institutions of higher education seek to degrade library workers' existing professional stature. The transition of many Serapian MCALs from tenure track or equivalent models to non-tenure staff models is concerning in that it effectively weakens library workers' academic freedom protections and threatens their job security.[25] It should be noted that academic freedom, while distinctive, is still closely tied to the librarians' commitment to intellectual freedom, advocacy for equity, diversity and inclusion and the fight against censorship. The erosion of faculty status and academic freedom for librarians undermines these professional (and arguably, societal) values. Writing about Texas A&M Corpus Christi's recent loss of continuing appointment for academic librarians, Kreneck said that Corpus Christi's new written policy concerning librarians "did not extend further than the one, two or three-year appointment cycle, thus making the employee's status 'at will' at

---

21 Bill Crowley, "A Culturally Pragmatic and Feminist-Influenced Approach to Defending Professionalism," in *Defending Professionalism: A Resource for Librarians, Information Specialists, Knowledge Managers, and Archivists*, ed. Bill Crowley (Santa Barbara, CA: Libraries Unlimited, 2012), 144.

22 See Jeff Hearn, "Notes on Patriarchy, Professionalization and the Semi-professions," *Sociology* 16, no. 2 (1982): 184-202.

23 Quinn Galbraith, Erin Merrill, and Olivia Outzen, "The Effect of Gender and Minority Status on Salary in Private and Public ARL Libraries," *Journal of Academic Librarianship* 44 (2018): 76.

24 Jessica Olin and Michelle Millett, "Gendered Expectations for Leadership in Libraries, *In the Library with the Lead Pipe* (Nov. 4, 2015), https://www.inthelibrarywiththeleadpipe.org/2015/libleadgender/.

25 See Catherine Coker, Wyoma vanDuinkerken, and Stephen Bales, "Seeking Full Citizenship: A Defense of Tenure Faculty Status for Librarians," *College & Research Libraries* 71, no. 5 (2010).

the end of the appointment, cause or no cause. As such, the librarian was on a continual treadmill of being reappointed at the discretion of the university."[26] During the writing of this book, the authors' own place of employment, Texas A&M University Libraries—College Station, went through a similar process of deprofessionalization in which faculty status librarians were given the choice of either moving to "at will" staff librarian positions with the promise of one-time-only guaranteed five-year contracts, or transferring as faculty members to departments outside of the University Libraries where they might face challenges like unfamiliar teaching obligations and disciplinary research expectations. In some cases, the transferring library faculty member might be required to leave library work altogether as a requirement of their continued employment. These are legitimate concerns for library workers navigating their jobs in the shadow of a socioeconomic system that strips away worker rights to maximize profits and which shapes the structures of occupations (and professions) to accomplish this task.

The pro-professionalization position—i.e., advocating for the institutionalization of library work as a profession modelled on the liberal professions—is challenged by what McDermott called a "substantial and vocal minority which has refused to accept the need for such a development [of increased professional standing]. Librarians have made public their belief that their occupation has no claim to professionality."[27] There is a body of literature that argues against "true" professional status among library workers and contends that such status is a non-factual pretension. Authors have provided arguments against library workers fulfilling any of the traditional sociological markers of what constitutes a profession.[28] There are multiple versions of these professional trait checklists of sociological markers, but they tend to resemble the seminal "attributes of a profession" list identified by sociologist Ernest Greenwood. According to Greenwood, the necessary attributes of a profession include (1) a systematic body of theory, (2) a professional authority, (3) a sanction of the community, (4) a regulative

---

26 Thomas H. Kreneck, "Degrading Professional Librarian Status at Texas A&M University-Corpus Christi, 2007-2015 – A Policy History, *Progressive Librarian* 46 (2017/2018): 39.

27 See McDermott, "Professional Status of Librarians," 17-21; David Lonergan, "Is Librarianship a Profession?" *Community & Junior College Libraries* 15 (2009): 119-122.

28

code of ethics, and (5) a professional culture.[29] McDermott questioned whether library workers would even want professional status for their work if they knew all that was involved in being a "true" profession. For example, writing about the professional attributes of possessing an "enforceable code of ethics and standard of behavior" and the "sanction of the community," McDermott said:

> While [the American Library Association] does develop and maintain a code of ethics, it is not at all elaborated, and individual practitioners are not excluded from the profession for failing to live up to it. Professionals can be sued for malpractice. Is this what we want?"[30]

There is also evidence that many library workers see "librarianship" as more of an occupation than a profession, i.e., that library workers just don't see themselves as like physicians or lawyers, i.e., with the latter twos' stockpiles of esoteric knowledge and professional monopolies, but more as trained technicians with an emphasis on skills over a canon of knowledge. In a grounded theory study of academic librarians with less than two years of on-the-job experience, Sare, Bales, and Neville found that novice academic librarians tended to value the practical training they received in library school as opposed to the theoretical coursework.[31] Achieving a master's degree in library and information science (MLIS) may be seen by some current and potential library workers primarily as a means of meeting the threshold of a position (as many librarian positions require an MLIS) and to get a pay increase more so than as a means of boosting one's theoretical knowledge base, social standing, and institutional authority.

In addition to the practical arguments against library work as a profession, there are those who contest the liberal professions' value to society in general, at least as the professions are presently conceived. As ideological constructs, professionalism and the model of the professional are both aligned with capitalist society and historically connected to the religious ISA. Roman Catholic priest, philosopher, and social critic Ivan Illich wrote a great deal on the adverse effects of professionalization on society and its institutions in radical polemical

---

29   Ernest Greenwood, "Attributes of a Profession," *Social Work* 2, no. 3 (1957): 45-55.

30   McDermott, "Professional Status of Librarians," 20.

31   Laura Sare, Stephen Bales, and Bruce Neville, "New Academic Librarians and Their Perceptions," *portal: Libraries and the Academy* 12, no. 2 (2012): 190.

works such as *Medical Nemesis*, *Deschooling Society*, and *Tools for Conviviality*. The twentieth century, he declared, should be known as "The Age of Disabling Professions;" it is a century that

> [...] will be remembered as the time when politics withered, when voters, guided by professors, entrusted to technocrats the power to legislate needs, the authority to decide who needs what, and a monopoly over the means by which those needs shall be met. It will be remembered as the Age of Schooling, when people for one-third of their lives were trained how to accumulate needs on prescription and for the other two-thirds were clients of prestigious pushers who managed their habits.[32]

Illich held that one of the ways that professions maintain power over society is through the esotericization or mystification of knowledge and its restriction to a professional elite. Illich's "prestigious pushers" were the modern professionals, experts that tightly controlled and restricted knowledge and practice and, in the process, stripped their clients of their agency.

The modern liberal professions developed hand in hand with capitalism. And even though the professions are often presented as a check on the marketization of society, they are closely tied to the capitalist socioeconomic mode of production. In her influential book *The Rise of Professionalism*, sociologist Magali Sarfatti Larson took a neo-Marxist approach to link the rise of the modern professions to the development of corporate capitalism, a system which provided the bureaucratic ideal of "self-organization and self-assertion" for the former to model itself upon.[33] The monopoly of both knowledge and professional practice is, of course, an essential part of professionalism and professionalization. There is also intense capitalistic competition among professions for control over disciplinary spheres of influence, such as the twentieth century competition between psychiatrists and neurologists over the treatment of mental health care patients outside of hospital settings (the psychiatrists prevailed) or the encroachment of

---

32 Ivan Illich "The Need-makers," in *The Professions and Public Policy*, ed. Philip Slayton and Michael Trebilcock (Toronto: University of Toronto Press, 1978), 341.

33 Magali Sarfatti Larson, *The Rise of Professionalism: A Sociological Analysis* (Berkeley, CA: University of California Press, 1977), 145.

the clergy onto the professional turf of social workers in the attempt to remain relevant.[34]

Illich recognized that the modern professions originated with the priesthood and the jurists,[35] and that "A profession, like a priesthood, holds power by concession from an elite whose interests it props up."[36] Zola likewise traced the modern liberal professions to the prototype of the Christian ministry.[37] This elitist construct perpetuates existing power structures and, when applied to library work, accomplishes this task by controlling knowledge via the complementary ISAs of the (culturally ascendant) modern capitalist educational system, and the (legacy) religious system.

The assertion that the Serapian MCAL worker is a crypto-priest challenges the idea that library work is not a profession because it does not fulfill all of the classical traits of the professions. Although several of Greenwood's "attributes of a profession" are missing or disputed when considering Serapian MCAL work (e.g., a systematic body of theory, a sanction of the community), the argument against the library worker as a "true" professional loses some credibility when one looks past the simple calculus of trait lists and considers the practitioner as a successor to the clergy. The library worker, when viewed in terms of their ideological composition and functions may be seen as a professional in the historical sense of the term, particularly as to how ideology interpellates them into society as well as how they interpellate others. Even if library workers do not tick off every one of the professional traits on Greenwood's list, even if they are considered poseurs or wannabe members of the liberal professions in their promotion of library work as a profession, they inherit some of that historical role's ideological gravity. The push for making library workers "professional" in the sense that physicians or lawyers are "professional" is essentially an attempt to codify this preexisting but cloaked elite status.

---

34 Andrew Abbot, "Professionalism and the Future of Librarianship," *Library Trends* 46, no. 3 (1998): 433.

35 Ivan Illich, "Disabling Professions," in Ivan Illich, Irving Kenneth Zola, John McKnight, Jonathan Kaplan, and Harley Shaiken, *Disabling Professions*, (London: Marion Boyars, 2010), 16.

36 Illich, 17. The concept of the liberal professions was derived from the clergy itself, where ecclesiastics undertook vows and professed their faith to God.

37 Irving Kenneth Zola, "Healthism and Disabling Medicalization," in Illich, Zola, McKnight, Jonathan Kaplan, and Harley Shaiken, *Disabling Professions* (London: Marion Boyars, 2010), 41-67.

Cynicism versus Kynicism

It may seem that the above thinking about the Serapian MCAL dooms the library worker to the role of an ISA lackey—that despite whatever good intentions they have, the library worker perpetuates systems of exploitation and oppression that are structurally ingrained in capitalist systems and supported by religious legacies. Nevertheless, where there is thoughtful critique, there is the possibility for meaningful change. Although a deep cynicism exists among many library workers, this cynicism may be countered by a positive approach to intellectual and public service work referred to here as *Kynicism*[38] (hereafter, both modern Cynicism and Kynicism are capitalized to differentiate them from the common usage of the word cynicism).[39] The Kynical academic library worker understands that they are a crypto-priest, that crypto-priests are aligned with capitalism, and that they should struggle against this ideologically imposed role.

In his *Critique of Cynical Reason*, philosopher Peter Sloterdijk draws a distinction between the ancient, philosophical understanding of the term Kynic, often associated with the Greek philosopher Diogenes of Sinope (lived 412- 323 BCE), and what he defines as the modern Cynic (Sloterdijk used the change of initial consonants to differentiate between the two meanings). The modern Cynic, he wrote, is a disillusioned person that is part of the system of repression resulting from entrenched hegemonic power structures:

> Thus modern cynics—and there have been mass numbers of them in Germany, especially since the first world war—are no longer outsiders. But less than ever do they appear as a tangibly developed type. Modern mass cynics lose their individual sting, and refrain from the risk of letting themselves display.[40]

---

38 Andreas Huyssen, "The Return of Diogenes as Postmodern Intellectual," foreword to Peter Sloterdijk, *Critique of Cynical Reason*, trans. Michael Eldred (Minneapolis, MN: University of Minnesota Press, 1987), xi.

39 The Oxford English Dictionary defines a "cynic" as "A person disposed to rail or find fault; now usually: One who shows a disposition to disbelieve in the sincerity or goodness of human motives and actions, and is wont to express this by sneers and sarcasms; a sneering fault-finder." In Oxford English Dictionary, s.v. "cynic, n." accessed April 18, 2022, https://www.oed.com/view/Entry/46638?redirectedFrom=cynic#eid.

40 Peter Sloterdijk, *Critique of Cynical Reason*, trans. Michael Eldred (Minneapolis, MN: University of Minnesota Press, 1987), 4.

Modern Cynics may be counted on to support the status quo instead of challenging it—even if they find the status quo distasteful. Many modern Cynics, in fact, consciously work towards reproducing the status quo through their general attitude of resignation to the prevailing situation. For Sloterdijk, modern Cynics are "borderline melancholics who can keep their symptoms of depression under control and remain more or less able to work," existing in a state of "enlightened false consciousness."[41] Slovenian philosopher and sociologist Slavoj Žižek analyzed Sloterdijk's work to further distinguish between modern Cynicism and the notion of "Kynicism:"

> [Modern] Cynicism is the answer of the ruling culture to this kynical subversion: it recognizes, it takes into account, the particular interest behind the ideological universality, the distance between the ideological mask and the reality, but it still finds reasons to retain the mask. This cynicism is not a direct position of immorality—the model of cynical wisdom is to conceive probity, integrity, as a form of dishonesty, and morals as a supreme form of profligacy, the truth as the most effective form of lie. This cynicism is therefore a perverted 'negation of the negation' of the official ideology. Confronted with illegal enrichment, with robbery, the cynical reaction consists in saying that legal enrichment is a lot more effective, and moreover, protected by the law. As Bertolt Brecht puts in his *Threepenny Opera*: 'what is the robbery of a bank compared to the founding of a new bank?'[42]

For Žižek, the "enlightened false consciousness" of modern Cynicism is the recognition of disillusionment in oneself without taking action to address and remedy this disappointment. To be a modern Cynic is to discern the imposition of ideological structures on human reality and then do nothing more than criticize and complain. Žižek's Kynicism, in contrast to his articulation of modern Cynicism, means observing the existence of ideological structures, i.e., their materiality, and then struggling against these repressive structures. Kynicism is a *lived ideological critique* with the goal of human emancipation from oppressive ideology; the modern Kynic is a successor to the philosophical project of the ancient Greek and Roman Kynics.

---

41 Sloterdijk, 5.

42 Slavoj Žižek, *The Sublime Object of* Ideology (London: Verso, 1989): 29-30.

Diogenes of Sinope (412-323 BCE) is the paradigmatic Kynic. Before becoming a philosopher, he was exiled from his native Sinope (located in Anatolia on the coast of the Black Sea) for the crime of adulterating the state coinage.[43] Navia wrote that upon being exiled, the future philosopher asked the Oracle of Delphi what he should do with his life. She responded "Παραχαραττειν τό νόμισμα":

> [...] which literally means, 'Adulterate the currency.' After this, and with an understanding of the symbolic meaning of the oracular pronouncement. Diogenes returned to Athens where he began at once to do what Apollo had ordered him to do, that is, to wage a relentless war on the cultural and political 'currency' of his contemporaries.[44]

The Roman historian Diogenes Laertius (lived 3rd century CE) wrote that "On being asked what sort of person Diogenes was, Plato said 'A Socrates—gone mad.'"[45] The philosopher is remembered mostly because of the wild stories surrounding his life, such as how he lived in a clay pot in the Athenian forum or urinated on the leg of a rival that called him a dog, because that is what a dog would do (*kunos* is Greek for dog). Most of these antics were meant for shock value, but an important thing to consider about the ancient Kynics is that they were not misanthropes; that would have made them more akin to the modern Cynic than the modern Kynic. Diogenes lived and taught in the busy forum of Athens and his goal of seeking the truth, living that truth, and imparting that truth on his fellow persons, was a humanistic endeavor. Diogenes's primary philosophical legacy lies in his *uncompromising stance towards power and his trenchant and visible role in the negation of institutional power.* Diogenes' Kynicism, Sloterdijk wrote, "is a first reply to Athenian idealism," an idealism that "justifies social and world orders."[46] His antics, doing things like pissing on his colleagues' legs, masturbating in public, and being obnoxious during a personal visit from Alexander the Great, were effective ways (for the times, at least) to draw attention to the ridiculousness of the prevailing political and

---

43 Diogenes Laertius, *Lives of the Eminent Philosophers*, 6.20.
44 Luis E. Navia, *Diogenes of Sinope: The Man in the Tub* (Westport, CT: Greenwood Press, 1998), 11.
45 Diogenes Laertius, *Lives of the Eminent Philosophers*, 6.54.
46 Sloterdijk, *Critique of Cynical Reason*, 104.

social norms, a means of waking people up (the basic tenets of classical Kynicism have, in fact, been likened to Indian Buddhism).[47]

Conclusion: The Kynical Academic Library Worker

The Cynical library worker has essentially "checked themselves out." That is, while they have become aware of the impact of the ideological upon their work, they are jaded and do nothing to remedy the situation, preferring instead to collect their pay and not challenge the status quo. Such Cynicism may, in fact, lead to a library worker working actively to enforce the status quo and therefore the dominant power structures of society. It is the sincere hope of the present authors, however, that there are, in fact, few actual Cynical library workers and that the work ahead lies primarily in engendering a critical consciousness in those library workers who have not yet fully explored the role of the MCAL in society.

How might the MCAL worker imbedded in the Serapian MCAL behave like a modern Kynic? First, they must challenge their own ideological assumptions and predispositions to achieve a critical consciousness and reflexivity. They must become critical historians and cultural analysts. Writing on the topic of education, Nietzsche said that:

> It requires a totally new attitude of mind to be able to look away from the present educational institutions to the strangely different ones that will be necessary for the second or third generation. At present the labours of higher education produce merely the savant or the official or the businessperson or the philistine or, more commonly, a mixture of all four; and the future institutions will have a harder task—not in itself harder, as it is really more natural, and so easier; and further, could anything be harder than to make a youth into a savant against nature, as now happens? But the difficulty lies in unlearning what we know and setting up a new aim; it will be an endless trouble to change the fundamental idea of our present educational system that has its roots in the Middle Ages and regards the medieval savant as the ideal type of culture.[48]

---

47 Ian Cutler, "Old Dogs, New Tricks: A Cynical Legacy," *Think: Philosophy for Everyone* 4, no. 12 (2006), 90-91.

48 Friedrich Nietzsche, *Political Writings of Friedrich Nietzsche: An Edited Anthology*, ed. Frank Cameron and Don Dombrowsky, trans. Adrian Collins (London: Palgrave Macmillan, 2008), 70.

Working to achieve the new "attitude of mind" is not an easy task when one considers that the "conscious" academic library worker inhabits a strange space where they actively protest a system that provides them with their livelihood and bears the lion's share of responsibility for how they view themselves as professionals. Not only must they "unlearn" what reality is, they face the prospect of "endless trouble" to change this reality. "Endless trouble" is not really an overstatement if one considers that, to ultimately change an institution, one must transform the basic underlying structures of the society in which it operates. It is here that the "conscious" library worker might give up, becoming a Cynic as opposed to a Kynic. What transforms the "conscious" academic library worker into a Kynical academic library worker is the decision to work for revolutionary change, both within the Serapian MCAL and beyond, and to advocate for change loudly.

The ancient Kynics used the word *tuphos* (smoke) to mean the morass of mental confusion that people are mired in. The goal of the Kynic is to pierce this veil through lived philosophy, and their primary tool for doing this is *parrhêsia*, or freedom of speech. Kynical *Parrhêsia* is not freedom of speech in the sense that we often use it today. Instead, it is provocative dialogue performed in defiance of authority to expose the absurdities of that authority. Foucault referred to it as "fearless speech," a "verbal activity in which a speaker expresses his personal relationship to truth, and risks his life because truth telling as a duty to improve or help other people (as well as himself)."[49] *Parrhêsia* borders on transgressive speech: "So that you see that the parrhesiastic game is always at the frontier of the *parrhêsia*-contract, always close to a transgression either because the parrhesiast has said too many bad things, or because the interlocutor becomes angry."[50] Through *parrhêsia*, Foucault wrote, the Kynic forces their interlocuter to recognize that they are not what you think they are.[51] With the Kynical academic library worker, the role of parrhesiast requires constant

---

49 Michel Foucault, *Fearless* Speech, ed. Joseph Pearson (Los Angeles, CA: Semiotext(e), 2001), 19. Applied to the act of social criticism, *parrhêsia* is like Marx's famous injunction to engage in the "ruthless criticism of everything existing." In Karl Marx, "For a Ruthless Criticism of Everything Existing: M. to R., Kreuznach September, 1843," in *The Marx-Engels Reader*, ed. Robert C. Tucker (New York: Norton, 1972), 13.

50 Michel Foucault, *Discourse and Truth and Parrësia*, ed. Henri-Paul Fruchaud, Daniele Lorenzini, and Nancy Luxon (Chicago, IL: University of Chicago Press, 2019), 176.

51 Foucault, 176.

vocal critique of the institution and the profession as well as an intense, probing reflexivity.

The Kynical academic library worker is what McKnight described as a "post-professional" and a "modern heretic," that is, one of "those professional practitioners who support citizen competence and convert their profession into an understandable trade under the comprehensible command of citizens."[52] Illich advocated for a "convivial society," that "would be the result of social arrangements that guarantee for each member the most ample and free access to the tools of the community and limit this freedom only in favor of other members' equal freedom."[53] The Kynical academic library worker must work doggedly (pun intended) to puncture through the ideological morass of the Serapian MCAL and restructure their institutions to become prefigurative institutions, preferably at the highest administrative levels (an admittedly difficult task).

It should also be noted that, as de Acosta stated, ancient Kynicism was a dogma free organization (it was really not an organization at all), and that despite the basic ways in which their philosophy was *expressed through their actions*, there is arguably no Kynicism per se but "there are (or at least were) Cynic [i.e., Kynic], individuals."[54] The Kynical academic library worker is not required to subscribe to a political doctrine (although this is certainly possible). What they are required to do, however, is to always question the academic library as an institution (What is it telling us to do? Who is it telling us that we are?). In concert with fearless speech, the Kynical academic library worker actively works to implement material change in society. They must understand the ideological demands placed on people within that society, identify the symbols and rituals that instill those demands into individual subjects, and countermand those appeals through direct challenges and interventions. They are modern heretics and apostates, forsaking the sacred for the whole story.

---

52 John McKnight, "Professionalized Service and Disabling Help," in Ivan Illich, Irving Kenneth Zola, John McKnight, Jonathan Kaplan, and Harley Shaiken, *Disabling Professions* (London: Marion Boyars, 2010), 86.

53 Ivan Illich, *Tools for Conviviality*. (London: Marion Boyars, 2009), 12.

54 Alejandro de Acosta, "Cynical Lessons," *The Anvil Review* (blog), *The Anarchist Library*, July 2011, https://theanarchistlibrary.org/library/alejandro-de-acosta-cynical-lessons.

Authors' Biographies

Stephen Bales is a Professor in Global Languages and Cultures at Texas A&M University. He has a master's degree in Information Science and a PhD. in Communication and Information from the University of Tennessee—Knoxville. His research areas include the philosophy of librarianship, and ideology of the library. He sole-authored two monographs, *The Dialectic of Academic Librarianship: A Critical Approach and Social Justice* and *Library Work: A Guide to Theory and Practice*, and co-authored a third, *Transformative Library and Information Work: Profiles in Social Work*. He is General Editor of the *Journal of Radical Librarianship*.

Wendi Arant Kaspar is a Professor in International Affairs at Texas A&M University. She has a MLS from the University of Washington and a MS in Management from Texas A&M University – College Station. Her research interests include Human Resources and Management in Libraries, Innovation in Library Services, Outreach and Liaison. She has written numerous articles and book chapters and co-authored 3 monographs: *Guide to Ethics in Acquisitions*, *Leading Libraries: Creating a Service Culture* and *Library Storage Facilities: from Planning to Construction to Operation*. She has also been co-editor of 3 premier journals in librarianship, *Library Administration and Management*, *Journal of Academic Librarianship* and *College & Research Libraries*.

Image Copyright and Acknowledgments

Introduction

Figure 0.1   "Serapian ideological plexus, the reciprocal relationship between MCAL-Religion-State" by Stephen Bales. Copyright 2020 by Stephen Bales. Used with permission.

Chapter 1

Figure 1.1   "The Assyrian Empire and the Region about the Eastern Mediterranean, 750-625 B.C." from The Historical Atlas by William R. Shepherd, 1923. Courtesy of University of Texas Libraries (https://maps.lib.utexas.edu/maps/historical/shepherd/assyrian_empire_750_625.jpg). In the public domain.

Figure 1.2   "Library of Ashurbanipal 1500-539 BC, British Library" by Gary Todd, 2017, Wikimedia Commons (https://commons.wikimedia.org/wiki/File:Library_of_Ashurbanipal.jpg). CC BY 1.0.

Figure 1.3   "Thoth illustration from Pantheon Egyptien (1823-1825) by Leon Jean Joseph Dubois (1780-1846), 2018, flickr (https://www.flickr.com/photos/vintage_illustration/42794572881). CC BY 4.0.

Figure 1.4   "Cynocephalus, emblem of Thoth illustration from Pantheon Egyptien (1823-1825)" by Leon Jean Joseph Dubois (1780-1846), 2018, flickr (https://www.flickr.com/photos/vintage_illustration/41893681085). CC BY 4.0

Figure 1.5   "Sumerian cuneiform clay tablet" by Gary Todd, 2016, flickr (https://www.flickr.com/photos/101561334@N08/28211328681). CC BY 1.0.

Figure 1.6   "Clay counting tokens" by Marie-Lan Nguyen, 2009, Wikimedia Commons (https://commons.wikimedia.org/wiki/File:Clay_accounting_tokens_Susa_Louvre_n1.jpg). CC BY 2.5.

Figure 1.7   "Mosul Library Outside" by Herg-derg-editor, 2016, Wikimedia Commons (https://commons.wikimedia.org/wiki/File:Mosul_Library_Outside-e1424800354833.jpg). CC BY 4.0.

Figure 1.8	"Ninurta with his thunderbolts pursues Anzû stealing the Tablet of Destinies from Enlil's sanctuary" from Monuments of Nineveh, 2nd Series, 1853, edited by Austen Henry Layard, drawing by L. Gruner. Wikimedia Commons (https://en.wikipedia.org/wiki/Anz%C3%BB#/media/File:Chaos_Monster_and_Sun_God.png). CC BY 1.0.

Chapter 2

Figure 2.1	"The Athenian Empire at its Height (about 450 B.C.)" from The Historical Atlas by William R. Shepherd, 1923. Courtesy of University of Texas Libraries (https://maps.lib.utexas.edu/maps/historical/shepherd/athenian_empire_450.jpg). In the public domain.
Figure 2.2	"Clay tablet inscribed with linear B script" by vintagedept, 2010, Wikimedia Commons (https://commons.wikimedia.org/wiki/File:Clay_Tablet_inscribed_with_Linear_B_script.jpg). CC BY 2.0.
Figure 2.3	"La Canee muse lineaire A" by Ursus, 2012, Wikimedia Commons (https://commons.wikimedia.org/wiki/File:0726_La_Can%C3%A9e_mus%C3%A9e_lin%C3%A9aire_A.JPG). CC BY-SA 3.0.
Figure 2.4	"Metroon in Athens" by John Karakatsanis, 2010, Wikimedia Commons (https://commons.wikimedia.org/wiki/File:Ancient_Olympia,_Greece42.jpg). CC BY-SA 2.0.
Figure 2.5	"Temple of Artemis, Ephesus" by DenisDoukhan, 2016, Pixabay (https://pixabay.com/photos/ephesus-temple-of-artemis-1334571/). Free for commercial use; no attribution required.
Figure 2.6	"Map of Alexandria, 1575" by Goerg Braun and Frans Hogenberg. Courtesy of the Metropolitan Museum of Art (https://www.metmuseum.org/art/collection/search/587676). In the public domain.
Figure 2.7	"Great Library of Alexandria, O. von Corven, 19th century" by Igor Merit Santos, 2016, Wikimedia Commons (https://commons.wikimedia.org/wiki/File:The_Great_Library_of_Alexandria,_O._Von_Corven,_19th_century.jpg). CC BY-SA 4.0.
Figure 2.8	"Library at Pergamon" by Hugh Llewelyn, 2009, flickr (https://www.flickr.com/photos/vintage_illustration/42794572881). CC BY-SA 2.0.
Figure 2.9	"Porticas van Octavia" by Hugo DK, 2018, Wikimedia Commons (https://commons.wikimedia.org/wiki/File:Porticus_van_Octavia.jpg). CC BY-SA 4.0.
Figure 2.10	"Tempio di Apollo Palatino" by CCCP, 2012, Wikimedia Commons (https://commons.wikimedia.org/wiki/File:Tempio_di_Apollo_Palatino.jpg). CC BY-SA 2.5.

Figure 2.11	"Hadrian Library, Athens" by Andreas Trepte, 2008, Wikimedia Commons (https://commons.wikimedia.org/wiki/File:Hadrian_Library_Athen.jpg). CC BY-SA 2.5.
Figure 2.12	"Abbeye de Senanque" by Hans, 2016, Pixabay (https://pixabay.com/photos/abbaye-de-s%C3%A9nanque-monastery-abbey-1460366/). Free for commercial use; no attribution required.
Figure 2.13	"Abbey of Montserrat" by Bernard Gagnon, 2009, Wikimedia Commons (https://commons.wikimedia.org/wiki/File:Abbey_of_Montserrat_01.jpg). CC BY-SA 3.0.
Figure 2.14	"Ground Plan of a Monastery (St. Gall, Switzerland)" from The Historical Atlas by William R. Shepherd, 1923. Courtesy of University of Texas Libraries (https://maps.lib.utexas.edu/maps/historical/shepherd/monastery_st.gall_swiss.jpg). In the public domain

Chapter 3

Figure 3.1	"Map of Universities in Europe in the 16th Century" from The Public Schools Historical Atlas by Charles Colbeck. Longmans, Green; New York; London; Bombay. 1905. Courtesy of University of Texas Libraries (https://maps.lib.utexas.edu/maps/historical/colbeck/europe_universities_16_century.jpg). In the public domain.
Figure 3.2	"Comparative Hierarchy of Church and Higher Education Institution" by Stephen Bales. Copyright 2020 by Stephen Bales. Used with permission.
Figure 3.3	"Duke Humfrey's Library Interior, Bodleian Library, Oxford, UK" by David Duliff, 2015, Wikimedia Commons (https://commons.wikimedia.org/wiki/File:Duke_Humfrey%27s_Library_Interior_6,_Bodleian_Library,_Oxford,_UK_-_Diliff.jpg). CC BY-SA 3.0.
Figure 3.4	"Trinity College Library" by Brett Jordan, 2011, flickr (https://www.flickr.com/photos/x1brett/6382651341). CC BY 2.0.
Figure 3.5	"Radcliffe Camera" by Tom Murphy VII, 2005, Wikimedia Commons (https://upload.wikimedia.org/wikipedia/commons/b/b7/Radcliffe_Camera_%282005%29.jpg). CC BY-SA 3.0.

Chapter 4

Figure 4.1	"Macedonian Empire, 336-323 BC" from The Historical Atlas by William R. Shepherd, 1923. Courtesy of University of Texas Libraries (https://maps.lib.utexas.edu/maps/historical/shepherd_1911/shepherd-c-018-019.jpg). In the public domain.

Figure 4.2	"Bust of Serapis with kalathos on his head, Roman period, from Alexandria Egypt, Osiris, Sunken Mysteries of Egypt exhibition, Paris" by Carole Raddato, 2015, flickr (https://www.flickr.com/photos/carolemage/31013074656). CC BY-SA 2.0.
Figure 4.3	"The two-faced Osiris/Apis (Serapis) born from the lotus flower, om the Antinoeion at Hadrian's Villa, 131-138 AD, Vatican Museums" by Carole Raddato, 2015, flickr (https://www.flickr.com/photos/carolemage/29881393811). CC BY-SA 2.0
Figure 4.4	"Pluto Serapis and Persephone Isis at the Heraklion Museum" by Jebulon, 2015, Wikimedia Commons (https://commons.wikimedia.org/wiki/File:Pluto_Serapis_and_Persephone_Isis_Heraklion_museum.jpg). CC 1.0.
Figure 4.5	"Serapeum of Saqqara" by Ovedc, 2017, Wikimedia Commons (https://commons.wikimedia.org/wiki/Category:Serapeum_of_Saqqara#/media/File:By_ovedc_-_Serapeum_of_Saqqara_-_04.jpg). CC BY-SA 4.0.
Figure 4.6	"Plan of Alexandria c 30 BC Otto Puchstein 1890s" by Philg88, 2012, Wikimedia Commons (https://commons.wikimedia.org/wiki/File:Plan_of_Alexandria_c_30_BC_Otto_Puchstein_1890s_EN.svg). CC BY-SA 3.0.
Figure 4.7	"Pharos of Alexandria, Wonders of the Ancient World" 1899. Courtesy of New York Public Library (https://nypl.getarchive.net/media/pharos-of-alexandria-74fdb9). In the public domain.
Figure 4.8	"Seated scribe with papyrus scroll, Louvre" by Janmad, 2009, Wikimedia Commons (https://commons.wikimedia.org/wiki/File:Seated_scribe_with_papyrus_scroll_Louvre-white.jpg). CC BY 3.0.
Figure 4.9	"Exterior of Hodges Library" by Christopher Glass. Copyright 2022 by Christopher Glass. Used with permission.
Figure 4.10	"Hodges Desk" by Christopher Glass. Copyright 2022 by Christopher Glass. Used with permission.
Figure 4.11	"Information Commons at Hodges Library" by Christopher Glass. Copyright 2022 by Christopher Glass. Used with permission.
Figure 4.12	"Book stacks at Hodges Library" by Christopher Glass. Copyright 2022 by Christopher Glass. Used with permission.

Chapter 6

Figure 6.1	"Harry E. Widener Library, Harvard University, Cambridge, Mass." Detroit Publishing Co., 1914. Courtesy of the Library of Congress (https://www.loc.gov/item/2016814160/). In the public domain.

Image Copyright and Acknowledgments

Figure 6.2	"N.Y. Public Library - Schwarzman Building – exterior" by Bestbudbrian, 2014, Wikimedia Commons (https://commons.wikimedia.org/wiki/File:N.Y._Public_Library_-_Schwarzman_Bldg._-_exterior.jpg). CC BY-SA 3.0.
Figure 6.3	"Biblioteque Universitaire D'Aix-En-Provence" by Chrissharky, 2007, Wikimedia Commons (https://upload.wikimedia.org/wikipedia/commons/thumb/1/14/France_Aix-en-Provence_fac_de_droit.jpg/512px-France_Aix-en-Provence_fac_de_droit.jpg). CC BY 1.0.
Figure 6.4	"Main UL Building" by Cambridge University Library, 2015, Wikimedia Commons (https://commons.wikimedia.org/wiki/File:-Main_UL_building.jpg). CC BY-SA 4.0.
Figure 6.5	"Ghent University Library, Ghent Belgium" by Lukas Koster, 2007, flickr (https://www.flickr.com/photos/lukask/449343936). CC BY-SA 2.0.
Figure 6.6	"Obelisk in Evans Library" by Daniel Welch. Copyright 2022 by Daniel Welch. Used with permission.
Figure 6.7	"Learning Statue, Harold Cohen Library" by Rodhullandemu, 2018, Wikimedia Commons (https://commons.wikimedia.org/wiki/File:Learning_statue,_Harold_Cohen_Library.jpg). CC BY-SA 4.0.

Bibliography

Ancient and Medieval Sources

Ammianus Marcellinus. *History*. 3 vols. Translated by J.C. Rolfe. Cambridge, MA: Harvard University Press, 1935.

Anonymous. *The Greek Anthology*. 5 vols. Translated by W.H. Paton. London: William Heinemann, 1916.

Athenaeus, *The Learned Banqueters*. 6 vols. Edited and Translated by S. Douglas Olson. Cambridge: MA: Harvard University Press, 2006.

Aulus Gellius. *Attic Nights*. 3 vols. Translated by John C. Rolfe. Cambridge, MA: Harvard University Press, 1927.

Benedict. *The Rule of Benedict: An Invitation to the Christian Life*. Translated by George Holzherr and Mark Thamert. Collegeville, MN: Cistercian Publications, 2016.

Cassiodorus, *The Institutes*. In *The Early Middle Ages: 500-1000*. Edited by Robert Brentano, 54-61. London: Free Press.

Clement of Alexandria. *Exhortation of the Greeks*. Translated by G.W. Butterworth. Cambridge, MA: Harvard University Press, 1919.

Diodorus Siculus. *The Library of History*. 11 vols. Translated by C.H. Oldfather. Cambridge, MA: Harvard University Press, 1933.

Diogenes Laertius, *Lives of the Eminent Philosophers*. Translated by Pamela Mensch, Edited by James Miller. New York: Oxford University Press, 2018.

Epiphanius. *Treatise on Weights and Measures: The Syriac Version*. Edited by James Elmer Dean. Chicago, IL: University of Chicago Press, 1935.

Eusebius. *Preparation for the Gospel*. 2 vols. Translated by E.H. Gifford. Grand Rapids, MI: Baker Book House, 1903.

Isodorus of Seville. *The Etymologies*. Translated by Stephen A. Barney, W.J. Lewis, J.A. Beach, and Oliver Berghof Cambridge: Cambridge University Press, 2006.

Orosius. *Seven Books of History Against the Pagans*. Translated by Roy J. Deferrari. Washington, DC: The Catholic University of America Press, 1964.

Ovid, *Tristia*. 2nd ed. Translated by Arthur Leslie Wheeler. Revised by G. P. Gold. Cambridge, MA: Harvard University Press, 1996.

Pausanius. *Description of Greece*. 5 vols. Translated by W.H.S. Jones (Cambridge, MA: Harvard University Press, 1918).

Plato. "Apology." In *Complete Works*. Edited by John M. Cooper. Indianapolis, IN: Hackett. 1997.

Pliny the Elder 35.2.10, *Natural History*. 10 vols. Translated by H. Rackham. Cambridge, MA: Harvard University Press, 1952.

Plutarch. *Lives*. Translated by Bernadotte Perrin. Cambridge, MA: Harvard University Press, 1920.

Plutarch. *Moralia*. Edited by Frank Cole Babbitt. Cambridge, MA: Harvard University Press, 1936.

Rufinus of Aquileia. *History of the Church*. Translated by Philip R. Amidon. Washington, DC: Catholic University of America Press, 2016.

Strabo. *Geography*. 8 vols. Translated by Horace Leonard Jones. Cambridge, MA: Harvard University Press, 1917.

Suetonius, *Lives of the Caesars: The Deified Augustus*. 2 vols. Translated by J.C. Rolfe. Cambridge, MA: Harvard University Press, 1914.

Tacitus. *Histories*. 5 vols. Translated by John Jackson. Cambridge: MA: Harvard University Press, 1937.

Modern Sources

Abbot, Andrew. "Professionalism and the Future of Librarianship." *Library Trends* 46, no. 3 (1998): 430-443.

Abrahams, I., and C.E. Sayle. "The Purchase of Hebrew Books by the English Parliament in 1647." *Transactions of the Jewish Historical Society of England* 8 (1915-1917): 63-77.

Acosta, Alejandro de. "Cynical Lessons." *The Anvil Review* (blog). *The Anarchist Library*, July 2011. https://theanarchistlibrary.org/library/alejandro-de-acosta-cynical-lessons.

Adkins, D., and L. Hussey, "The Library in the Lives of Latino College Students." *Library Quarterly* 76, no. 4 (2006): 456-480.

Allred, John R. "The Purpose of the Public Library: The Historical View." *Library & Information History* 2, no. 5 (1972): 185-204.

Althusser, Louis. *For Marx*. Translated by Ben Brewster. New York, NY: Verso, 1996.

———. *Lenin and Philosophy and Other Essays*. Translated by Ben Brewster. New York: Monthly Review Press, 2001.

———. *On the Reproduction of Capitalism: Ideology and Ideological State Apparatuses*. Tanslated by G.M. Goshgarian. London: Verso, 2014.

Aman, Mohammed. "Egypt, Libraries In." In *Encyclopedia of Library and Information Science*. 73 vols. Edited by Allen Kent and Harold Lancour, 574-588. New York: Marcel Dekker, 1972.

American Library Association. "Library Bill of Rights." Amended January 29, 2019. https://www.ala.org/advocacy/intfreedom/librarybill.

Bacon, Francis. *The Letters and the Life of Francis Bacon*. 7 vols. Edited by James Spedding. London: Longman, 1861-1874.

Bailey, Alvin R., ed. *Public Library Advisory Board Handbook*. Austin, Texas: Texas State Library Development Division, 1992.

Baker, Drew and Nazia Islam. "From Religion Class to Religion Classification and Back Again: Religious Diversity and Library of Congress Classification." *Theological Librarianship* 13, no. 1 (April 2020): 27-37.

Bakos, Jan. "Monuments and Ideologies." *Human Affairs* 1, no. 2 (1991): 106-119.

Bakunin, Michael. *God and the State*, New York: Dover, 1970.

Bales, Stephen Edward. "Aristotle's Contribution to Scholarly Communication." PhD. Diss, University of Tennessee, Knoxville (2008). https://trace.tennessee.edu/cgi/viewcontent.cgi?article=1539&context=utk_graddiss.

———. *Dialectic of Academic Librarianship*. Sacramento, CA: Library Juice Press, 2015.

———. "The Academic Library as Crypto-temple: A Marxian Analysis." In *Class and Librarianship: Essays at the Intersection Information, Labor and Capital*. Edited by Eric Estep and Nathaniel Enright, 5-24. Sacramento, CA: Library Juice, 2016.

Bales, Stephen, and Tina Budzise-Weaver. *Transformative Library and Information Work: Profile in Social Justice*. Cambridge, MA: Chandos, 2020.

Bales, Stephen E., and Lea Susan Engle. "The Counterhegemonic Academic Librarian: A Call to Action. *Progressive Librarian*, 40 (2012): 16-40.

Band, Erster. *Keilschriftexte Aus Assur Religiösen Inhalts*. Leipzig, J.C. Hinrichs'sche Buchhandlung, 1919.

Barker, Rod. "Ancient Libraries: The Early Evolution of Cataloging and Finding Tools." *Cataloguing Australia* 24, no. 1/2, (1998): 3-12.

Barthes, Roland. *Mythologies*. Translated by Annette Lavers. New York: Hill & Wang, 1972.

Battles, Matthew. *Libraries: An Unquiet History*. New York: W.W. Norton, 2003.

Bäuml, Franz H. "Varieties and Consequences of Medieval Literacy and Illiteracy." *Speculum* 55, no. 2 (1980): 237-265.

Bendall, Lisa Maria. *Resources Dedicated to Religion in the Mycenaean Palace Economy*. Oxford: Oxford University School of Archaeology, 2007.

Berman, Sanford. *Prejudices and Antipathies: A Tract on the LC Subject Heads Concerning People*. Metuchen, NJ: Scarecrow, 1970.

Berthoud, J. "*The Italian Renaissance Library.*" Theoria: A Journal of Social and Political Theory 26 (1966): 61-80.

Bivens-Tatum, Wayne. *Libraries and the Enlightenment.* Los Angeles, CA: Library Juice Press, 2012.

Black, Alastair, Simon Pepper, and Kaye Bagshaw. *Books, Buildings, and Social Engineering: Early Public Libraries in Britain from Past to Present.* New York: Ashgate, 2009.

Black, Jeremy, and Anthony Green. *Gods, Demons and Symbols of Ancient Mesopotamia: An Illustrated Dictionary.* Austin, TX: University of Texas Press, 1992.

Blake, William. *The Continental Prophecies.* Edited by D.W. Dörrbecker. Princeton, NJ: Princeton University Press, 1995.

Bogatyrev, Sergei. "The Patronage of Early Printing in Moscow." *Canadian-American Slavic Studies* 51 (2017): 249-288.

Bommas, Martin. "Isis, Osiris, and Serapis." In *The Oxford Handbook of Roman Egypt.* Edited by Christina Riggs, 419-435. Oxford: Oxford University Press, 2012.

Bowers Sharpe, Krista. "'Commonsense' Academic Reference Service: Neoliberal Discourse in LIS Article." *Library Quarterly* 89, no. 4 (2019): 298-315.

Bowersock, G.W. *Julian the Apostate.* Cambridge, Harvard University Press, 1978.

Boyd, Timothy W. "Libri Confusi." *The Classical Journal* 91, no. 1 (1995): 35-45.

Bradbury, Ray. *Something Wicked This Way Comes.* New York: Simon & Schuster, 2017.

Brough, Kenneth. "The Colonial College Library." In *Reader in American Library History.* Edited by Michael H. Harris, 31-32. Washington, DC: National Card Register Company, 1971.

Brouzas, Christopher G. "Libraries in Ancient Athens: A Condensation of a Paper." *The Classical Outlook* 29, no.1 (1951): 13-15.

Budge, E.A. Wallis. trans. *The Book of the Dead: The Chapters of Coming Forth By Day.* London: Kegan Paul, Trench, Trubner & Co., 1898.

Bundy, Mary Lee and Paul Wasserman. "Professionalism Reconsidered." *College & Research Libraries* 29, no. 1 (1968): 5-25.

Buzás, Ladislaus. *German Library History, 800-1945.* Translated by William D. Boyd and Irmguard H. Wolfe. Jefferson, NC: McFarland & Company, 1986.

Casson, Lionel. *Libraries of the Ancient World.* New Haven, CT: Yale University Press, 2001.

Castleden, Rodney. *Mycenaeans.* New York: Routledge, 2005.

de Cervantes Saavedra, Miguel. *Don Quixote de la Mancha.* Translated by Milan Kundera. Oxford: Oxford University Press, 1999.

Cheyfitz, E. "The Corporate University, Academic Freedom, and American Exceptionalism." *South Atlantic Quarterly* 108, no. 4 (2009): 702-722.

Christ, Karl. *The Handbook of Medieval Library History*. Edited and Translated by Theophil Otto. Metuchen, NJ: Scarecrow Press, 1984.

Clanchy, M.T. *From Memory to Written Record: England, 1066-1307*. Cambridge, MA: Harvard University Press, 1979.

Clayton, Howard. "The American College Library." In *Reader in American Library History*. Edited by Michael H. Harris, 120-137. Washington, DC: National Card Register Company, 1971.

Coker, Catherine, Wyoma vanDuinkerken, and Stephen Bales. "Seeking Full Citizenship: A Defense of Tenure Faculty Status for Librarians." *College & Research Libraries* 71, no. 5 (2010): 406-420.

Coldstream, J.M. *Geometric Greece*. 2nd ed. London: Routledge, 2003.

Cornforth, Maurice. *Materialism and the Dialectical Method*, 4th ed. New York: International Publishers, 1977.

Coulson, Charles L. H. *Castles in Medieval Society: Fortresses in England, France, and Ireland in the Central Middle Ages*. Oxford: Oxford University Press, 2003.

Courtenay, William J. *Rituals for the Dead: Religion and Community in the Medieval University of Paris*. Notre Dame, IN: University of Notre Dame Press, 2016.

Cowley, W.H. and Donald T. Williams. "The Meaning of Higher Education." *The Educational Forum* 33, no. 4 (1969): 497-509.

Craig, Maurice. *Dublin: 1660-1860*. Dublin: Hodges, Figgis & Co., 1952.

Critten, Jessica. "Ideology and Critical Self-reflection in Information Literacy." *Communications in Information Literacy* 9, no. 1 (2015), 145-156.

Crowley, Bill. "A Culturally Pragmatic and Feminist-Influenced Approach to Defending Professionalism." In *Defending Professionalism: A Resource for Librarians, Information Specialists, Knowledge Managers, and Archivists*. Edited by Bill Crowley, 133-149. Santa Barbara, CA: Libraries Unlimited, 2012.

Cutler, Ian. "Old Dogs, New Tricks: A Cynical Legacy." *Think: Philosophy for Everyone* 4, no. 12 (2006): 89-94.

Dalby, Andrew. "The Sumerian Catalog." *Journal of Library History* 21, no. 3 (Summer, 1986): 475-485.

Dalley, Stephanie. "The Sassanian Period and Early Islam, c. AD 224-651." In *The Legacy of Mesopotamia*. Edited by Stephanie Dalley, 163-181, Oxford: Oxford University Press, 1998.

Davidson, Linda Kay and David M. Gitlitz. *Pilgrimage: From the Ganges to Graceland: An Encyclopedia*. 2 vols. Santa Barbara, CA: ABC CLIO, 2002.

Davies, John K. "Greek Archives: From Record to Monument." In *Ancient Archives and Archival Traditions: Concepts of Record-Keeping in the Ancient World*. Edited by Maria Brosius, 323-343. Oxford: Oxford University Press, 2003.

D'A Desborough, V.R. *The Greek Dark Ages*. New York, St. Martin's Press, 1972.

Drogin, Marc. *Biblioclasm: The Mythical Origins, Magic Powers, and Perishability of the Written Word*. Savage, MD. Rowman & Littlefield Publishers, 1989.

Dupré, Louis. *The Enlightenment and the Intellectual Foundations of Modern Culture*. New Haven, CT: Yale University Press, 2004.

Eco, Umberto. *The Name of the Rose*. Translated by William Weaver. Boston, MA: Mariner Books, 2014.

Eliade, Mircea. *The Forge and the Crucible: The Origins and Structures of the Academy*. 2nd ed. Translated by Stephen Corrin. Chicago: University of Chicago Press, 1978.

———. *The Sacred and the Profane: The Nature of Religion*. Translated by Willard R. Trask. San Diego, CA: Harcourt, 1987.

———. *Images and Symbols: Studies in Religious Symbolism*. Translated by Philip Mairet. Princeton, NJ: Princeton University Press, 1991.

Engels, Friedrich. *Socialism: Utopian and Scientific*. Translated by Edward Aveling. New York: International Publishers, 2004.

———. *Feuerbach: The Roots of the Socialist Philosophy*. Translated by Austin Lewis. New York: Mondial, 2009.

Ettarh, Fobazi. "Vocational Awe and Librarianship: The Lies We Tell Ourselves." In *The Library with the Lead Pipe* (Jan. 10, 2018). https://www.inthelibrary-withtheleadpipe.org/2018/vocational-awe/.

Firth, Simon. *Symbols: Public and Private*. Ithaca, NY: Cornell University Press, 1973.

Fisher, Max. "'Fighting Reality': Life as an Atheist in Saudi Arabia." *Washington Post*. Nov. 21, 2012. https://www.washingtonpost.com/news/worldviews/wp/2012/11/21/fighting-reality-life-as-an-atheist-in-saudi-arabia/.

Fleming, Willard C. "The Attributes of a Profession and Its Members." *Journal of the American Dental Association* 69 (Sep. 1964): 390-395.

Foucault, Michel. *Fearless* Speech. Edited by Joseph Pearson. Los Angeles, CA: Semiotext(e), 2001.

—-. *Discourse and Truth and Parrësia*. Edited by Henri-Paul Fruchaud, Daniele Lorenzini, and Nancy Luxon. Chicago, IL: University of Chicago Press, 2019.

Fraser, Nancy. "From Progressive Neoliberalism to Trump — and Beyond." *American Affairs* 1, no. 4 (2017): 46–64.

Fraser, P.M. *Ptolemaic Alexandria*. 3 vols. Oxford: Clarendon Press, 1972.

Freeman. Geoffrey, T. "The Library as Place: Changes in Learning Patterns, Collections, Technology, and Use." In *Library as Place: Rethinking Roles, Rethinking* Space, 1-24. Washington, DC: Council on Library and Information Resources, 2005. https://www.clir.org/wp-content/uploads/sites/6/pub129.pdf.

Freshwater, Peter. "Books and Universities." In *The Cambridge History of Libraries in Britain and Ireland*, 3 vols. Edited by Giles Mandelbrote and K. A. Manley. Cambridge, NY: Cambridge University Press, 2006.

Galbraith, Quinn, Erin Merrill, and Olivia Outzen. "The Effect of Gender and Minority Status on Salary in Private and Public ARL Libraries." *Journal of Academic Librarianship* 44 (2018): 75-80.

Gardiner, Alan H. "The House of Life." *Journal of Egyptian Archaeology* 24, no. 2 (1938), 157-179.

Gates, Jean Key. *Introduction to Librarianship*. 2nd ed. New York: McGraw-Hill, 1976.

Geertz, Clifford. *The Interpretation of Cultures*, New York: Basic Books.

Gelfer-Jørgensen, Mirjam. "Towers and Bells: The Symbolism of Torah Finials." *Studia Rosenthaliana* 37 (2004): 37-54.

Gintis, Herbert. "The Nature of Labor Exchange and the Theory of Capitalist Production." *Review of Radical Political Economics* 8, no. 2 (1976): 36-54.

Giroux, Henry A. *Neoliberalism's War on Higher Education*. 2nd ed. Chicago, IL: Haymarket Books, 2014.

Goethe, Johann Wolfgang von. *West-Östilicher Diwan*. Stuttgard: Stuttgard Cottaische Bucandlung, 1819.

Goldsborough, Reid. "Toward a Universal Library." *Tech Directions* (2008): 14.

Gormley, Dennis M. "A Bibliographic Essay of Western Library Architecture to the Mid-Twentieth Century." *Journal of Library History* 9, no. 1 (January, 1974): 4-24.

Gould, Eric. "The University, the Marketplace, and Civil Society." In *The Business of Higher Education*, 3 vols. Edited by John C. Knapp and David J. Siegel, 1-29. Santa Barbara, CA: ABC CLIO, 2009.

Graff, Harvey J. "On Literacy in the Renaissance: Review and Reflections." *History of Education* 12, no. 2 (1983): 69-85.

Grafman, Jordan, Irene Cristofori, Wanting Zhong, and Joseph Bulbulia. "The Neural Basis of Religious Cognition." *Current Directions in Psychological Science* 29, no. 2 (2020): 126-133.

Gramsci, Antonio. *Selections from the Prison Notebooks of Antonio Gramsci*. Edited and translated by Quinton Hoare and Geoffrey Nowell Smith. New York: International Publishers, 1978.

Greenwood, Ernest. "Attributes of a Profession." *Social Work* 2, no. 3 (1957): 45-55.

Grendler, Paul F. *Books and Schools in the Italian Renaissance*. Hampshire, UK: Variorum, 1995.

Grendler, Paul F. "The Universities of the Renaissance and Reformation." *Renaissance Quarterly* 57, no. 1 (Spring, 2004): 1-42.

Guthro, Clem. "The 21st Century Academic Library: Six Metaphors for a New Age." *Library Leadership & Management* 33, no. 2 (2019): 1-12.

Haas, Christopher. *Alexandria in Late Antiquity: Topography and Social Conflict*. Baltimore: MD: John Hopkins University Press, 1997.

Hadas, Moses. *The Greek Ideal and Its Survival*. New York: Harper & Row, 1960.

Handis, Michael. "Myth and History: Galen and the Alexandrian Library." In *Ancient Libraries*. Edited by Jason König, Katerina Oikonomopoulou, and Greg Woolf, Cambridge, 364-376. Cambridge University Press, 2013.

Handler, Susan. "Architecture on the Roman Coins of Alexandria." *American Journal of Archaeology* 75, no. 1 (1971): 57-74.

Hankins, James. "Religion and the Modernity of Renaissance Humanism." In *Interpretations of Renaissance Humanism*. Edited by Angelo Mazzocco, 137-153. Leiden: Brill, 2006.

Harris, Michael H. "State, Class, and Cultural Reproduction: Toward a Theory of Library Service in the United States." *Advances in Librarianship* 14 (1986): 211-252.

Harris, William V. *Ancient Literacy*. Cambridge, MA: Harvard University Press, 1989.

Hart, George. *Routledge Dictionary of Egyptian Gods and Goddesses*. 2nd ed. London: Routledge, 2005.

Haskins, Charles Homer. *The Rise of the Universities*. Ithaca, NY: Great Seal Books, 1957.

―――. *The Renaissance of the Twelfth Century*. New York: New American Library, 1976.

Hearn, Jeff. "Notes on Patriarchy, Professionalization and the Semi-professions." *Sociology* 16, no. 2 (1982): 184-202.

Hebron, Stephen. *Dr. Radcliffe's Library: The Story of the Radcliffe Camera in Oxford*. Oxford: Bodleian Library, 2014.

Heinsohn, Gunnar. "The Rise of Blood Sacrifice and Priest-kingship in Mesopotamia: A 'Cosmic Decree'?" *Religion* 22, no. 2 (1992): 109-134.

Hendrickson, Thomas. "The Serapeum: Dreams of the Daughter Library." *Classical Philology* 111, no. 4 (2016): 453-464.

Jackson, Sidney L. *Libraries and Librarianship in the West: A Brief History*. New York: McGraw-Hill, 1974.

Hill, Jane A., Philip Jones, and Antonio J. Morales. "Comparing Kingship in Ancient Egypt and Mesopotamia: Cosmos, Politics, and Landscape," In *Experiencing Power, Generating Authority: Cosmos, Politics, and the Ideology of Kingship in Ancient Egypt and Mesopotamia*. Edited by Jane A. Hill, Philip Jones, and Antonio J. Morales, 3-30, Philadelphia: University of Pennsylvania Museum of Archaeology and Anthropology, 2013.

Hood, M.S.F. "The Tartaria Tablets." *Antiquity* 41, no. 2 (1967): 99-113.

Horn, Walter and Ernest Born. *The Plan of St. Gaul*, 3 vols. Berkeley, CA: University of California Press, 1979.

Howson, Richard and Kylie Smith. "Hegemony and the Operation of Consensus and Coercion." In *Hegemony: Studies in Consensus and Coercion*." Edited by Richard. Howson and Kylie Smith, 1-15. New York: Routledge, 2008.

Humanists International. "The Right to Apostasy in the World." Accessed May 14, 2022. https://humanists.international/get-involved/resources/the-right-to-apostasy-in-the-world/.

Huyssen, Andreas. "The Return of Diogenes as Postmodern Intellectual." Foreword to *Critique of Cynical Reason*, by Peter Sloterdijk. Translated by Michael Eldred, ix-xxv. Minneapolis, MN: University of Minnesota Press, 1987.

International Federation of Library Associations. "Statement on Privacy in the Library Environment." https://www.ifla.org/publications/ifla-statement-on-privacy-in-the-library-environment/.

Illich, Ivan. "The Need-makers." In *The Professions and Public Policy*. Edited by Philip Slayton and Michael Trebilcock, 341-346. Toronto: University of Toronto Press, 1978.

———. *Tools for Conviviality*. London: Marion Boyars, 2009.

———. "Disabling Professions." Ivan Illich, Irving Kenneth Zola, John McKnight, Jonathan Kaplan, and Harley Shaiken. *Disabling Professions*, 11-39. London: Marion Boyars, 2010.

Irwin, Raymond. "Ancient and Medieval Libraries." In *Encyclopedia of Library and Information Science*. 73 vols. Edited by Allen Kent and Harold Lancour, 399-415. New York: Marcel Dekker, 1968-.

Jacob, Margaret C. *The Secular Enlightenment*. Princeton, NJ: Princeton University Press, 2019.

Jastrow, Jr., Morris. "Did the Babylonian Temples Have Libraries." *Journal of the American Oriental Society* 27 (1906): 147-182.

Jiménez, E. "Cities and Libraries." In *Cuneiform Commentaries Project*. Edited by E. Frahm, E. Jiménez, M. Frazer, and K. Wagensonner. 2013. https://ccp.yale.edu/introduction/cities-and-libraries.

Johnson, Elmer D. *History of Libraries in the Western World*. Metuchen, NJ: Scarecrow Press, 1970.

Jones, Ray. *The Lighthouse Encyclopedia: The Definitive Resource*, 2nd ed. Guilford, CT: Globe Pequot Press, 2013.

Jursa, Michael. "Cuneiform Writing in Neo-Babylonian Temple Communities." In *The Oxford Handbook of Cuneiform Culture*. Edited by Karen Radner and Eleanor Robson, 184-204. Oxford: Oxford University Press, 2011.

Kallendorf, Craig. "The Ancient Book." In *The Book: A Global History*. Edited by Michael F. Suarez, S.J. Woudhuysen, and H.R. Woudhuysen, 39-53. Oxford: Oxford University Press, 2013.

Kane, Laura Townsend. "Access Versus Ownership." In *Encyclopedia of Library and Information Science*. 2nd ed. 4 vols. Edited by Miriam A. Drake. New York: Marcel Dekker, 2003.

Kelley, Donald R. *Renaissance Humanism*. Boston, MA: Twayne Publishers, 1991.

Kibre, Pearl. "Scholarly Privileges: Their Roman Origins and Medieval Expression." *The American Historical Review* 59, no. 3 (1954): 543-567.

Kingsley, Charles. *Hypatia*. New York: Garland Publishing, 1975.

Krapivin, Vassily. *What is Dialectical Materialism?* Translated by Galina Sdobnikova. Moscow: Progress Publishers, 1985.

Kreneck, Thomas H. "Degrading Professional Librarian Status at Texas A&M University-Corpus Christi, 2007-2015 — A Policy History." *Progressive Librarian* 46 (2017/2018): 12-49.

Kuntz, Blair. "Stolen Memories: Israeli State Repression and Appropriation of Palestinian Cultural Resources." *Journal of Radical Librarianship* 7 (2021). https://journal.radicallibrarianship.org/index.php/journal/article/view/54.

Larson, Magali Sarfatti. *The Rise of Professionalism: A Sociological Analysis.* Berkeley, CA: University of California Press, 1977.

Lazar, Aryeh. "Cultural Influences on Religious Experience and Motivation." *Review of Religious Research* 46, no. 1 (2004): 64-71.

Leeb, Claudia. "Marx and the Gendered Structure of Capitalism. *Philosophy and Social Criticism* 33, no. 7 (2007): 833-859.

Leitch, Donovan. "Riki Tiki Tavi." Recorded January 1970–February 1970. Epic 44601, 1970. Vinyl long playing record.

Lévi-Strauss, Claude. *Sociologie et Anthropologie par Marcel Mauss.* Paris: Presses Universitaire de France, 1950.

Levine, Gregory J. "On the Geography of Religion." *Transactions of the Institute of British Geographers* 11, no. 4 (1986): 428-440.

Lewis, David W. "Library as Place." In *Academic Librarianship Today.* Edited by Todd Gilman, 161-176. Lanham, MD: Rowman & Littlefield, 2017.

Library of Congress. *Library of Congress Subject Headings.* 43rd ed. Washington, DC: Policy and Standards Division, Library of Congress, 2021. https://www.loc.gov/aba/publications/FreeLCSH/freelcsh.html.

Logan, Robert K. *The Alphabet Effect: A Media Ecology Understanding of the Making of Western Civilization.* Creskill, NJ: Hampton Press, 2004.

Lonergan, David. "Is Librarianship a Profession?" *Community & Junior College Libraries* 15 (2009): 119-122.

Lopez-Vidriero, Maria Luisa. *The Polished Cornerstone of the Temple: Queenly Libraries of the Enlightenment.* London: The British Library, 2005.

Lovatt, Roger. "College and University Book Collections and Libraries." In *The Cambridge History of Libraries in Britain and Ireland.* 3 vols. Edited by Elisabeth Leedham-Green and Teresa Webber, 152-177. Cambridge: Cambridge University Press, 2006.

Lowe, Dunstan. "Twisting in the Wind: Monumental Weathervanes in Classical Antiquity." *Cambridge Classical Journal* 62 (2016): 147-169.

Pae, Taavi, Helen Sooväli-Sepping, and Egle Kaur. "Landmarks of Old Livonia — Church Towers, Their Symbols and Meaning." *Journal of Baltic Studies* 41, no. 4 (December 2010): 431-448.

Pankl, Elisabeth and Jenna Ryan. "Information Commons and Web 2.0 Technologies: Creating Rhetorical Situations and Enacting Habermasian Ideals in the Academic Library." In *Handbook of Research on Computer Mediated Communication*. Edited by Sigrid Kelsey and Kirk St. Amant, 845-855. Hershey, NY: Information Science Reference, 2008.

Perdue, Leo G. "Sages, Scribes, and Seers in Israel and the Ancient Near East: An Introduction." In *Scribes, Sages, and Seers: The Sage in the Eastern Mediterranean World*. Edited by Leo G. Purdue, 1-35. Gottingen: Vandenhoeck & Ruprecht, 2008.

Richardson, Cyril C. "The Foundations of Christian Symbolism." In *Religious Symbolism*. Edited by F. Ernest Johnson, 1-22. New York: Institute for Religious and Social Studies, 1955.

McCarthy, James and Scott Prudham. "Neoliberal Nature and the Nature of Neoliberalism." *Geoforum* 35 (2004): 275-283.

McCook, Kathleen. *A Place at the Table: Participating in Community Building*. Chicago: American Library Association, 2000.

McDermott, Judy C. "The Professional Status of Librarians: A Realistic and Unpopular Analysis," *Journal of Library Administration* 5, no. 3 (1984): 17-21.

Mckenzie, Judith. *The Architecture of Alexandria and Egypt: 300 BC — AD 700*. New Haven: Yale University Press 2004.

Mckenzie, Judith, Sheila Gibson, and A.T. Reyes. "Reconstructing the Serapeum in Alexandria from the Archaeological Evidence." *Journal of Roman Studies* 94 (2004): 73-121.

McKnight, John. "Professionalized Service and Disabling Help." In Ivan Illich, Irving Kenneth Zola, John McKnight, Jonathan Kaplan, and Harley Shaiken. *Disabling Professions*, 69-91. London: Marion Boyars, 2010.

Machlup, Fritz. *Knowledge: Its Creation, Distribution, and Economic Significance*, 2 vols. Princeton, NJ: Princeton University Press, 1982.

Malone, Caroline Marino and Walter Horn. In Walter Horn and Ernest Born, "The Plan of St. Gall & Its Effect on Later Monastic Planning." In The Plan of St. Gaul: *A Study of the Architecture & Economy of, & Life in a Paradigmatic Carolingian Monastery*, 3 vols., 315-359. Berkeley, CA: University of California Press, 1979.

Manchester, William. *A World Lit Only by Fire: The Medieval Mind and the Renaissance: Portrait of an Age*. Boston, MA: Little Brown and Company, 1992.

Margolin, Jean-Claude. *Humanism in Europe at the Time of the Renaissance*. Translated John L. Farthing. Durham, NC: Labyrinth Press, 1989.

Marx, Karl. "Contribution to the Critique of Hegel's Philosophy of Right." In Karl Marx and Friedrich Engels, *On Religion*, 41-58. New York: Schocken Books, 1964.

———. "For a Ruthless Criticism of Everything Existing: M. to R., Kreuznach September, 1843." In *The Marx-Engels Reader*. Edited by Robert C. Tucker. New York: Norton, 1972.

———. *Capital: A Critique of the Political Economy*. Vol. 1. Translated by Ben Fowkes. London: Penguin Books, 1976.

Marx, Karl, and Friedrich Engels. *The German Ideology*, Amherst, NY: Prometheus Books, 1998.

Martin, Mies. "Using Cultural Studies to Rethink Library Research." Houghton, MI: Michigan Technological University, 2013. .https://www.academia.edu/7023923/Using_Cultural_Studies_To_Rethink_Library_Research.

Matthews, Victor H. "El-Amarna Texts." In *Near Eastern Archaeology: A Reader*. Edited by Suzanne Richard. Winona Lake, IN: Eisenbrauns, 2003.

Max, Gerald E. "Ancient Near East." In *Encyclopedia of Library History*. Edited by Wayne A. Wiegand and Donald G. Davis, Jr., 23-31. New York: Routledge, 1994.

Maxwell, Nancy Kalikow. *Sacred Stacks: The Higher Purpose of Libraries and Librarianship*. Chicago, IL: American Library Association, 2006.

Mellon, Constance. "Library Anxiety: A Grounded Theory and Its Development." *College & Research Libraries* 47 (1986): 160-165.

Mies, Maria. *Patriarchy and Accumulation on a World Scale: Women in the International Division of Labour*. London: Zed Books, 1986).

De Montalembert, Count. *Monks of the West*. 2 vols. Edinburgh: William Blackwood and Sons, 1861.

Moore, John C. *A Brief History* of Universities. Cham, Switzerland: Palgrave Macmillan, 2019.

Morenz, Ludwig D. "Texts before Writing: Reading (Proto-)Egyptian Poetics of Power." In *Experiencing Power, Generating Authority: Cosmos, Politics, and the Ideology of Kingship in Ancient Egypt and Mesopotamia*, edited by Jane A. Hill, Philip Jones, and Antonio J. Morales, 121-149. Philadelphia: University of Pennsylvania Museum of Archaeology and Anthropology, 2013.

Morsch, Lucile M. "Foundations of the American Public Library." In *Bases of Modern Librarianship: A Study of Library Theory and Practice in Britain, Canada, Denmark, The Federal Republic of Germany and the United States*. Edited by Carl M. White, 29-41. Oxford: Pergamon Press, 1964.

Mross, Emily and Christian Riehman-Murphy. "A Place to Study, a Place to Pray: Supporting Student Spiritual Needs in Academic Libraries." *College & Research Libraries News* 79, no. 6 (2018): 327-330.

Murphy, Lauren. "Beware Greeks Bearing Gods," *Amphora* 2 (2021): 29-54.

Murray, Mary. *The Law of the Father: Patriarchy in the Transition from Feudalism to Capitalism*, New York, NY: Routledge, 1995.

MyAggieNation.com. "Cushing Memorial Library and Archives." Updated November 18, 2013. https://myaggienation.com/campus_evolution/building_history/cushing-memorial-library-and-archives/article_1b7181bc-118f-11e3-8a87-0019bb2963f4.html.

Nadeau, Ray. "The Progymnasmata of Aphthonius in Translation." *Communications Monographs* 19, no. 4 (1952): 264-285.

Navia, Luis E. *Diogenes of Sinope: The Man in the Tub.* Westport, CT: Greenwood Press, 1998.

Neill, Thomas P. and Raymond H. Schmandt. *History of the Catholic Church.* 2nd ed. Milwaukee, WI: Bruce Publishing Company, 1965.

Nichols, Charles L. *The Library of Rameses the Great.* Berkeley: Peacock Press, 1964.

Nietzsche, Friedrich. *Political Writings of Friedrich Nietzsche: An Edited Anthology.* Edited by Frank Cameron and Don Dombrowsky. Translated by Adrian Collins. London: Palgrave Macmillan, 2008.

Novak, D. "The Place of Anarchism in the History of Political Thought," *The Review of Politics* 20, no. 3 (1958), 307-329.

O'Connor, Frances and Becky S. Drury. *The Female Face in Patriarchy: Oppression as Culture.* East Lansing, MI: Michigan State University Press, 1999.

Olin, Jessica, and Michelle Millett. "Gendered Expectations for Leadership in Libraries. *In the Library with the Lead Pipe* (Nov. 4, 2015), https://www.inthelibrarywiththeleadpipe.org/2015/libleadgender/.

Olivier, J.P. *Les Scribes de Cnossos: Essai de Classement Des Archives D'un Palais Mycénien, Incuanubala Graeca.* Rome: Edizioni Dell'Ateneao, 1967.

–––. "Cretan Writing in the Second Millennium B.C." *World Archaeology* 17, no. 3 (February 1986): 377-389.

Ollman, Bertell. *Dance of the Dialectic: Steps in Marx's Method.* Urbana, IL: University of Illinois Press, 2003.

Olmstead, A.T. *History of Assyria.* New York: Charles Scribner's Sons, 1923.

Olson, Carl. "The Sacred Book." In *The Book: A Global History.* Edited by Michael F. Suarez, S.J. Woudhuysen, and H.R. Woudhuysen, 19-38. Oxford: Oxford University Press, 2013.

Online Library Learning Center. "A Library Tour," Accessed March 11, 2022. https://www.usg.edu/galileo/skills/unit03/libraries03_01.phtml.

Oppenheim, A. Leo. "—Assyriology—Why and How?" *Current Anthropology* 1, no. 5/6 (1960): 409-423.

–––. *Ancient Mesopotamia: Portrait of a Dead Civilization.* Chicago: University of Chicago Press, 1964.

–––. "The Position of the Intellectual in Mesopotamian Society." *Daedalus* 104, no. 2 (Spring, 1975): 37-46.

Otto, Rudolf. *The Idea of the Holy: An Inquiry into the Non-rational Factor in the Idea of the Divine and Relation to the Rational.* Translated by John W. Harvey. London, Oxford University Press, 1958.

De Paravincini, Frances. *Early History of Balliol College.* London, Trubner & Company, 1891.

Parsons, Edward Alexander. *The Alexandrian Library, Glory of the Hellenic World: Its Rise, Antiquities, and Destructions.* Amsterdam: Elsevier Press, 1952.

Paul, Shalom M. "Heavenly Tablets and the Book of Life." *Janes* 5 (1973): 345-354.

Pedersén, Olof. *Archives and Libraries in the Ancient Near East: 1500-300 B.C.* Bethesda, MD: CDL Press, 1998.

Pinner, H.L. *The World of Books in Classical Antiquity.* Leiden: A.W. Sijthoff, 1948.

Polastron, Lucien X. *Books on Fire: the Destruction of Libraries throughout History.* Translated by Jon E. Graham. Rochester, VT: Inner Traditions, 2004.

Popowich, Sam. *Confronting the Democratic Discourse of Librarianship: A Marxist Approach.* San Diego, CA: Litwin Books, 2019.

Porcaro, David S. "Sacred Libraries in the Temples of the Near East." *Studia Antiqua* 2, no. 1 (2002), 63-70.

Posner, Ernst. *Archives in the Ancient World.* Cambridge, MA: Harvard University Press, 1972.

Potts, D.T. "Before Alexandria: Libraries in the Ancient Near East." In *The Library of Alexandria: Centre of Learning in the Ancient World*, edited by Roy MacLeod, 19-33, London: I.B. Tauris & Co., 2010.

Pruyser, P.W. *The Play of Imagination: Toward a Psychoanalysis of Culture.* New York: International Universities Press, 1983.

Raber, Douglas, "Librarians as Organic Intellectuals: A Gramscian Approach to Blind Spots and Tunnel Vision." *Library Quarterly* 73, no. 1 (2003): 33-53.

Rait, Robert S. *Life in the Medieval University.* Cambridge, Cambridge University Press, 1918.

Rambusch, Robert E. "Contemporary Architecture and Catholic Faith." In *Christian Faith and the Contemporary Arts.* Edited by Finley Eversole, 205-211. New York, NY: Abingdon Press, 2021.

Rashdall, Hastings. *The Universities of Europe in the Middle Ages.* Oxford: Clarendon Press, 1936.

Rayward, W. Boyd. "Information Revolutions, the Information Society, and the Future of the History of Information Science." *Library Trends* 62, no. 3 (Winter 2014): 681-713.

Redford, Donald. "Ancient Egyptian Literature: An Overview." In *Civilizations of the Ancient Near East.* Edited by Jack M. Sasson, 2223-2241. New York: Charles Scribner's Sons, 1995.

Reed, Henry Hope. *The New York Public Library: Its Architecture and Decoration.* New York: W.W. Norton, 1986.

Reynolds, L.D. and N.G. Wilson. *Scribes & Scholars: A Guide to the Transmission of Greek & Latin Literature.* 2nd ed. Oxford: Clarendon Press, 1975.

Richardson, Ernest Cushing. *Biblical Libraries: A Sketch of Library History from 3400 BC to AD 150.* Hamden, CT: Archon Books, 1963.

———. *Some Old Egyptian Librarians*. Berkeley, CA: Peacock Press, 1964.

Robathan, Dorothy M. "The Catalogues of the Princely and Papal Libraries of the Italian Renaissance." *Transactions and Proceedings of the American Philological Association* 64 (1933): 138-149.

Robinson, Andrew. "Writing Systems." In *The Book: A Global History*. Edited by Michael F. Suarez, S..J. Woudhuysen, and H.R. Woudhuysen, 3-18. Oxford: Oxford University Press, 2013.

Rowe, Alan. *Discovery of the Famous Temple and Enclosure of Serapis at Alexandria*. Le Caire: Imprimerie De L'institute Francais, 1946.

Rubin, Rachel and Richard Rubin. "Justifying Professional Education in a Self-Service World." In *Defending Professionalism: A Resource for Librarians, Information Specialists, Knowledge Managers, and Archivists*. Edited by Bill Crowley, 20-30. Santa Barbara, CA: Libraries Unlimited, 2012.

Rudy, Willis. *The Universities of Europe, 1100-1914: A History*. Rutherford, NJ: Fairleigh Dickinson University Press, 1984.

Russell, Bertrand. *History of Western Philosophy*. London: Routledge, 2004.

Sallaberger, Walther. "The Management of Royal Treasure: Palace Archives and Palatial Economy in the Ancient Near East." In *Experiencing Power, Generating Authority: Cosmos, Politics, and the Ideology of Kingship in Ancient Egypt and Mesopotamia*. Edited by Jane A. Hill, Philip Jones, and Antonio J. Morales, 219-255. Philadelphia, PA: University of Pennsylvania Museum of Archaeology and Anthropology, 2013.

Sandys, John Edwin. *A History of Classical Scholarship: From Antiquity to the Modern Era*. 3 vols. London: I.B. Taurus, 2011.

Sare, Laura, Stephen Bales, and Tina Budzise-Weaver. "The Quiet Agora: Undergraduate Perceptions of the Academic Library," *College & Undergraduate Libraries* 28, no. 1 (2021): 18-36.

Sare, Laura, Stephen Bales, and Bruce Neville. "New Academic Librarians and Their Perceptions of the Profession." *portal: Libraries and the Academy* 12, no. 2 (2012): 179-203.

Satija, M.P. "Briefs on the 19th (1979) to the 23rd Edition (2011) of Dewey Decimal Classification." *DESIDOC Journal of Library & Information Technology* 33, no. 4, (July 2013): 277-288.

Saunders, Daniel. "Neoliberal Ideology and Public Higher Education in the United States." *Journal for Critical Education Policy Studies* 8, no. 1 (2010): 42-77.

Savage, Ernest A. *The Story of Libraries and Book Collecting*. New York: Burt Franklin, 1969.

Schachner, Nathan. *The Medieval Universities*. New York: A.S. Barnes and Co., 1962.

Schaudig, Hanspeter. "The Ancient Near Eastern Ruler." In *Uruk: First City of the Ancient World*. Edited by Nicola Crüsemann, Margarete van Ess, Markus Hilgert, and Beate Salje. Translated by Timothy Potts, 111-115. Los Angeles, CA: Getty Publications, 2013.

Schmandt-Besserat, Denise. *How Writing Came About*. Austin, TX: University of Texas Press, 1996.

Schneider, Tammi J. *An Introduction to Ancient Mesopotamian Religion*. Grand Rapids, MI: William B. Eerdmans, 2011.

Schoenfeld, Eugen. "Militant and Submissive Religions: Class, Religion and Ideology." *The British Journal of Sociology* 43, no. 1 (1992): 111-140.

Schroll, Sister Mary Alfred. *Benedictine Monasticism as Reflected in the Warnefrid-Hildemar Commentaries on the Rule*. New York: Columbia University Press, 1941.

Schwinges, Rainer. *Studenten und Gelehrte : Studien zur Sozial- und Kulturgeschichte deutscher Universitäten im Mittelalter*. Leiden: Brill, 2008.

Shores, Louis. *Origins of the American College Library*. Hambden, CT: Shoe String Press, 1966.

Shubert, Steven Blake. "Oriental Origins of the Alexandrian Library." *Libri* 43, no. 2 (1993): 142-172

Sickinger, James P. *Public Records and Archives in Classical Athens*. Chapel Hill, NC: University of North Carolina, 1999.

Slaughter, Sheila, and Larry L. Leslie. *Academic Capitalism: Politics, Policies, and the Entrepreneurial University*. Baltimore, MA: John Hopkins University Press, 1997.

Sloterdijk, Peter. *Critique of Cynical Reason*. Translated by Michael Eldred. Minneapolis, MN: University of Minnesota Press, 1987.

Sly, Dorothy. *Philo's Alexandria*. London: Routledge, 1996.

Smith, Steven B. "Althusser and the Overdetermined Self." *The Review of Politics* 46, no. 4 (1984): 516-538.

Spinoza, Benedict. *Ethics*. Translated by W.H. White. Revised by A.H. Stirling. London: Wordsworth, 2001.

Staikos, Konstantinos Sp. *The History of the Library in Western Civilization*, 4 vols. Translated by Timothy Cullen. New Castle, DE: Oak Knoll Press, 2004.

Takács, Sarolta A. *Isis and Sarapis in the Roman World*. Leiden: Brill, 1995.

Texas A&M University Libraries, "Our Vision, Mission & Values." Accessed March 11, 2022. https://library.tamu.edu/about/vision.html.

Thompson, Anthony. *Library Buildings of Britain and Europe: An International Study, with Examples Mainly from Britain and Some from Europe and Overseas*. London: Butterworths, 1963.

Thomas, Rosalind. *Literacy and Orality in Ancient Greece*. Cambridge: Cambridge University Press, 1999.

Too, Yun Lee. *The Image of the Library in the Ancient World*. Oxford, Oxford University Press, 2010.

Townsend, Pete. "Won't Get Fooled Again." With The Who. Recorded April 1971-May 1971. Decca 088 113 056-2, 1971. Vinyl long playing record.

Trecentale Bodleianum: A Memorial Volume. Oxford: Clarendon Press, 1913.

Trubowitz, Sidney. "The Spirit of the Library." *Public Libraries* 57, no. 4 (2018): 7-8.

Turner, Victor. *The Forest of Symbols: Aspects of Ndembu Ritual.* Ithaca, NY: Cornell University Press, 1967.

UTC Library Wiki. "Library Building Project." Accessed March 11, 2022. https://wikilib.utc.edu/index.php/Library_Building_Project#The_Facts.

Vais, Gheorge. "The House of Books: The Metamorphosis of the Library Space." *Philobiblon* 17, no. 1 (2011): 15-25.

Vanstiphout, H.L.J. "Lipit-Estar's Praise in the Edubba." *Journal of Cuneiform Studies* 30, no. 1 (1978): 33-61.

Veenhof, Klaas. "Introduction." In *Cuneiform Archives and Libraries: Papers Read at the 30e Rencontre Assyriologique Internationale Leiden, 4-8 July 1983*, Edited by Klaas Veenhof, 1-36. Leiden: Nederlands Historisch-Archaeological Instituut, 1986.

Ventris, Michael and John Chadwick. *Documents in Mycenaean Greek: Three Hundred Selected Tablets From Knossos, Pylos, and Mycenae with Commentary and Vocabulary.* Cambridge: Cambridge University Press, 1956.

Vincent, J. *LGBT People and the UK Cultural Sector: The Response of Libraries, Museums, Archives and Heritage Since 1950.* Farnham, UK: Ashgate, 2014.

De Vleeschauwer, H.J. "History of the Western Library." 2 vols. In *Mousaion.* Pretoria: University of South Africa, 1963.

———. "Afterword: Origins of the Mouseion of Alexandria." Afterword to *The Oral Antecedents of Greek Librarianship.* By H. Curtis Wright. Provo, UT: Brigham Young University Press, 1977.

Wace, A.J.B. "Recent Ptolemaic Finds in Egypt." *Journal of Hellenic Studies* 65 (1945): 106-109.

Waerzeggers, Caroline. "The Pious King: Royal Patronage of Temples." In *The Oxford Handbook of Cuneiform Culture.* Edited by Karen Radner and Eleanor Robson, 725-751. Oxford: Oxford University Press, 2011.

Weitmeyer, Mogens. "Archive and Library Technique in Ancient Mesopotamia." *Libri* 6, no. 3 (1956): 217-238.

Welch, D'arne. "Sixteenth-Century Humanism and the Education of Women." *Paedagogica Historica* 24 (1984): 244-257.

Wendel, Carl. *Die Griechisch-römische Buchbeschreibung Verglichen mit der des Vorderen Orients.* Halle, 1949.

Whitehouse, David. "Library of Alexandria Discovered." *BBC News*, 12 May 2004. http://news.bbc.co.uk/2/hi/science/nature/3707641.stm.

Williams, Raymond. *Marxism and Literature.* Oxford: Oxford University Press, 1977.

Womack, Mari. *Symbols and Meaning: A Concise Introduction*, Walnut Creek, CA: Altamira Press, 2005.

Wycherley, R.E. *The Athenian Agora: Results of Excavations Conducted by the American School of Classical Studies at* Athens. Princeton, NJ: American School of Classical Studies at Athens, 1957.

Younger, John G. and Paul Rehak, "Minoan Culture: Religion, Burial Customs, and Administration." In *The Cambridge Companion to the Aegean Bronze Age*. Edited by Cynthia W. Shelmerdine Cambridge, 165-185. NY: Cambridge University Press, 2008.

Žižek, Slavoj. *The Sublime Object of* Ideology. London: Verso, 1989.

Zola, Irving Kenneth Zola. "Healthism and Disabling Medicalization." In Ivan Illich, Irving Kenneth Zola, John McKnight, Jonathan Kaplan, and Harley Shaiken. *Disabling Professions*, 41-67. London: Marion Boyars, 2010.

Index

abstraction[s],
    concrete, 9
    sacred, 7, 121
    simple, 6-8, 108, 154, 158
Albertus Magnus, 85, 148
Alcuin, 69, 70
Alexander III (the Great), 51, 52, 55-7, 111, 180
Alexandrian acropolis, 113
Althusser, Louis, 11, 127-1, 135-9
Ambrose of Milan, 75
American Library Association Library Bill of Rights, 172
Anatolia, 54, 180
Antiquae Consuetudines Canonicorum Regularium, 72
Apis Bull of Memphis, 104, 105
Aphthonius, 113, 116
apostasy, 125
Archaic and Classical Greek collections, 47, 50, 56
Archaic period, 46
Aristotle, 21, 49, 52-4, 81, 147, 148
Ark of the Covenant, 153
Asinius Pollio, 58
Assuru, 24 *see also*, Nabû
Assyria, 16, 18, 20, 32, 36-7
Augustine of Hippo, 75, 114
Augustus, 58-60
Aulus Gellius, 49, 54
Authentica Habita, 83

Bacon, Francis, 93, 148, 157
Bakunin, Mikhail, 126-7
Barbarossa, Frederick (Holy Roman Emperor), 83
Benedict's Rule (Rule of Saint Benedict), 71
biblioclasm[s], 73, 75
bibliomania, 111
Biblioteque Universitaire D'Aix-En-Provence, 155-6, 159
Bodleian Library, 80, 93

Boethius, 75
book burning, 73
book culture, 71, 75
Borges, Jorge Luis, 1
Borsippa (Nebo temple), 18
Bronze Age, 9, 124, 166, 167
Bruni, Leonardi, 88
Buddhism, 149, 181

Callimachus of Cyrene, 52
Cambridge University, 92
Cambridge University Library, 155
capitalism, 4, 87, 96-7, 102, 146, 176
    neoliberal, 11, 98, 123-31, 163-4
    power of, 100, 101
    and religion, 154, 161, 178
Cassiodorus, 70, 71, 75
Catholic Counter-Reformation, 91-3 *see also*, Reformation
Cecil H. Green Library, 151
censorship, 92, 173
Centrale Bibliotheek der Rijksuniversiteit te Gent, 156, 157
chained books, 85, 93
chaos, 24, 25
Charlemagne, 69
Chartres Cathedral, 154
Christianity, 75, 106, 148-9, 157, 161
clay tablets, 18, 21, 32, 36, 38, 45
Cleopatra VII, 114, 117
colonial empires, 97
cosmic mountain, 118, 135, 150 *see also*, Eliade, Mircea
cosmos, 5, 24, 87, 115, 122, 138, 146-7, 150, 153, 159-0
crypto-priest[s], librarian/library worker as, 77, 141-2, 153, 169, 177-8
crypto-religious institution[s], 2, 160-1
crypto-religious ritual[s], 159
crypto-religious symbolism/symbology/symbols, 138, 143, 153

crypto-temple
  academic library as, 2-3, 11, 55, 77, 87, 96, 102, 104, 108, 119, 122-3
  Serapian MCAL as, 139, 142, 161, 164
cuneiform, 31, 33, 37, 46
Cushing Memorial Library and Archives, 150
cynical library worker, 165, 181 see also kynical library worker
Cynicism, 11, 178-81 see also, kynicism

Dante, 87-8
Darwin, Charles, 97
declericalization, 3, 165
deep belief, 126, 132, 135, 142
Demetrius of Phalerum, 52, 55
democracy, 6, 7, 42, 99
Dewey Decimal Classification (DDC), 122, 147-50
Dewey, Melvil, 148, 170
Diadochi, 57, 59
dialectical materialism, 4, 5
Dietzgen, Joseph, 4, 5
Diocletian, 86
Diodorus Siculus, 40, 110
Diogenes Laertius, 47, 180
Diogenes of Sinope, 178, 180
Dionysius, 111
divination/divinatory texts, 19, 33, 36
divine kingship, 167
divine origin of written language, 22, 40
Dominicans, 85
Donovan Leitch, 165

Early Modern Period, 10, 87, 94, 96
Eastern Orthodox Church, 146
Ebla, 20, 33
Eco, Umberto, 65
Egypt
  ancient, 9, 21, 27, 38-40, 166-7
  conquest of, 51, 104, 107, 114
  proto-libraries of, 121
Eliade, Mircea, 29, 115, 118, 143, 145, 159
emancipation, 90, 91, 179
endoxa (esteemed opinions), 53, 54
Engels, Friedrich, 4, 8
Enlightenment, 10, 22, 87, 90-5
Enlil, 24, 41
Erasmus, 88
Euclid, 52

faculty-staff divide, 170
fallacy of anachronism, 21
Flavius Josephus, 146
Foucault, Michel, 182

Franciscans, 85
free market, 98, 99
freedom
  academic, 85, 90, 173
  intellectual, 172-3
  of speech, 182
Fromm, Erich, 124

gatekeeper[s], 15, 74, 121, 152, 166-8
Geertz, Clifford, 133-4
gender equality, 173
Germany, 92, 178
globalization, 100
Gramsci, Antonio, 127-8
Great Chain of Being, 147-8
Great Harbor of Alexandria, 109-10
Great Library of Alexandria, 9, 15, 19, 21, 50-2, 54-5, 73, 76, 111, 117, 142
Great Library of Nineveh, 16
Great Lighthouse of Pharos, 110
Great Museum of Alexandria, 52
Greco-Roman period, 26, 77, 158
Greece, 46-7, 57
Greek book trade, 111
Greek Dark Age, 46, 76
Greek thesis (for the origin of the Great Library of Alexandria), 55-6, 107
Greek tragedians (Aeschylus, Euripedes, Sophocles), 47
Greenwood, Ernest, 174
guild system in Europe, 81
Gutenberg, Johannes, 89

Hades (Greek god), 104, 106
Hadrian (Roman emperor), 60
Harold Cohen Library, 158
Harris, Michael H., 127-8
Haskins, Charles Homer, 80, 82
Hegel, Georg Wilhelm Friedrich, 5
hegemonic consent, 10, 104
hegemony, 4, 107, 128
  Christian, 75, 131
  by dominant classes and cultures, 154, 167
  Greek cultural and political, 56, 105
Hellenistic period, 42
Hellenization (in the post-Alexandrian world), 56
Heraclitus, 47
hierarchy(ies)
  academic, 122
  Church (religious), 86, 131, 146, 164
  MCAL, 3, 87, 138, 170
  and patriarchy, 146-7, 171
  sociocultural, 136, 141, 169, 171
hieroglyphic[s], 25, 44-6, 113

hierophany, 143
historicization, 14
Hodges Library, 11, 118-22, 131, 134
Holy of Holies, 28, 121, 146, 153-4
Homer, 49
House of Life (Per Ankh), 39
Humanism, 10, 65, 87, 101, 121
    Renaissance, 88, 90, 91

iconography, 27, 36, 84
idealism, 5, 180
ideograms, 31
ideological state apparatus (ISA), 11, 14, 127-9, 131, 135-6, 141, 145, 164, 168, 170, 175, 178
ideology, 136
    capitalist, 164
    Marxist, 127
    material, 124, 128, 133, 139-42, 147, 153
    neoliberal, 98, 99
    religious, 10, 11, 50, 102, 108, 124, 126, 129, 137-9, 142
    of the sacred, 3, 165
Illich, Ivan, 175-7, 183
Illiteracy, 46, 64
imago mundi, 115, 122, 145-6, 159
information commons model, 120-1
initiation, 159, 160
Inquisition, 73, 91
Internet, 143, 151, 168
interpellation, 124, 135-9, 143, 153, 164
Iron Age, 9, 31, 32
Isidorus of Seville, 49
Isis, 106
Italy, 70, 92

Jastrow, Morris, 16-18, 36
Jesus Christ, 157
Judaism, 24, 149
Julian the Apostate, 75
Julius Caesar, 117

Kant, Immanuel, 90
Keynesianism, 98
King Eumenes II, 54
King Perseus of Macedonia, 58
King Seleucus, 49
King Lipit-Estar, 23
Kipling, Rudyard, 165
Kynical academic library worker, 11, 102, 161, 165, 178, 182-3
Kynicism, 11, 178-81, 183

laicus (layperson), 64
Larson, Magali Sarfatti, 176

late antiquity, 10, 26, 62-5, 75
Late Modern Period, 10, 96, 97, 102
Late Roman empire, 86, 122, 146
Late Uruk period, 30
Latin language, 32, 64, 84
Latin literature and poetry, 59-60, 80
lay students, 83
Layard, Austen Henry, 36
Lenin, Vladimir Ilyich, 4, 127, 132
Lévi-Strauss, Henri, 135
library anxiety, 138-41
Library of Congress Classification System (LCC), 147-50
Library of Congress Subject Headings (LCSH), 149-50
Library of Palatine Apollo, 60
Library of Pergamum, 15, 54, 58, 117
Library of the Serapeum, 15, 54, 59, 115-17
Library of Trinity College, Dublin, 94
limit situation, 140
literacy, 56, 88, 159
    of Greeks, 45-6, 50
    in the Middle Ages, 64-5, 74, 76
    among women, 89, 91
Lucullus, 58
Lukàcs, György, 127

Machiavelli, Niccolò, 88
Manchester, William, 62
Manetho of Sebennytus, 52, 104
Marcellinus, Ammianus, 113
Marduk, 24
Marduk temple, 18
Marx, Karl, 4-6, 14, 97, 102
Marxist theory, 127 *see also*, dialectical materialism
Max, Gerald E., 29
Maxwell, Nancy Kalikow, 168-9
MCAL see modern capitalist academic library
Mesopotamia, 3, 9, 18, 21, 31, 35, 121, 166
Mesopotamian Tablet of Destinies, 24
Metroon, 47-8
Middle Ages, 15, 32, 64, 168
    Christianity and control of knowledge, 75-7, 87
    Early, 63-5, 70
    High, 64, 82
    Late, 74, 77, 81, 85, 87, 102, 148
modern capitalist academic library (MCAL), 2, 14, 98, 108, 123, 164
modern liberal professions, 170, 176-7
modern university system, 83, 100
modes of production, 14, 97, 101, 129, 131, 164, 176

Morsch, Lucile M., 97-8
Museum of Alexandria, 52, 111, 152
Mycenaean civilization, 44
mysterium fascinans, 141
mysterium tremendum, 140, 141
mythical geography, 145-7

Nabû, 23-7, 37
Neo-Babylonian era, 35
Neo-Babylonian Sippar, 20
neoliberalism, 10, 98-101, 163
Nicholas of Cusa, 88
Nicholas V, 89
Nietzsche, Friedrich, 97, 181
Ninurta, 41
Nisaba, 23, 26
North Carolina State University Libraries, 153
numinous, 118, 139, 140

Ollman, Bertell, 4, 14
Oppenheim, A. Leo, 15, 17-19, 21, 31, 36
Origen, 75
Orosius, 114-5
Osiris, 40, 104-6
otherness, 141
Otto, Rudolf, 139-41
overdetermination, concept of, 139
Ovid, 57-8
Oxford library, 94, 96
Oxford University, 81, 85, 93, 95

pagan[s], 63, 73-6, 88, 114, 157
Palestine, 74
palimpsest, 142
papyrus, 21, 38, 40, 47 *see also*, scrolls
parchment, 21, 47
Parthenon, 154
patriarchy, 86-7, 122, 131, 146-7, 173
Paul, Shalom M., 24
Paulus Aemilius, 58
Pausanius, 61
Penn State Harrisburg Libraries, 153
Peripatetic philosophy, 52-4, 115
Petrarca, Francesco, 88
Philo of Byblos, 26
pilgrimage, 159, 160
Pisistratus, 49, 58
Plan of Saint Gall, 68
Plato, 21, 180
Plutarch, 55, 104
Polastron, 73, 74
Polycrates tyrant of Samos, 49, 58
Pont du Gard aqueduct, 155
Porphyry, 148

Porticus Octaviae (Portico of Octavia), 58
positivism, 128
priesthood, 10, 24, 48, 50, 164, 177
professionalism, 11, 171, 175-6
professionalization of library work, 165, 171-6
Prometheus, 32, 41
proto-library, 21, 31-3, 36-8, 40, 47-9, 51, 55-6, 74, 167
Ptolemaic thesis, 55, 56, 107
Ptolemy I Soter, 51, 52, 55-6, 104-8, 111, 167
Ptolemy II Philadelphus (The Sister Lover), 111, 114
Ptolemy III Euergetes (The Benefactor), 110-12

Ra, 25, 26, 40, 158
Radcliffe Camera, 94-5
Rambusch, Robert E., 156
Rameses II, 40
Ramesseum, 40
Rashdall, Hastings, 87
Rassam, Hormuzd, 36
rationalism, 90
Reformation, 90-93
religious dread, 140
Renaissance
    European, 10, 87-91, 95, 102
    Italian, 63, 65, 87, 91
    Medieval, 10, 80
    twelfth century, 87, 102
repressive state apparatus (RSA), 128-9, 137, 139
Richardson, Ernest Cushing, 18-21, 28, 133, 168
ritual, 10, 14, 29, 84, 104, 132-4, 159, 166
Roman Catholic Church, 80, 122
Roman Empire, 62-3, 76, 86, 122, 146
Rushd, Ibn, 81

sacred space[s], 14, 29, 62, 111, 115, 141, 145, 153, 156, 159
Saddam Hussein, 132
Saint Jerome (patron saint of librarians), 157
Saint Mark the Evangelist, 157
salvation, 71, 89, 97
Santa Maria de Montserrat Abbey, 66
Scala Naturae (Ladder of Being), 148
Schelling, Friedrich Wilhelm Joseph von, 90
Schleiermacher, Friedrich, 90
scientific pluralism, 128
Scientific Revolution, 90
scribe[s], 15, 19, 23-6, 32, 37-44, 68-72, 121, 167-8, 172
script[s], 23, 25, 27, 30-1, 33, 44-6
scriptoria, 35, 66-71, 77, 152

scriptorium, 39, 68, 70, 72, 85
scrolls, 21, 24, 55, 117, 38, 111, 116, *see also* papyrus
Second Temple of Jerusalem, 146
secular clergy, 3, 81, 82
secularization, 14, 83, 89, 102
Sénanque Abbey, 66
Serapeum, *see also*, Serapian library
    Alexandrian, 10, 11, 51, 61, 109, 114, 122
    Library of the Serapeum, 15, 54, 59, 115-17
    temples, 107-15
Serapian ideological plexus (SIP), 3, 10, 30, 108, 122, 165, 167-9
Serapian information institution, 10, 104
Serapian library, 10, 104, 142, 164
Serapis, 3, 10, 51, 104-11, 114-5, 122
Seshat, 26
Shulgi (King of Ur III), 167
Sloterdijk, Peter, 178-80
social order, 135, 160
Socrates, 112, 180
Spinoza, Benedict, 4-5
Stephen A. Schwarzman Library, 154-5
Sterling C. Evans Library, 150
Strabo of Pontus, 52
Straton of Lampsacus, 52
stream of tradition, 15, 33, 37, 42, 50, 76, 121, 153
structuralized society, 124
student strikes, 82
Sumerians, 16, 23, 30-1, 118
syllabograms, 31
symbol[s], 33, 39, 107-8, 132-3, 157
    and modern capitalist academic library, 14, 161, 164
    religious, 11, 134, 164
symbolism, 145, 158
    ideological, 117, 140
    religious, 4, 10, 104, 107, 139
syncretism, 86

Tablet of Destinies, 24, 40, 41
Temple of Artemis, 47
Temple of Athena Nikephoros, 55
Temple Library of the Serapeum, 15, 115-17
Temple of Solomon, 153, 156
Temple of the Palatine Apollo, 60
Texas A&M University Libraries, 150-1, 153, 174
Theocritus, 52
Theodoric the Great, 70
Theophrastus, 52
theoretical inquiry, 55
Thomas Aquinas, 85, 148

Thoth, 25-28, 39-42
Thuringia (Germany), 92
Timon of Phlius, 52
Timotheus, 104
Titus Flavius Pantainos, 61
transcendence, 140
Turner, Victor, 134
twelfth century CE, 10, 66, 72, 77, 80-1, 86-7, 101, 107
Tzetzes, John, 117

Universal Decimal Classification, 122
universal library, 151
University Church of St. Mary the Virgin, 95
University of Bologna, 81
University of Georgia, 151
University of Liverpool, 158
Uruk, 30, 31, 166

vocational awe, 7, 101

wax tablets, 21 *see also*, clay tablets
Widener Library (Harvard), 138, 151
Williams, Raymond, 130, 160
Windham, Henry Penruddocke, 91
Wollstonecraft, Mary, 91
women, 24, 89, 91, 146-7, 173
writing, 22-5, 27-8, 30-3, 38, 41, 44-6, 56, 64, 76

Xerxes, 49

Yun Lee Too, 142

Zeus, 61, 106, 110
ziggurat, 118, 134
Žižek, Slavoj, 179
Zola, Emile, 177
Zu, 40-42
Zweistrombegriff, 56

Printed in the USA
CPSIA information can be obtained
at www.ICGtesting.com
CBHW082011071123
1712CB00005B/12

9 781634 000970